AF605908

Timing and Rulership in *Master Lü's Spring and Autumn Annals (Lüshi chunqiu)*

SUNY series in Chinese Philosophy and Culture
David L. Hall and Roger T. Ames, editors

Timing and Rulership in *Master Lü's Spring and Autumn Annals (Lüshi chunqiu)*

James D. Sellmann

State University of New York Press

"Four Seasons" drawings by Enyo Yang Kowalski, the author's aunt

Published by
State University of New York Press, Albany

Printed in the United States of America

For information, address the State University of New York Press,
State University Plaza, Albany, NY 12246

Production by Judith Block
Marketing by Fran Keneston

Library of Congress Cataloging-in-Publication Data

Sellmann, James D. (James Daryl)
Timing and rulership in Master Lü's Spring and Autumn annals (Lüshi chunqiu) / James D. Sellmann.
p. cm. (SUNY series in Chinese philosophy and culture)
Includes bibliographical references and index.
ISBN 0–7914–5231–X (alk. paper) — ISBN 0–7914–5232–8 (pbk. : alk. paper)
1. Lè shi chun qiu. I. Title. II. Series.

PL2663.L83 S45 2002
181'.112—dc21

2001031195
CIP

10 9 8 7 6 5 4 3 2 1

For my wife, Roni

Contents

Acknowledgments

The philosophical anthology *Lüshi chunqiu* (*Lü-shih ch'un-ch'iu*) contains an abundance of information concerning pre-Qin (before 221 B.C.E.) culture and thought. I began to study the *Lüshi chunqiu* (hereafter LSCQ) in 1980 while researching the etymology for *daoshi* (Daoist priest) in the LSCQ's expression *youdao zhi shi* (scholars who comply with the Way). From 1982 to 1983, I translated the LSCQ under the guidance of Yang Youwei in Taiwan. Without his assistance, this book would not be possible. A longer draft of this manuscript was presented to the University of Hawaii in partial fulfillment of the requirements for the doctorate in Chinese Philosophy in 1990. The University of Guam granted me sabbatical leave (1998–99) to revise the manuscript.

I am very grateful for the advice and guidance given by Roger T. Ames. He suggested that I focus the study of the LSCQ on proper timing. His influence is readily apparent. This book could not have been completed without the further contribution of the following scholars: Eliot Deutsch guided me through the intricacies of extrinsic and intrinsic timing; Ken Kipnis encouraged me to study comparative political theory; Angus C. Graham and James Landers rectified my translations of the LSCQ and commented on the manuscript; David W. Chappell offered suggestions for improving the manuscript; and Henry Rosemont Jr. contributed helpful insights on revising the manuscript for publication. The anonymous reviewers for State University of New York Press made suggestions for shortening the text. Of course, I am solely responsible for the errors remaining in this book.

I must acknowledge support from family members and friends. Colleagues, friends, and classmates entertained numerous hours of discussion. Mary Ann Santangelo fostered my budding mind, and more recently provided electronic library support. Enyo and Edward Kowalski brought China closer to home, and my Aunt Enyo prepared the cover design. Richard W. Sellmann provided much needed financial support. My wife, Roni, used her art of *fengshui* to create my work environment and encouraged me to see this project to its conclusion. Christopher and Angela reminded me that there is no work without play. I am indebted to them all.

The editor of *Asian Culture Quarterly* published by the Asian-Pacific Cultural

Center, Taipei, Taiwan, ROC, granted permission to reprint material from my articles: "The *Lüshi chunqiu* on the Ruler's Use of Proper Timing," *Asian Culture Quarterly* 27:1 (spring 1999): 59–71; "Eco-Ethics: A New Perspective from Guam," *Asian Culture Quarterly* 21:3 (autumn 1993): 47–51; "Seasonality in the Achievement of *Hsing* in the *Lü-shih ch'un-ch'iu*," *Asian Culture Quarterly* 18:2 (summer, 1990) 42-68. *The Journal of Asian Philosophy* allowed me to use material from my article "The Origin and Role of the State According to the *Lüshi chunqiu*," *Journal of Asian Philosophy* 9:3 (1999): 193–218. See their web site: http//www.tandf.CO.UK.

A Note Concerning Conventions Used in This Book

All dates mentioned in the body of the text are from before the common era (B.C.E.) unless otherwise stated. I have merely repeated the traditional dates. Because of the growing volume of archaeological evidence, these traditional dates will be revised by the experts, but there is no consensus at this time, so I have relied on the traditional dates.

I employ the Pinyin system of Romanization. However, to assist the reader who may be more familiar with the Wade–Giles system, I have included that system of romanization in parentheses for a few key names and concepts when they first appear. I have not modified the spelling of the names of those authors who are published and well known in the West under their own unique Romanized name, such as Fung Yu-lan or Kung-chuan Hsiao (instead of Feng Youlan and Gongquan Xiao). I realize that this is inconsistent and may confuse the beginning student, but I do not have the right to change a person's name. To save time, energy, ink, and paper, I abbreviate *Lüshi chunqiu* as LSCQ. Because there is no way of telling how many authors or editors had a hand in the construction of LSCQ, I have found it convenient to anthropomorphize the text. For instance, I say "the text describes," rather than "the authors or editors describe."

Chapter 1

Introduction: The *Lüshi chunqiu*'s Background and Foreground

In the third century before the common era (B.C.E.; all dates are B.C.E. unless noted otherwise), the kingdoms on the central plains of China encountered a period of intense warfare. Out of the various feudal principalities turned kingdoms, only one would stand as victor and unifier. In 256 B.C.E., the Qin army vanquished the vestiges of the imperial house of Zhou, officially terminating that dynasty. At that time, Qin was not prepared to do battle with the remaining seven kingdoms. *Master Lü's Spring and Autumn Annals* (*Lüshi chunqiu* or *Lü-shih ch'un-ch'iu*) was written during a lull in Qin's battles when the child king, Zheng (259–210 B.C.E.), reigned (traditional reign 246–221). Zheng unified the empire and became the self-proclaimed first-generation emperor of Qin (Qin shihuangdi, or Ch'in Shih Huang-ti, reigned as emperor from 221–210). *Lüshi chunqiu* was completed in 241 B.C.E. at the estate of Lü Buwei (Lü Pu-wei), the prime minister of Qin and tutor to the child king, Zheng. A decade after the completion of the *Lüshi chunqiu*, King Zheng began the ensuing nine years of fervent warfare that led to unification of the empire in 221. Before the political unification, *Lüshi chunqiu* created a philosophical consolidation.[1] The *Lüshi chunqiu* performed an important function in the literary and political education of the young King Zheng. It provided a philosophical understanding of and justification for a unified empire that left its mark on the young king, and on the subsequent Han philosophy. After unifying the empire, Qin shihuangdi established the insignia of water for the imperial emblems, employing concepts from *Lüshi chunqiu*'s *yingtong* (Responding and Identifying) chapter, which describes the succession of dynasties according to the timely cycle of the five phases (*wuxing*) to justify his new dynasty.[2]

To study the *Lüshi chunqiu* is to enter into the tumultuous but progressive times of the Warring States period (403–221 B.C.E.)—commonly referred to as the pre-Qin period because of the fundamental changes that occurred after the Qin unification. The struggle among the eight most powerful states climaxed in unification under one centralized ruler, establishing the rudiments of a dynastic system that persevered for more than 2,000 years. About a century before the military and political unification of the kingdoms, a unified composite philosophy and literature had begun to flower in such works as the *Guanzi* and *Shizi*.[3] That eclectic, discriminating, selective, and consolidating trend in philosophical literature blossomed with the *Lüshi chunqiu*, and it continued to bear fruit in the Han dynasty (206 B.C.E.–220 C.E.) in the *Huainanzi* and the *Chunqiu fanlu*. The authors of those texts appropriate the unified amalgamated strategy, philosophical concepts, and even whole passages from the *Lüshi chunqiu*. The *Guanzi*, *Shizi*, and *Lüshi chunqiu* express the possibility of political unification implicitly by setting an example of diverse positions working in harmony with each other, that is, a consolidated philosophy, and explicitly by proposing the unification of the empire. A major theme running through the *Lüshi chunqiu* is the idea of "the proper timing" required to bring about and maintain a unified empire. Proper timing is a constituent process for securing victory in battle and a bountiful harvest, two important aspects in the ancient art of rulership. The idea of proper timing is an important component in divination, and it continued to dominate philosophy in the Han dynasty.[4]

The concern for proper timing in achieving social and political order, specifically how to achieve such an order and to obtain its beneficial results for human life, instructs classical Chinese philosophy, especially in the Warring States period (403–221 B.C.E.). Pre-Qin philosophy has a social and political orientation. The predominant theme of self-cultivation, typical of *daojia* (Daoist or Taoist), *rujia* (Literati or Confucian),[5] and Mohist thought, which interpreters as diverse as James Legge and Donald Munro are prone to psychologize, given their own cultural commitments, is directed toward the achievement of harmony, both natural and social. To attempt an unbiased study of pre-Qin philosophy, the modern interpreter must be self-conscious of the themes that color one's own philosophical world. For example, contemporary philosophers, such as Fung Yu-lan and Thomé Fang, who discuss ancient Chinese metaphysics and ontology, study the *Yijing* (*I ching* or *Book of Changes*), but they rarely acknowledge the original context and function of that text: it was consulted at court for timely guidance in the art of rulership, and even in its popular usage the text is directed toward lending counsel for one's own life or the well-being of one's family within the temporal social context. The *Lüshi chunqiu* is typical as a classical pre-

Qin text in that it is primarily concerned with discourses directed at influencing social and political order in a timely fashion. At a glance, these discourses appear disjointed because of their diversity, but coherence emerges as a "temporal orientation for maintaining order."

More will be said below, but a brief description of the *Lüshi chunqiu* (hereafter LSCQ) will show that the text commands an important understanding of the world, and it holds a crucial position during what would prove to be a decisive time in pre-Qin social and political philosophy. The text is not only a product of its day, but it also helps shape an era. The LSCQ was compiled by the retainers and guest scholars at Lü Buwei's estate during his appointment as prime minister of Qin (249–237 B.C.E.). The work was completed by 241 or, according to another reckoning, by 238. It is one of the few pre-Qin texts that dates itself. The date, though not precise, is given in the *xuyi* chapter.[6] It is one of the few philosophical texts to avoid the infamous "burning of the books" contained in private collections in 213 B.C.E. The LSCQ was completed toward the end of the classical age of philosophy after the Eastern Zhou dynasty (traditional dates 770–256 B.C.E.). In its day, the LSCQ was a unique phenomenon, because books of its size, more than 100,000 characters, were rare. It marks a fixed date for and a developed form of the unified composite movement in Qin and subsequent Han philosophy. As a compendium or an anthology of classical knowledge, the LSCQ provides a resource for cultural and philosophical material.[7] Studying this text, one sees that it either focuses on social and political topics organized under a seasonal scheme, or discusses the importance of proper timing in ruling a state.

To the extent that the LSCQ is representative of many pre-Qin philosophers, this study has a bearing on the reevaluation of other classical pre-Qin texts.[8] The LSCQ's integral, this-worldly, temporal approach provides one with insights that might occasion a reevaluation of one's own tradition. In the pre-Qin context, "time," rooted in historical circumstance, is didactic and heuristic; that is, "time" is not an objective condition but a historical interpretation with moral and cosmic "lessons." In the principal pre-Qin philosophies, there is no conception of an interpretation or a "theory" divorced from context and performance. Although the expression "theory and action are one" (*zhixing heyi*) was coined relatively late by Wang Yangming (1472–1529 C.E.), the assumption that theory entails praxis is pervasive in pre-Qin Literati and Daoist texts.[9] Pre-Qin philosophy proffers an alternative to the atemporal approach in European and American social contract theory. The temporal nature of theory and praxis provides a different perspective for legal reform, constitutional interpretation, and environmental ethics.

"Proper timing" or "season" (*shi*) is a central concern in the diverse philosophies of the LSCQ, and this concept has been undervalued or ignored in the Chinese, Japanese, and European commentarial literature on the LSCQ. The art of rulership generated in numerous chapters of the LSCQ has as a unifying feature the presupposition that order is based on a programmatic understanding of human life in its social, political, and cosmic contexts. Although the connection between ethical and political policy and cosmic order may be apparent, in pre-Qin and Han philosophy, cosmic harmony is a core concept. The LSCQ is one of China's earliest extant texts that develops a "temporal cosmology."

A word about terminology is in order. Generally speaking, there are two different yet interrelated senses of "proper timing"—intrinsic and extrinsic.[10] Proper timing is an event-in-context where the extrinsic perspective underscores the context and the intrinsic outlook emphasizes the event. The former is morphological, the latter genetic. *Extrinsic timing* is the more familiar. When human actions are performed in accordance with either natural or social conditions, there is a timely fit. Extrinsic timing is best described as a "timely action" that appropriately agrees with seasonal and historic circumstances. The execution of policy and the enactment of ritual, coinciding with the seasons and social or historic conditions, constitute timely actions. Agricultural and military operations easily fit the extrinsic model. For example, planting in the spring and harvesting in autumn, or moving troops in the proper season or when the socioeconomic, political, and historical conditions are right.

The second sense of proper timing is the quality of an action that is achieved creatively and spontaneously with a timing intrinsic to the act itself. *Intrinsic timing* does not depend on a given order. It is not determined by external conditions, though it may depend on them. Intrinsic timing is associated with the proper fit between the action and its performer; it is a qualitative experience. The actual act of planting or the act of battle that is executed with creative power exemplifies the model of acting with proper intrinsic timing. For heuristic purposes, it is instructive to distinguish between the two models of timing. It is equally instructive to notice how they meld together to create an event-in-context. For example, sports, especially ball games, appear to fit the extrinsic model of timing, and art forms, such as modern dance or painting, lean toward the intrinsic. But the distinction begins to blur. Certain dances (a waltz, for example), where each step accords with the music, evidence extrinsic concerns not found in a game of handball. Even in the most extrinsically controlled contexts, such as football or square dancing, the performer brings an intrinsic quality to the event. A human articulation of time is found in the performance of acts that harmonize and creatively appropriate both the extrinsic and intrinsic elements.

In this context, "proper timing" should not be thought of as a formal abstraction but as a selective abstraction that integrates both extrinsic and intrinsic experiences of timing. The term *proper timing* is meant to summon up images that integrate both intrinsic timing and extrinsic timely actions. "Proper timing" is that overall experience of performing actions with an intrinsic quality and extrinsic correspondence. This integration of extrinsic and intrinsic timing is due to the dynamic nature of the Chinese language and its philosophy.

There is a tendency to explain classical pre-Qin philosophy by employing the terminology of classical Greek and Roman thinkers, or modern Western philosophers. This approach does not do justice to the pre-Qin worldview.[11] Joseph Needham and others have proposed that Chinese philosophy needs to be conceptualized in dynamic and organic terms.[12] Angus Graham and Sarah Allan argue that English terms do not adequately capture the dynamic character of the Chinese language.[13] The student of pre-Qin philosophy must keep these *dynamic* and *organic* assumptions in mind. In particular, the *dynamic* nature of pre-Qin philosophy should *not* be thought of as a teleological process—"things" are not developing along the lines of Aristotelian causes; they do not culminate into a Whiteheadean process of creativity or any other end. The dynamic character of the pre-Qin outlook is rooted in the plethora of particular foci that maintain a complex network of processes in and through their mutual interaction. In the context of this work the word "organic" should *not* be thought of in terms of traditional Western organic theory in which the whole organism is greater than the sum of its parts or organs. With these caveats in mind, I will employ the term *organic* as a shorthand for the foci-field net, that is, the complex network of particulars, made up of other particulars, contributing to coherent organizations or "fields," which in turn are parts of other "fields."[14] The pre-Qin world is hylozoistic—a living world empowered with *qi*. The relationships obtaining between the particular foci constitute "field cosmology." The foci-field model is notably different from the traditional Western understanding of the part/whole, organ/organism relationship. The pre-Qin organic world is an emergent order of particular foci changing through their mutual interrelatedness with each other, that is, the field. The interrelationships establish patterns of continuity. Agriculture may have originally sponsored the model; that is, a seed, piece of root, or stalk, the focus, generates a plant as a field, then the plant as a focus propagates a host of other plants—a field—which in turn engenders a seed, root, or stalk, and the dynamic ongoing process continues.

Lü Buwei and the LSCQ

Lü Buwei's life and the compilation of the LSCQ exemplify many aspects of proper timing.[15] The historical background behind the LSCQ and Lü Buwei's motivations for having that anthology compiled are intriguing. It is necessary to put the work in a historical context to gain a full appreciation of it, its sponsor's art of timing, and the philosophy of proper timing contained therein. One is immediately confronted with two obstacles in attempting to reconstruct Lü Buwei's lifetime. First, there is a lack of material on his family and early life before coming into contact with the hostage prince, Zichu (or Yiren), in the State of Zhao between 265–260 B.C.E. Second, there are problems of credibility and textual corruption or intentional alteration in the scant historical material we have concerning Lü Buwei's life, especially his "Biography" in the *Shiji* (*Records of the Historian*). It appears that the original material was altered.[16]

The reign of the self-proclaimed first-generation emperor of Qin (221–210) created radical social, cultural, political, and economic changes. Substantial hardship and unnecessary death were inflicted on the people in the undertaking of imperial construction projects such as the imperial highways, palaces, and tombs, and in joining the territorial walls to constitute a great wall. Shihuangdi imposed censorship against the Literati class. This is seen in the promulgation of Li Si's notorious edict, implementing the destruction of private libraries and the execution of scholars.[17] These hardships, and their later exaggeration, created a good deal of animosity against the First Emperor and those associated with him. Time did not heal this wound. Because of the enmity and the didactic nature of ancient (and modern) historiography in China, there has been a tendency by some historians to read anachronistically the tyranny of the Qin dynasty (221–206) back into his earlier reign as King Zheng (traditional reign 246–221—Zheng, in fact, took the throne in the fifth month of 247, when his father died). The anachronistic interpretation is especially problematic, because King Zheng was but a child, without any real control, during the first nine years of his reign (ca. 247–238). He began to wield power after donning the cap and sword of adulthood in 238. There is a tendency to attack anyone associated with Qin shihuangdi as though the early associates were responsible for his tyranny after unifying the empire.[18]

These peculiar interpretations of Qin history generate misunderstandings of the LSCQ. Although it is not the object of this book to labor over the diverse interpretations of the LSCQ, especially the inadequate ones, nevertheless one questionable interpretation is well worth noting, because it really distorted the purpose and content of the LSCQ and reemerged recently. This is the view first proposed by the Song scholar, Gao Sisun, elaborated by the Ming scholar, Fang Xiaoru, and finally synthesized by Kung-chuan Hsiao, proposing that the LSCQ was directed against *fajia* (so-called Legalist) doctrine, particularly the policies of Qin shihuangdi.[19] Such an interpretation can only be based on a selective reading and misquoting of the text coupled with an anachronistic interpretation that the LSCQ opposes policies that were not instituted for at least two decades after the LSCQ's publication. The hypothesis that the LSCQ is anti-Qin ignores the fact that Lü Buwei had power at court and further ignores the long-standing attraction for *fajia* thinkers, such as Shang Yang and later Li Si, at the Qin court. Lü Buwei's "businesslike" approach to politics is not at all at odds with *fajia* procedures. Most devastating to the hypothesis that the LSCQ is an anti-*fajia* text is the *fajia* material contained in the LSCQ itself and, as Hu Shi has argued, some of that *fajia* material may have been written by Li Si himself, especially the *chajin* chapter.[20] Regardless of which date one accepts for the compilation of the LSCQ (241 or 238), the text was completed about two decades before Shihuangdi unified the empire and, with Li Si's aid, imposed severe policies. At the date of its compilation, severe restrictions had not yet been imposed. The LSCQ was written when the Shihuangdi-to-be was still a child king. Moreover, if the *Shiji* story were correct (though we have reason to believe it is a later interpolation), Lü was not only King Zheng's prime minister but also his father. This would make it even more unlikely that Lü Buwei opposed court policy, especially when he made a lot of the policy himself during the child king's early reign.[21] Thus to describe the LSCQ as an anti-*fajia* and anti-Qin work is to impose an anachronism that greatly oversimplifies the content and nature of the LSCQ. Because of these historiographical concerns, scholars approach the history of the state of Qin before and during unification (221), especially the life of Lü Buwei, with a critical eye.

There is another pre-Qin and Han cultural bias to interpret the growth of Qin, west of the central plains, as the ascent of an uncivilized, basically barbaric people, and to see Qin's unification of the empire as an attack on the vestiges of the civilized Zhou dynasty. Because the state of Lu, in the East, was the home of Confucius, it came to be idealized as a cultural center along with the state of Qi. Though Qi was of a tribal, not a royal family, origin, like Qin, nevertheless Qi was noted for sponsoring the Jixia academy, and it became known as a center of political power and learning. Thus, some ancient and modern historians have promoted the impression that the state of Qin was backward and uncultured, which is far from the truth.

To fully apprehend Lü Buwei's relationship to the state of Qin and his sponsorship of the LSCQ, and to further comprehend the essential gravity of "proper timing" in the LSCQ, one must appreciate the place of "timing" in Lü's meteoric rise from merchant to prime minister. Lü Buwei was from Puyang (originally part of Wei). By the time he came into contact with the Qin prince, Zichu (or Yiren), held hostage in Zhao, he was known as a wealthy merchant from Yangdi, the capital of the state of Han. Lü Buwei was probably born into the merchant class, which was prospering during the Warring States period. Since he was already a renowned wealthy merchant when he met Zichu between 265 and 260, he was probably in his twenties or early thirties. So Lü Buwei was probably born sometime between 295 and 280. The story recounted in the *Zhanguoce* (*Intrigues of the Warring States*) relates that after Lü Buwei became aware of the Qin prince held hostage in Zhao, he returned home to ask for his father's advice about the yield from investing in agriculture, jewels, or "establishing a ruler."[22] Of course, he was told that political investments promise a much higher return than jewels or produce. As with most investment advice, the higher risk taken for the higher yield is not mentioned—in the end, it cost Lü his estate and his life. The story gives the impression that Lü Buwei was young because he is seeking his father's counsel, and he appears to be searching for his own career—so he may have been in his twenties when he met the Qin prince.

Zichu, like most political hostages of the day, was only a prince in title. He had no real hope of inheriting the Qin throne. However, in 265, Zichu's father, Lord An Guo, became heir apparent to the Qin throne. Lord An Guo had taken his favorite concubine, Lady Huayang, as his legal wife. Zichu was the son of a secondary wife, Lady Xia. However, the legal wife, Lady Huayang, remained childless.

Lü Buwei's rise to power began with the risky investment in gifts and bribes to influence Lady Huayang's family to assist in convincing her to adopt Zichu as her legitimate heir.[23] The gifts, bribes, and heavy persuasions paid off. Lady Huayang adopted Zichu, and she convinced Lord An Guo to establish him as their heir apparent. Before leaving Zhao, Zichu took a fancy to Lü Buwei's concubine, and asked for her hand. When she bore a son, Zichu took her as his legal wife. The son, his legitimate heir, became King Zheng upon Zichu's death in 247.

The *Shiji* adds that Lü's concubine was already pregnant when she went to Zichu. Because this part of the story is not contained in the other sources, especially the *Zhanguoce*, and because it is hardly believable, it is rejected as a later interpolation to slander the First Emperor and Lü Buwei.[24] Because of the literary disdain for the merchant class in ancient China, it is not too surprising that Lü Buwei is made out to be self-serving, driven by profit and power. Even if we strip away the scholar-literati bias, it is apparent that Lü Buwei was an opportunist, an "entrepreneur," intimately involved in the perilous adventures of court intrigue for whom timing was of the utmost significance.

Once Zichu was safe within the Qin court, uneducated, he was in need of a tutor. Of course, Lü Buwei was at hand to be appointed. This may be significant in understanding Lü Buwei's motivation in sponsoring the compilation of the LSCQ. First as tutor to Zichu and later as his minister, and subsequently in serving as the prime minister to the child King Zheng, Lü Buwei found himself in the role of court tutor. One of the prime minister's duties was to supervise the ruler's education, especially a young ruler. Faced with the responsibility of providing his rulers with a basic education and an understanding of their complex role as king, Lü Buwei, in part, devised the idea of the LSCQ in order to fulfill this twofold educational requirement.

King Zhao of Qin, in the fifty-sixth year of his reign, 251, died. Lord An Guo died in 250, after only one year of rule; he was posthumously titled King Xiaowen. After a little more than a decade of involvement with Zichu, Lü Buwei's plans yielded large returns. In 249, Zichu, enthroned as King Zhuangxiang, appointed Lü Buwei as assistant chancellor and enfeoffed him as marquis Wenxin (*wen* meaning "cultured," as in literature, *xin* meaning "credibility") with the revenues of 100,000 households in Henan and Loyang. The title "Wenxin" implied that Lü Buwei, at least, had the ambition, if not the actual practice, of compiling a great literary work at that time. Zhuangxiang's reign was also short lived,[25] lasting only three years—officially, it was only a few days after ending the three-year mourning period. So Zheng became King of Qin at about the age of twelve (thirteen by Chinese custom) in 247. King Zheng appointed Lü Buwei prime minister with the title Zhongfu ("second father," or "uncle"), emulating the title and relationship often mentioned in the LSCQ concerning Duke Huan of Qi and his famous minister Guan Zhong, whose name was used for the title of the anthology, *Guanzi*, compiled by the scholars at the Jixia academy in Qi.

Lü Buwei was quite adept at manipulating the times and circumstances of his day to maneuver himself into one of the most influential positions in Qin. The *Shiji* introduces an additional motivation for Lü Buwei to sponsor the compilation of the LSCQ, namely, intellectual competition. Lü Buwei was faced with the practical issue of educating the crown prince, Zichu, and then the child king, Zheng. He was one of the most powerful men in the Warring States period and undoubtedly sensitive to, or at least aware of, the need to propagate learning. Though the *Shiji* makes Lü Buwei appear to be attempting to corner the education market, it was certainly the style of the times for great statesmen and rulers to keep protégés and guest scholars in residence. The *Shiji* reports that: "Thinking it would be shameful not to equal them when Qin was so powerful, Lü Buwei also invited guests and treated them handsomely, until he had three thousand protégés."[26] At this time there were numerous teachers and their books circulating about the various centers of learning in the different states. Lü Buwei wanted to show his prowess again, or so the *Shiji* continues:

> Lü Buwei also had his guests record all their knowledge, compiling more than two hundred thousand words divided into the "Eight References" (*balan*), "Six Discussions" (*lulun* or *liulun*), and the "Twelve Chronicles" (*shierji*). Believing that this work dealt with everything in heaven and earth, comprising all ancient and modern knowledge, he entitled it *Master Lü's Spring and Autumn Annals*. It was displayed at the gate of the Xianyang market, with a thousand pieces of gold hung above it. Itinerant scholars and protégés from other states were invited to read it, and the gold was offered to anyone who could add or subtract a single character.[27]

We have a fairly good idea when the text was produced. The *xuyi* (Postscript) chapter, which appears at the end of the *shierji* section of the LSCQ, begins by stating that it was "in the eighth year of Qin" (ca. 241 or 238) that Lü Buwei was asked about the meaning of the *shierji*. A few years after its publication, Lü Buwei was dismissed from office in 237, apparently because he was implicated in the Lao Ai revolt of 238. Lü Buwei was later banished to Shu, where he either died in exile or committed suicide in 235 rather than face the hardship of banishment.

The LSCQ was undoubtedly compiled by guest scholars under the patronage of Lü Buwei while he was assistant chancellor, and then the prime minister of Qin between 249 and 238 B.C.E.—most likely it was completed by 241. In part, Lü Buwei's motivation to have the text written was his competition with other centers of learning that were producing books, displaying the cultural and literary heritage of the respective sponsor's state. It is likely that Lü Buwei sought to compile a viable handbook on the arts of rulership that could serve as curriculum in his role as court tutor. Lü Buwei's business sense, his able planning, and his administrative abilities perhaps made him sensitive to the issue of "critical timing." The role of proper timing was certainly important in everyday affairs, trade, agriculture, and warfare. Lü Buwei's sensitivity is not only seen in the fact that the LSCQ was produced at a crucial time during the Warring States period, but also in the content and the formal structure of the LSCQ itself. A discussion of the character and structure of the LSCQ is required to grasp the importance of proper timing within its structure, its selective, consolidated philosophy, and the diverse but amalgamated approaches toward achieving social and political order.

Season Timing (*chunqiu*) and the Nature of the LSCQ

The LSCQ is a rather long and complex text. It contains more than 100,000 characters, nearly twice the size of the *Zhuangzi*, making it one of the largest texts of its day. It is composed of three "volumes," containing a total of 160 chapters. It can be described as an anthology with a unifying theme. Lü Buwei had the means to support literally thousands of guest scholars at his estate, and he called upon them to record whatever knowledge they had in order to compile the text known as *Master Lü's Spring and Autumn Annals*. Lü's guests came from various backgrounds, and hence their contributions touch upon a wide range of topics: political philosophy, geography, music, court ritual, medicine, history and legend, military arts, farming techniques, and so on. Overall, the work functions as a political handbook with the recurring image of unifying and ruling an empire.

The LSCQ's content is eclectic, that is, discriminating and selective, drawn from various sources but united in a unique manner, and not easily classified. In the dynastic histories, historians list the LSCQ under the bibliographical classification of *zajia* (unified eclectic "school" or unclassified literature—regrettably mistranslated as "miscellaneous"). The misunderstanding and depreciation of *zajia* as a bibliographical label led some scholars, such as A. Wylie and B. Watson, to discount the value and coherence of the LSCQ.[28] As a bibliographic category, *zajia* should not be understood to mean "miscellaneous."[29] As a bibliographic category *zajia* means "unclassifiable under standard headings," such as poetry, or *rujia* (Literati), *daojia* (Daoist), *Mojia* (Mohist), and so on.[30] The authors of the LSCQ borrowed material broadly from almost the entire pre-Qin corpus, making it unclassifiable under the standard headings. They unified, or consolidated and amalgamated, that composite material into an eclectic synthetic or syncretic philosophy. Thus the term *zajia* should be understood to have two different meanings. When *zajia* is used as a label for such texts as the *Shizi*, *Huainanzi*, or the LSCQ, then it should be understood to be a label used to denote "an eclectic unified approach to philosophy," that is, a distinctive philosophy drawn from various sources metamorphosized and amalgamated together.[31] Otherwise, as a bibliographical heading, *zajia* means "unclassifiable under the standard headings," such as poetry, history, and so on. When Liu Xiang implemented the *zajia* label in his bibliography, *Qilue*, also published in the *Hanshu*, he defined it as uniting the teachings of the *ru*, Literati, with the Mohists, and unifying the *mingjia* and the *fajia*, noting that this approach was used in the administration of the various states and was a necessary part in the art of rulership. The LSCQ unifies *rujia*, *Mojia*, *mingjia*, and *fajia*, and it blends in *daojia*, *yinyangjia*, *nongjia* (Agriculturalists), *bingjia* (Militarists), *xiaoshuojia* (small talk, or lesser [known] discussions), and *zonghengjia* (political strategy not classified under the other labels).[32]

The LSCQ is unquestionably eclectic, that is, selective, in its variety of sources and can be understood as a pastiche or montage of collated ideas, concepts, phrases, passages, and anthologized chapters, but the text does exhibit cohesiveness. The diverse contents are combined into a practical approach concerned with proper timing for the art of rulership. Although the LSCQ may lack a clear logical structure across the diversity of chapters and its three volumes, nevertheless it evidences a kind of coherence because the congruity is aesthetic as well as theoretical, dependent in important measure upon image, metaphor, allusion, rhetorical effect, and seasonal or timely placement in addition to discursive and expository treatises. Complementing the rhetoric, an expository style is developed in the LSCQ that is uncommon for many pre-Qin works, and various types of logical arguments are employed. This coherence is peculiar in that, in the absence of a clearly demarcated theory/praxis distinction and under the sway of proper timing as a central concern, seemingly inconsistent positions can be juxtaposed without necessarily violating the integrity or coherence of the text. Said simply, where proper timing is a factor in correctly managing the kingdom, it can mediate and render coherent opposing positions that would otherwise be incompatible. This model of coherence is apparent in the title of the work and its tripartite structure.

The title *Lüshi chunqiu* is composed of two parts: the first part, Lüshi, denotes the sponsor, the Lü clan estate (because the expression "the Lü clan" is awkward, and "Mister Lü" is anachronistic, I render Lüshi as "Master Lü," in the sense of a master or lord of the manor, not a philosophical master or *zi*). The second part, *chunqiu*, emulates and rivals other state's records, especially the ever-popular *Chunqiu* (*Spring and Autumn Annals*) of the state of Lu, denoting that the text is an important historical record for practicing virtuous rulership. The state of Lu, located in the southwestern part of what is now Shantung province, was noted as a cultural center of the Zhou dynasty, especially because it was the home of Kongzi (Confucius). The historical annals for the state of Lu were recorded by the state historians on a seasonal basis: spring, summer, autumn, and winter. In fact, it was common for all of the states to have monthly annals called *Chunqiu*.

The expression *chunqiu* ("spring and autumn") denotes the whole year—pivotal agricultural and administrative activities occur during these seasons—and as such, *chunqiu* became a shorthand title for "state histories," especially that of the state of Lu and, by extension the name for the era from 722–481, which the state of Lu records cover. Because these seasonal chronicles recorded the timely and untimely behavior, and the policies of the rulers and statesmen, *chunqiu* came to mean a "moral critique." Along these lines, the *Spring and Autumn Annals* of the state of Lu was given an ethical interpretation in the famous *Zuozhuan commentary*. Regardless of Kongzi's (Confucius') actual role in the preparation of the *Chunqiu*, the work became an important text for those who followed his teachings. In this context, *chunqiu* came to mean a comprehensive study of appropriate and timely actions for the achievement of social and political order. In imitation, this same purpose is pursued by the *Lüshi chunqiu* and the *Chunqiu fanlu*, which use the phrase *chunqiu* in their titles. The title *chunqiu* was used by later scholars who compiled the historical records of both states and statesmen, such as the *Yanzi chunqiu* and the *Wu Yue chunqiu*.

The *Chunqiu* of the state of Lu was studied as a historical model for initiating appropriate and timely administrative actions for social and political order. Likewise, the LSCQ provided a similar guide for the king of Qin. The LSCQ contains the monthly seasonal rituals (*chunqiu*) that an emperor requires. The *shierji* section is organized under lunar-monthly chapter headings. The LSCQ contains various descriptions of historical events with moral criticisms appended to the stories, constituting a didactic history. It typifies this genre of historical writing as a heuristic record replete with moral examples. This notion of history as moral example is a major factor in the *chunqiu* structure of the *Lüshi chunqiu*.

Both the title of the LSCQ and its tripartite structure disclose a concern for proper timing. The "spring and autumn" (*chunqiu*) part of the title of *Lüshi chunqiu* is probably derived from the *shierji*, the first of the extant three volumes in the received redactions, because it gives the most explicit concern for administering social and political order within the confines of the seasonal cycles (*chunqiu*) of the year. The LSCQ is composed of three volumes or books: *shierji* (Twelve Chronicles), *balan* (Eight References), and *lulun* (Six Discussions). D. C. Lau proposes the possibility that these three volumes are separate attempts to prepare a manuscript for Lü Buwei, which were finally put together to constitute the work, the LSCQ.[33] This helps account for the apparent lack of continuity and transition among the three separate volumes. However, it does not help explain the apparent interrelated numerical arrangement of the three volumes, or why there is not far more repetition.

The first volume is known as the *shierji*, the Twelve Chronicles, or more appropriately the Chronicles of Rulership for the Twelve Lunar-Months of the Year. The *shierji* is divided into twelve monthly sections, three months for each season, and each "month" is subdivided into five chapters. That is, the four seasons are divided into three-month periods—for example, early, middle, and late spring, and so forth, totaling twelve months—which are subdivided into one chapter directing the ritual for the month and an additional four (weekly) chapters, which loosely guide the attitude and intellect of the ruler and ministers, yielding a total of sixty chapters. The twelve opening chapters of each monthly section constitute the *yueling* (Monthly Commands) chapter of the *Liji* (*Book of Rites*).[34] These opening chapters present a general aesthetic guideline for the monthly rituals. This aesthetic order of the rites provides a coherence for the subsequent chapters falling under that "month," so that the structure of the *shierji* (Twelve Chronicles) taken as a whole cannot be understood without reference to the paramount concern for proper timing in administrative activities, especially planting, weeding, and harvesting, education, the self-cultivation of the ruler and ministers, military matters, funeral rites, and other such affairs of court.[35]

It is the programmatic concern for proper timing that lends coherence to the opposing philosophies contained in the LSCQ. The concern for timing has been overlooked by those scholars, who propose that the LSCQ is only an encyclopedic collection of contradictory material.[36] From a quick synopsis of the *shierji* chapters, one is left with the impression that the material under the spring season is generally *daojia*, life affirmative, and considered an extant source of Yang Zhu's thought; the autumn material is chiefly military arts, or *bingjia*; the summer chapters deal with *rujia* subjects, such as ritual music and education; the winter chapters discuss Mohist frugal funerals and *fajia* administrative policy. Argumentative and rhetorical style, that is, concerns of the *mingjia* (so-called school of names), is evident in all of the chapters, and some *nongjia* (Agriculturalist), and *yinyang wuxing* (five phases) ideas are expressed in the monthly ritual chapters. This is just a general overview. There is some mixture of various materials and quotations from the various teachers or their works throughout the respective sections; notably, there is a Mohist chapter in the spring section. This overview does capture, in part, what can be called the standard of extrinsic timing—the more rigid formulation where policy is altered and philosophy is applied according to the changing seasons.

In the second chapter of the late summer section, entitled *yinlü* (Tones of the Twelve Pipes), the correspondences between the months of the year and the pitch pipes are given. In the concluding passage of that chapter, the ruler is provided with a guide on which administrative policy to institute during the months correlated with the respective pitch pipes. Musical harmony is employed as a model for correlating the seasons and political policy. For example, the text states that:

> In the month corresponding to the *jiazhong* pipe, the second month, the active energy tends to be encompassing, plentiful, harmonious, and equally distributed. The ruler should practice being generous of virtue, and put aside criminal punishments; never initiate affairs to harm any living creature.
>
> In . . . the sixth month, the plant life is thick and flourishing, and the passive [energy] for the first time will begin to push its destruction of life (*xing* lit. punishment).
>
> In the month corresponding to the *yize* pipe, the seventh month, the ruler should organize judicial standards and strengthen criminal punishments; he should select soldiers and sharpen the weapons, preparing for war. During this month he should interrogate and punish those who were unjust so as to appease those who live in the far off corners of the state.[37]

This passage displays an extrinsic model of timely action where policy is made to correspond to the seasonal changes of the year, and it is informed by an intrinsic timing of musical harmony. When policy is shaped according to proper timing, there is no preassigned controlling principle of unity, but rather there is an aesthetic sense of coherence that emerges out of the context. There is an extrinsic timing that matches the season and an intrinsic timing that allows for improvisation. This reflects back on the character of the text as a whole. The text incorporates a diversity of teachings that might appear to be inconsistent with each other, especially if practiced simultaneously. But when considered from a temporalized perspective, where different times require different programs, the amalgamated array of material and the various views and policies contained in the LSCQ can be construed as having a different order of coherence. My point is that temporality extends the possibilities of coherence and, to some degree, ameliorates differences.

The second volume of the LSCQ, the *balan*, Eight References or Eight Panoramic Views, is composed of eight sections with eight chapters each (minus one chapter).[38] Because Sima Qian's description of the LSCQ begins by mentioning the *balan*, it is thought that the original text opened with it.[39] When Chinese scholars abbreviate the title of the LSCQ, they call it *Lülan*. Although the significance of proper timing is not as apparent in the structure of the *balan* the way it is in the seasonal arrangement of the *shierji*, the role and function of administering social and political policy in a timely fashion are addressed in various chapters of the *balan*. The opening *lan* begins with a chapter titled *youshi* (There Was a Beginning). Although the chapter is chiefly devoted to cosmological and geological speculations, it is concerned with the temporal "inception" of cosmic order that maintains a link with the other volumes, in that each volume begins with a temporal "source" or initiating. That is, the spring season opens the *shierji*; the *youshi* (There Was a Beginning) chapter initiates the *balan* section, and the *kaichun* (Opening Spring) chapter begins the *lulun* section. Though cosmogonic speculation was dawning in the late pre-Qin period, nevertheless we must remain sensitive to the traditional organic "self-so" (*ziran*) cosmology, where particulars co-create each other in a natural field of *tian* or *dao*. The *youshi* chapter is concerned with a cosmology of particular places, not cosmogonic origins. The character *shi*, "to begin," is a cognate with *tai*, "the pregnant womb," suggesting *creatio ab initio* rather than *ex nihilo*; that is, this being a heuristic model, one should imagine a spiral cycle, not a closed circle, an emergent beginning in the midst of an ongoing process, such as spring beginning again. The *balan* volume discusses various topics relevant to maintaining social and political order. In addition to various references to proper timing spread throughout the *balan*, there are two chapters entirely devoted to that topic, namely, the *shoushi* (Awaiting the Right Time) and the *yuhe* (Opportunities for Meeting). These are discussed in detail in Chapter 4.

The role of timing is more apparent in the structure of the third volume, which opens with a chapter titled *kaichun* (Opening Spring). The third volume is composed of six sections, called *lulun* (or *liulun*, Six Discussions), consisting of six chapters each. Since the *lulun* is chiefly concerned with techniques for farming, it naturally makes frequent reference to seasonal activity. Without timely management of affairs, the planting, growing, and harvesting of crops would be a disaster. Like the *shierji*, the *lulun* begins with a chapter discussing the significance of starting things properly in the spring. The final chapter of the *lulun*, entitled *chashi* (Examining Seasonality), discusses in detail the seasonal factors to be considered in planting, caring for, and harvesting the various grains to obtain a bountiful and nutritious crop.

Despite the numerical and temporal organization of the LSCQ, its eclectic, consolidated approach to diverse topics has made it difficult to interpret. Some scholars have raised a number of significant criticisms against the LSCQ. There are features that challenge any presumption that it has integrity as a text. It is possible to argue one or more of the following positions, namely, that: (1) the three volumes or "books" that compose the LSCQ have no relation to each other; (2) the contents of the three respective volumes seem randomly organized, probably due to its many authors; (3) the chapter titles are ambiguous or have no relationship to a chapter's content; and (4) the three volumes lack internal consistency, as do a number of chapters. That is, the text in whole and in part is unsystematic and unrelated. Although it would be a time-consuming, trivial exercise to explain the significance of every ambiguous chapter title in relation to its content, especially since the LSCQ, like all ancient texts, has surely suffered from copiers' errors and the corruptions of time, nevertheless, the reader may take note that in the ensuing chapters in this book the passages cited from the LSCQ do bear a relationship to their respective chapter titles, and that there is a good deal of internal consistency within the subsections of the LSCQ. Burton Watson holds a modified position that the three volumes reveal a formal structure, but this structure is only carried out in the content of the *shierji*.[40]

In spite of these legitimate concerns, there is evidence to allow for a degree of coherence within the text. Central to the structure and content of the LSCQ is the concern for timely action and the articulation of timing in social and political policy. In an important sense, the LSCQ lacks the systematicity of a conventional Western text in that it does not develop one central unifying theme in a discursive, logical manner. But perhaps the requirement for a work to be linear and systematic in the development of its thesis is a culture specific bias. An anthology is not expected to be directed by only one theme, and the LSCQ is an anthology. It is too simple to dismiss the LSCQ as a mere hodgepodge of materials, lacking any logical structure. It does not have an imposed structure. Rather, the architecture of the text is emergent, correlating the specific content with temporal context. The content of any chapter, or even the work as a whole, must be viewed from the perspective of attempting to affect social and political order in a world that is constantly changing, in a pluralistic society comprised of various ethnic groups with life plans and life styles whose members are assumed to have no universalizable human nature that guarantees commensurate conduct. At yet another level, the meaning of the content and the text depend on the reader's own cultural and historical setting. Beginning from the presumption of the actual diversity of human life and the cosmic transformations that attend it, the LSCQ as a political handbook contains material advocating that administrative affairs be conducted with appropriateness and proper timing. The numerical structure of the chapters further emphasizes the temporal harmony of heaven, earth, and human beings as each volume of the LSCQ acts as a kind of "almanac" or "clock" for gaging action.[41]

The LSCQ's Impact

The LSCQ undoubtedly influenced the young King Zheng and his adoption of the *yinyang wuxing* symbols of water and LSCQ's justification for the overthrow of dynasties in establishing the Qin empire. The impact of the LSCQ on subsequent East Asian history, philosophy, and literature cannot be underestimated.

The LSCQ played an important role in structuring the administrative and political arrangements of the Qin dynasty (221–206). Though it was short lived, the Qin unification laid the foundation for the Han dynasty (206 B.C.E.–220 C.E.) and thereby all subsequent dynasties. The political and legal structure of the Han owes much to the Qin, and the ritual orientation of the Han court is borrowed from the same material that is included in the leading chapters of the *shierji*, namely, the "monthly commands." Those chapters impact later Daoist ritual. The proposal for maintaining political order through ritual that integrates the emperor on cosmic, social, legal, and moral levels set a program for the rulers and ministers of the Han. Xu Fuguan has shown, in his three volumes on Han intellectual history, how the LSCQ influenced Han scholarship and politics.[42] The political organization of the Han dynasty served "Chinese" culture for more than 2,000 years, laying the organizational structure for the subsequent dynastic institutions.

Whether the writers of the LSCQ actually wrote the "monthly commands" chapters of the *shierji* or only borrowed them from another source to structure the chapters of the *shierji* is a question that cannot be definitely answered at this time. Because it is a question of historical origins, it is not relevant to the impact of the LSCQ on subsequent intellectual history. The fact is that the LSCQ contains the earliest extant source of the "monthly commands" material, assuming that the *yueling* (Monthly Commands) chapter of the *Liji* is extracted from the LSCQ. The *Liji* is commonly understood to have been anthologized in the Han. The *Huainanzi*'s *shize* (Seasonal Patterns) chapter basically contains the same material. Because of its impact on Han court ritual, the "monthly commands" material was guaranteed a place in subsequent imperial ritual. Later approaches to self-cultivation, ritual, and even magic in Tang, Song, Ming *lixue* (so-called Neo-Confucianism), *xuanxue* (studies in profundity in later Daoism), and Daoist religion all have their roots in Han practices and in the cosmological reflections contained in the LSCQ. Notably, the imperial courtly pursuit of seasonal ritual and the practice of assigning auspicious names to the reign periods show a basic concern both to accord with the seasons, and to strive to constitute the appropriate time. The rituals of liturgical Daoism possess this concern for mutually interrelated, timely, seasonal activity and proper timing in ritual performance. Many of the rituals of early liturgical Daoism are based on the seasonal program of court ritual.[43]

Not only did the unified eclectic social and political thought contained in the LSCQ have a major impact on Qin and Han philosophy, but it also played an important role in setting the genre of early Han literature. Its amalgamated eclecticism influenced Dong Zhongshu (179–104 B.C.E.) and Prince Huainan,

Liu An (ca. 179–122 B.C.E.). Dong Zhongshu's *Chunqiu fanlu* is more like the LSCQ in that both of these works sponsor a centralized political structure, celebrating unity in the face of diversity. Although Liu An's *Huainanzi* borrows much from the LSCQ and owes much to its syncretic approach, nevertheless the *Huainanzi* advocates a decentralized political structure, celebrating diversity in the face of unity. The LSCQ was considered important enough that Gao You (fl. 205–212 C.E.), a late Han scholar, wrote a commentary for it and other important works such as the *Huainanzi*. After the Han dynasty, the LSCQ was often used as a citation in commentaries, especially Li Shan's (d. 689 C.E.) *Wenxuanzhu* (*Commentary on the Anthology of Literature*) and dynastic encyclopedias, such as Li Fang's (925–996 C.E.) *Taiping yulan* (*Imperially Reviewed Encyclopedia of the Taiping Era*).

The genealogy of our present editions of the *Lüshi chunqiu* traces their redactions back to the Song and Yuan dynasties. It was chiefly due to philological concerns among Qing dynasty scholars that interest was revived in the LSCQ, and now this revival has stimulated a number of Chinese, Japanese, and Western scholars to advance the study of this historically significant text.

The Mythification of History

It has been a common practice in the Euro-American tradition to attempt a reconstruction of ancient cultures through the study of mythology.[44] The generally received interpretation proposes that archaic Chinese cultures developed along similar lines as Indo-European culture, from mythology to philosophy.[45] Archaic Shang and Zhou religio-philosophy is based on the veneration of historical clan ancestors. Systematic *myths* begin to emerge late in the pre-Qin period, culminating in the Han dynasty. Chinese cultures develop in their own ways, distinct from Indo-European cultures.[46]

The received interpretation concerning the development of Indo-European cultures and philosophy is that they developed highly rational, historical, and naturalistic worldviews after moving through different forms of religion and more "primitive" modes of expression, for example, myth, magic, nature worship, and so on. Giambattista Vico began the division of history into three parts, borrowing from an ancient Egyptian model of the three ages, namely, the age of the gods, heros, and humans.[47] G.W.F. Hegel employs this general scheme in his historical dialectic of Absolute Spirit where it develops through art, is negated by religion, and is finally realized in philosophy. Max Müller develops the nature worship theory, which offers an empirical basis through the interpretation of ancient mythology and language to support the claim that "primitive religion" arose out of people's confrontation with a hostile environment. Human fear and respect for the elements develop into a system of nature worship, which in time deifies the forces of nature. This polytheism is revealed in the mythology and ritual of "primitive religion," so that the religion is further rationalized into what Müller called a henotheism; that is, "a king/father god" dominates the polytheistic pantheon—either at different seasonal rites or over periods in the historical development of the mythic literature. Through higher levels of abstraction, monotheism comes into practice. With further advances in reason, monotheism transforms into monism, and philosophy is born. Müller's analysis certainly has explanatory force for the general development of religio-philosophy found in the *Vedas* and the *Upanishads*. It can be applied to the development of Babylonian, Egyptian, Ionian, and Roman culture, and to philosophy as well. Francis M. Cornford and others attribute the birth of Ionian philosophy to Thales, because he sought a naturalistic interpretation of the world that opposed the traditional religio-mythical appeal to supernatural forces or gods. Setting aside the question of the adequacy of this "rationalization" of pre-Socratic philosophy, there has been a general tendency in cross-cultural and historical studies to export these universal indexicals and to see all civilizations as being dependent on a universal or transcendent principle. When such principles are not readily apparent in other cultures, they are "excavated" or constructed by implication to justify and lend credence to claims that another culture is in fact civilized.

The peculiar and even ironic consideration is that this received interpretation of the development of culture and philosophy is heavily influenced by the archaic, mythological worldview that it attempts to explain. Two recurring features of the myths, from the Indus River to the Tiber, are a cosmogony establishing a purpose (*telos*) for that culture, and the assumption of the universality of the traditional myth. If other peoples lack similar myths, it is an indication of their primitive, uncultured, or maybe even nonhuman status. Note that the received historical interpretation harbors implicit teleology in proposing that rational philosophy develops after religion and its primitive superstitious origins in mythical explanation. The modern interpreters of the past, like the ancient myths, attempt to reconstruct the "origin" of our world of philosophy and science in the cosmogonic myths. The received interpretation is believed to have universal application to cultures or at least to all "developed" cultures. Although the general pattern of progress from myth to philosophy appears to fit the archaic traditions of Persia, India, and the Mediterranean, it does not follow that all archaic cultures display similar developments, as Max Müller,

Carl Jung, Mircea Eliade, Derk Bodde, and others propose. *Contra* such generalizations, Clifford Geertz argues that universalism, especially structuralism, leads to cultural arrogance.[48] John S. Mbiti argues against the ethnocentric assumptions in Western academic theories, which attempt to account for the origin of religion and philosophy, because such theories assume that the West is a higher culture, while the so-called Third World nations are still at the mythological, "primitive" stage.[49]

The evolutionary approach "from myth through religion to philosophy" has wide appeal among academics, and Chinese and non-Chinese Sinologists adopt it to explain the development of archaic China. The earliest Shang records and objects of material culture are devoid of any complex mythology or even individual systematic myths. Cosmogonic myths are certainly absent.[50] This inconvenient lack of systematic myth, however, has not prevented scholars from speculating that an archaic mythology existed before the extant ancient literature historicized and humanized the ancient gods.[51] Derk Bodde claims that the ancient "Chinese" myths and gods are different from the post-classical ones in that the ancient tradition lacks a developed "systematic mythology," and the individual myths are very "fragmentary and episodic."[52] He warns against concluding that there were no myths in ancient China. China's ancient history and myths exhibit euhemerization. Bodde turns the process of euhemerization on its head to account for the absence of early archaic myths and for the presence of what he claims are "historicized" and "humanized" accounts of the clan ancestors.[53] Bodde quotes Henri Maspero, who also reverses euhemerization.[54] This approach is unacceptable, distorting the interpretation of pre-Qin culture and thought.

Bodde criticizes Bernhard Karlgren who argues that the Zhou literature praises the ancients because of their ancestral heritage. The ancient sage emperors were clan ancestors, not gods or demigods. Karlgren advocates the conventional understanding of euhemerization as an evolution from actual events and persons to mythological explanation, correctly explaining the extant literature of ancient China. The predominant "this-worldly" perspective, along with the organic worldview and the overwhelming concern for historical records, suggests that archaic Shang and Zhou culture heros were most likely actual historical ancestors, or composites of the ancient lineage.

From the archaeological discoveries of the archaic Shang and Zhou material culture—the sacrificial vessels and oracle bones—and their extant literature, there is a stronger case to be made for an "ancestor veneration" basis for Shang and Zhou religio-philosophy. The development of Zhou culture presents the possibility that systematic myth could develop as a cultural response after people lose their common roots in a shared ancestry, and so the various clans seek a common purpose in systematizing their once-disparate clan histories—the myths attempt to make these people children of the same culture hero, rather than their respective traditional ancestors. Hence with the destruction of the feudal lords of the Zhou, the destruction of the ancestral lineages and ancestral temples, the Han peoples developed mythology.

For the study of ancient China, archaeology provides fertile ground for reconstructing the tradition. In the archaic Shang dynasty, the two predominant objects of material culture—the oracle bones and the bronze sacrificial vessels—reveal that the Shang royal family's socio-spiritual concerns focused on ancestor veneration. The oracle bones were primarily used to contact deceased emperors, ancestors of the royal family, to petition them concerning weather conditions, prospects for the hunt, military campaigns, impending dangers, especially attacks at night, and sickness.[55] The bones were used to keep records, and the excavation of a Shang bone "library" confirmed the traditional lineage of the Shang rulers given in the *Shiji*, which was compiled much later in the early Han dynasty, showing the accuracy of later historical consciousness, especially concerning ancestral/dynastic lineage.

What we have in the archaic Shang is evidence of a royal family ancestor cult, where the deceased emperor is the composite embodiment of the dynastic lineage and viable heritage, and the ancestors are not beyond this world. They reside among the living and are contacted and revered through the rites and oracles. Sarah Allan and Emily Ahern argue that Chinese gods are actually deceased people.[56] With increased and more complex economic and military contacts with other peoples, the historical, this-worldly perspective of the Shang was modified in the Zhou with a plurality of ancestral lineages, possibly drawing on the various clan ancestor cults. Although the culture heros, Yao, Shun, Yu, and Tang, are described as superhuman and inventing the artifacts of culture, they and their accomplishments are presented as natural historical events. The extant literature shows that actual, not reverse, euhemerization was an ongoing process. Culture heros and actual ancestors are mythologized and deified, especially, after the fall of the grantee houses of Zhou.[57]

Mircea Eliade disregards the possibility that euhemerization or "mythicization of historical personages" might account for the development of archaic myth, even though he acknowledges that this process is at work in modern Yugoslavian epic.[58] Douglas K. Wood provides an example from Nikolai Berdyaev's understanding of the philosophy of history concerning the mythification of history, claiming that history is mythology, not objective empirical science.[59] For Berdyaev, we must examine both the religio-philosophical assumptions and the mythification of history to understand a philosophy of history. The "mythicization" of history is crucial in understanding the archaic Shang conception of time.

Against Eliade's "universalism," the pre-Qin conception of time (*shi*) is not tied to static ontology concerned with returning to the cosmogonic beginnings. For the majority of pre-Qin thinkers, time plays a crucial role in their understanding of the dynamic, process cosmology, so that reality or any thing is only realized through its co-creative temporal relationships. Time is not a mere container of events but is instead "the critical time" that makes or breaks the constituting factors of a situation. For many pre-Qin philosophers, time is socially constructed. In this sense, time is ontological and cosmological. Time concerns the existential nature of things.

Chapter 2

The LSCQ's Programmatic Conceptions of *Xing*: Cultivating Desires in the Process of Life

The nature and orientation of the LSCQ as an art of rulership text explicated in this chapter examine how its unified eclectic philosophy presents significant concepts such as *xing* 性 (*hsing*) and its concomitant concept, *ming* 命.[1] *Xing* conventionally rendered as "human nature," I translate as "human character" or "characteristics," because "human nature" carries metaphysical baggage not contained in pre-Qin philosophy. Although *ming* usually means "mandate," or "edict," it can denote something similar to "fate." In relation to *xing*, *ming* means "the conditions of life," and so I translate it as "natural relations" or "decreed conditions" of life. The temporal orientation of the LSCQ, especially in the *shierji* section, impacts significantly both the achievement conceptions of human character (*xing*) and the methods to maintain social and political order. Human character and political order are developed and preserved by employing proper timing.

Responsible policy for maintaining social and political order is generally based upon some interpretation of the meaning of human life. The *shiwei* (Appropriately Displaying Majesty) chapter of the LSCQ alludes to the need, after converting disorder, to discuss human character in developing a program for social and political order.[2] Presumably, a well-ordered society facilitates the fulfillment of human desires and tendencies—both the physical and sensual desires and the cultural tendency for person making and maturity. Many of the diverse political philosophies contained in the LSCQ have these concerns too. Most political philosophies are based on some conception of human possibilities and self-realization in developing their respective proposals for a well-ordered society.

The LSCQ contains various conceptions of human character and different viewpoints on the possibilities of self-realization achievable through the temporal context of social and political order. The LSCQ's teachings presuppose that human character undergoes a developmental process, accommodating an ever-changing environment. For many pre-Qin texts, people are *sui generis*. Hence humanity is not defined in terms of a universal nature but rather person making is illuminated temporally in a nomenclature of historical characteristics such as virtue and psychological tendencies such as likes and dislikes.

In contrast to the Parmenidean, Platonic, and Christian response to change as the contingent, less real, evil, and chaotic, the principal pre-Qin thinkers, such as Kongzi (K'ung Tzu, Confucius), Mozi (Mo Tzu), and Zhuangzi (Chuang Tzu), celebrate change, especially growth and maturity, as the root of all enjoyment and the natural, harmonious balance of life. Promoting these dominant cultural trends, the LSCQ's consolidated material acknowledges that the world is constituted through complex processes of change and transformation. Those processes are presented in terms of a network of correlative bipolar interpenetrating forces. An amalgamated yinyang five phases (*wuxing*) cosmology is blended into various chapters of the LSCQ, especially the lead chapters of the *shierji* that were appropriated by the Literati (Confucians) in the *Liji's yueling* (Monthly Commands) chapter. We can explicate the LSCQ's various conceptions of human character and appreciate their impact on its social and political theories and policies.

The contemporary philosopher, Tang Junyi (T'ang Chün-yi), proposes that change is the natural condition of human character, identifying creative transformation as the most sublime feature of human character. Tang Junyi acknowledges that, in reference to inanimate objects, *xing* refers to seemingly fixed properties, or propensities, but human character may undergo "boundless change."[3] Roger T. Ames comments that "*[x]ing* . . . denotes a human capacity for radical changeability that is qualitatively productive."[4] It is not an overgeneralization to conclude that pre-Qin philosophers maintain that human character is an achievement in process.

This process orientation leads many pre-Qin thinkers to espouse a unity of correlative opposites, so that humans and nature become one. The interpenetration and integration of self and the myriad things are expressed by both Mengzi and Zhuangzi:

> Mengzi said: "The myriad things are here in me." (*Mengzi*, 51/7 A/4).

> Heaven and Earth were born with me, and the myriad things are one with me. (*Zhuangzi*, 5/2/52–53).

This interpenetration of nature and oneself gave rise to the expression *tianren heyi* (nature and humans harmonize as one), signifying nonduality. Humans and nature are mutually defining through the co-dependent interaction of nature influencing human life and people altering nature through labor, agriculture, warfare, ritual, and so forth. What binds the correlativity of people and their world is *ming*—the natural relationships one is situated in which influence the processes of one's life. Tang Junyi identifies *ming* as the "interrelationship or mutual relatedness of Heaven, that is, nature, and man."[5] Tang stresses the nonduality or unity of nature and people.[6]

If we take this correlativity of *tian* (heaven or nature) and *renxing* (human character) as our guideline, then character (*xing*) can be expressed in terms of one's natural environment (*tian*), and the environment can be described anthropomorphically by appeal to humans.[7] This nondual relationship is captured in the *Zhongyong* expression: *tianming zhiwei xing*—"the natural condition of life is what is meant by human character."[8] That "human character is interdependent with nature" is often overlooked in discussions of *xing*. Passages from the LSCQ and its earliest commentator, Gao You, both recognize the mutual relationship of *tian* and *xing*. The *zunshi* (On Venerating the Teacher) chapter employs the expression *tian xing* (natural character).[9] Gao You's commentary defines *tian* (nature) in some contexts to mean *xing* (character).[10] The correlativity of humans and nature means that *xing* is the dynamic process of human development.[11] Because neither nature nor humans can constitute one's *xing* alone, it should *not* be thought of as a fixed, pregiven structure or form, but rather it is "received" by people in that each person is born into an ongoing environmental process from which one appropriates one's condition. The term *character* is not intended to connote any type of potentiality, or pregiven substance; it is used to highlight the *process* and developmental aspect of human life. This process perspective of *xing* 性 is rooted in its phonetic element *sheng* 生 which means "to give birth to," "to raise," or "the process of life."[12] D. C. Lau argues that the two traditional interpretations of *xing* pivot around the weight assigned to the radical or phonetic of the character *xing*.[13] The traditional interpretation focuses on the "heart-mind" radical (*xin*) as the human discursive moral ability, where the modern conviction beginning with Fu Sinian stresses the phonetic "life" (*sheng*) and reads *xing* as a developmental process.[14] Both interpretations have their shortcomings. Most contemporary espousers of them fall into some model of innateness or essentialism.[15]

In some chapters of the LSCQ, we find expressions such as *xing* is "received from" or "bestowed by" *tian*.[16] These expressions emphasize that human character is a correlative concept that must be understood in terms of its relation to nature. We find statements to the effect that people cannot "alter" or produce *xing*.[17] To say that humans cannot make or alter their character (*xing*) is not to contend that it is fixed or predetermined; rather, it means that people are limited to working with and refining the conditions and circumstances that are co-dependent on nature, cultural history, and personal characteristics. Although many of the chapters of the LSCQ present a programmatic conception of *xing* as an achievement, we can expect to find some passages that highlight contrasting views to this position, focusing on the environmentally dependent aspect of life.

The LSCQ's Seasonal Arrangement of Traditional Theories on *Xing*

The LSCQ is an anthology and a handbook for guidance in the art of rulership. The *shierji* section is organized according to the four seasons. Its chapters are correlated with the seasons so that they could be consulted on a monthly and weekly basis. That the LSCQ is arranged as a book of counsel is an important aspect that cannot be overlooked. For the LSCQ, the intended audience is understood to be the ruler and the ministers who require wisdom regarding how to rule and when to institute a specific type of policy, perform a ritual, or take action on state matters. The LSCQ, especially the *shierji*, is arranged to provide seasonal, timely advice; in a sense, it is similar to an almanac, but it lacks a daily calendar. Keeping the imperial frame of reference in mind, let us approach the LSCQ with the question: what is the appropriate relationship between human character (*xing*) and the art of ruling a well-ordered, chiefly agrarian society?

Examining the *shierji*, a discernable pattern begins to emerge. First, the leading "monthly ordinance" chapter sets the general topic in a flaccid manner for the subsequent four chapters given under each lunar month of the four seasons. For example, the *shierji* opens with the monthly ordinance for early spring, which is followed by four chapters describing how a ruler develops an impartial attitude toward promoting life. Second, there are noteworthy correlations between the seasons and the major philosophies of that era. In the spring section, we find *daojia*, mostly Yang Zhu, Huanglao, and Laozhuang,[18] and other materials that affirm the seasonal policy presented in the "monthly ordinance" chapters, focusing on "cultivation," especially the ruler's self-cultivation.[19] In the summer, we find predominately *rujia*, masters of rituals, and Xunzi style discussions on court music, and respect for one's teacher. The autumn section is chiefly concerned with military matters. The winter section elaborately discusses frugal funerals in the Mohist vein and other administrative topics in a *fajia* tone. The cultivation of human character is discussed under each season.

Proper timing is the ruler's primary concern in conducting affairs of state. Following the seasonal model, the ruler has a general guide for the performance of timely actions. The Shang and Zhou conception of "time" should be heuristically represented as a bipolar spiral to capture the continuous ongoing processes of change along with the cycles of the seasons. The climatic conditions of any season will vary, and the capable ruler can prevent what is untimely. The ruler's success in achieving social and political order is measured by the ability to not only respond in a timely fashion, but also to creatively articulate the season by orchestrating the masses and the myriad things. The ruler creates a climate for social and political harmony.

It is especially futile to classify the LSCQ under a single orientation of thought, because it borrows from the various teachings and seeks to harmonize them under a seasonal program. Although the LSCQ appears to have one very general theme, namely, its writers want to give advice concerning proper timing in the art of rulership, one must be wary of attributing an overarching systematic focus to the text. For example, take the contrast between Hu Shi's classification of the LSCQ's political philosophy as "utilitarian" and the advice given to the ruler in the *zhongji* chapter. Hu Shi argues that the LSCQ subscribes to a type of utilitarianism.

> The political thought of the LSCQ is based on a naturalism of "modeling heaven and earth." It fully developed the thought of venerating the process of life; it emphasized the essential desires to establish a type of utilitarian (*aili zhuyi*) political philosophy.[20]

Hu Shi contends that the LSCQ holds a Xunzi-like position, grounding political order in the fulfillment of human desire. The Mohists and Daoists emphasize *wuyu* (being without desires). The Literati, Xunzi in particular, advocate fulfilling human desires through social organization. The desire for attaining happiness, goods, or benefit underlies any type of utilitarianism. Hu Shi highlights a predominant motif in the LSCQ's consolidated political thought. The programmatic conception of achieving a refined character is rooted in a predominantly foci-field perspective in which human society and political order are derived from the fulfillment of human desires, and the political order is designed to fulfill human appetites.[21] Hu Shi's interpretation is based on chapters in the *lisilan*. Important as those chapters are, there are other positions represented in the text.

The *zhongji* (Emphasis on Oneself) chapter, from the early spring section, proposes a different approach to cultivating desire. The *zhongji* chapter counsels the ruler on how to fulfill one's own life and maturing character by examining the psychological point that people are biased to prefer what will immediately fulfill their livelihood.

> Chui was a man of utmost dexterity. People do not prefer Chui's fingers, but rather they prefer their own fingers. This is because they gain benefit by possessing them. People do not prefer the jade of Mount Kun, nor the pearls of the Jiang (Yangzi) and the Han rivers, but rather they prefer their own grey jadeite and tiny pearls. This is because they benefit by possessing them.
>
> Now my life is my possession, and it benefits me greatly indeed. In assessing what is honored or base even the position of the Son of Heaven is inadequate to compare with this. In assessing what is heavy or light even the wealth of possessing the whole empire cannot replace it. In assessing safety and risk, if you lose it one morning, till the end of your days you can never regain it. The above three cases are what those who possess the Way consider seriously. There are those who consider it carefully, but on the contrary they harm it (life). This is because they did not penetrate into the depths of the reality of their character and natural relations (*xingming zhi qing*). Not penetrating into the depths of the reality of your character and natural relations, no matter how seriously you consider it, what is the advantage?![22]

Hu Shi cites material that portrays the ruler employing the masses by manipulating their desires. The *zhongji* chapter points out that human desire, to a certain extent, cannot be manipulated. In the *weiyu* (Constituting Desires) chapter, it is assumed that the masses desire the position of the Son of Heaven as the most worthy and the empire as the greatest wealth, but in the *zhongji* chapter, the ruler should recognize that his own life is more important than possessing the empire. The adept ruler must change policies with the seasons. Under the spring section, the ruler, in Daoist-like fashion, is psychologically detached from affairs of state. In selecting personnel in the winter months, the ruler adopts an administrative *fajia*-like attitude and finds ministers who are willing to die in service to the state.

There is an emergent coherence that arises from this seasonal approach for classifying various social and political theories. If one can accept that there are patterns or "periods" in both individual and social development, maturation, and decay, then one wants to ascertain these different patterns and the means to properly respond to them. The seasonal arrangement of the *shierji* presents both a determinative, extrinsic model of seasonal change, requiring human responses, and a nondirective, intrinsic model of integrity in articulating time through self-cultivation, the performance of court ritual, and promulgating edicts.

The Spring: A Daoist Conception of *Xing*

The LSCQ contains a wide variety of seemingly disparate perspectives on *xing*, but its writers did not seek to systematically combine them into a comprehensive theory. The LSCQ's composite chapters present various traditional pre-Qin views of *xing* not as comprehensive constructs for a science of humanity but rather as various examples of how people could behave and how a ruler can effectively deal with people under different conditions. The LSCQ's diverse stories and materials highlight the multifaceted aspects of human character and the wide potentialities that human behavior will admit. Out of this pastiche a programmatic conception of human character (*xing*) emerges. These various conceptions of *xing* are programmatic in that they approach human character not as a given but as an achievement. Much of the guidance given to the ruler by the LSCQ is directed toward the ruler's self-cultivation in areas especially considered crucial for maintaining social and political order.

The teachings of *daojia* are of special interest in the study of the LSCQ. Although it has been popular to interpret "Daoism" as a system of metaphysics or ontology, it is important to keep in mind the fact that Zhou dynasty *daojia*, especially Huanglao and Laozhuang, had a social and political orientation. Because the chapters of the LSCQ were consulted as a political handbook, they naturally focus on the more practicable social and political aspects of the *daojia* teachings. According to the *xuyi* (Postscript) of the LSCQ, the *shierji* is an attempt to implement the teachings of the Yellow Emperor (Huang Di).

> A worthy person asked about the meaning of the *shierji*. Lord Wenxin (Lü Buwei) replied: "I received the teachings which the Yellow Emperor instructed Zhuan Xu with—there is a great circle above; there is a great square below, and the one who is able to take them as standards can be the father and mother (i.e., the ruler) of the masses."[23]

This is an important aspect of Huanglao philosophy—the one who achieves and maintains the status of being a ruler does so by emulating the natural bipolar relationship of heaven and earth. The art of rulership presented in various chapters of the LSCQ is an emergent order orchestrated by the ruler conducting social and political policy according to the general tendencies responsive to the demands of the hierarchical yet correlative harmony of heaven/earth, yin/yang, circle/square, above/below, and ruler/subject.

The analysis of *xing*, which is introduced in the spring section of the LSCQ, is framed within the context of practicable Laozi and Zhuangzi techniques, such as *wuwei*, overriding gross self-interest with a spirit of detached impartiality, and preserving one's life and kingdom by avoiding indulgence of the senses and desires. Because the hermit Yang Zhu was concerned with the preservation of one's life, the *bensheng*, *zhongji* and *guisheng* chapters that discuss *yangsheng* (cultivating the fulfillment of life) are considered repositories of Yang Zhu-like material.

A Ruler who Complies with the *Dao*. The *Daodejing* sets the criteria for a sage ruler who complies with the *dao*:

> Only when one can manage the empire with the same attitude with which he respects himself can he be entrusted with the empire.
>
> Only when one can organize the empire with the same attitude with which he loves his own person can he be commissioned with the empire. (*Laozi* 13)

Passages such as this account for the general impracticality of Laozi's teaching, because the Daoist sage ruler who is entrusted with the empire must hold a high degree of personal integrity to orchestrate rulership. The impracticability is twofold: first, who can really achieve such a high degree of integrity; second, there is always the possibility that the orchestrator may not, in fact, be the person on the throne. The sage ruler may be a hermit who sets the empire in harmony. This is accomplished in typical Daoist fashion, without anyone taking special notice. The *renjianshi* (In the Human World) chapter of the *Zhuangzi* actually says as much: "By being inwardly direct, I can be a companion of nature. Being a companion of nature, I know that the Son of Heaven and I are equally the Son of Heaven."[24] The impracticality of this perspective is based on an overgeneralization. The sage ruler could be anyone, or everyone. Aside from the sage's own realization and personal integrity, no one else can say what a sage is to do. There are no practical procedures one can follow. Hence those LSCQ passages influenced by a Laozhuang aesthetic do not provide a "science" of order. Rather, they offer an "art" of rulership, outlining general approaches to ruling, requiring policies and procedures to be reconfigured and transformed to accommodate the uniqueness of the present situation.

A number of the LSCQ's spring chapters present clear cases of the Lao-zhuang sage ruler who possesses the empire without necessarily holding the throne. The LSCQ contains a good portion of *Zhuangzi* chapter 28, *rangwang* (On Abdicating the Throne). These passages reveal that the sage ruler who complies with the *dao* is an anarchist. This kind of anarchy does not propose a total abdication of rulership, though it rejects certain forms of "governance," especially coercive control.[25] Daoist anarchy promotes an aesthetic culinary approach to rulership—ruling as one cooks small fish (*Laozi* 60). The state does not coerce or command the masses. It is assumed that the people of an agrarian society will find a natural way to organize themselves without state intervention, and that the state best serves the people in an administrative function primarily in interstate and military affairs.

The LSCQ's *guisheng* (On Venerating the Process of Life) chapter is noted as representing a Yang Zhu "nurturing life" position, and it echoes the *Daodejing* passage cited above. The author of the *guisheng* chapter adds the following comments after the story of Yao attempting to abdicate the throne to the sage Zizhou Zhifu, who refuses on the grounds of a deep-seated illness:[26]

> The empire is of extreme importance, and yet he would not let it harm his life. How much less, then, any other thing! Only he who does not let the empire harm his life can be entrusted with it.[27]

There is a practicable side to this notion that the sage ruler is not vexed or harmed in acting as a ruler. Namely, if one is, in fact, on the throne and one wishes to rule in the manner of a sage ruler who complies with the *dao*, then one's art of rulership promotes the fulfillment of one's own life, thus correlatively the people's lives will be fulfilled.

The *guisheng* chapter draws a bodily analogy of the state in which the offices of state (*guan*) are managed by the ruler as the sense organs (*guan*) are managed by the heart-mind.

> In the sage's profound consideration of the empire, nothing is valued more than life. The eyes, ears, nose, and mouth are the servants of life. . . . If they harm life, they must be stopped. If what resides within these four organs (*guan*) does not desire what is beneficial to life, then do not act on it.
>
> Observing it from this perspective, the eyes, ears, nose, and mouth do not get to proceed on their own authority; there must be something they are controlled by (i.e., the heart-mind). By way of illustration, it is like the official functions (*guanzhi*); they do not get to proceed on their own authority; there must be something they are controlled by (i.e., the ruler). This is the art of valuing life.[28]

Spring is the season of eros. The desires, stimulated by the senses, require nurturing and cultivation if they are to benefit the fulfillment of life. Once the ruler cultivates his desires, he is in a position to cultivate the "organs" of state. The proper operation of the officials assists in employing the masses to fulfill their desires and earn a living.

"Cultivating *Xing*" for the Fulfillment of Life. The LSCQ's second chapter, *bensheng* (Life as Basic), provides an interesting blend of Laozi-like and Mengzi-like material on self-cultivation by *yang xing* (cultivating one's character). The *bensheng* chapter is important not only in that it begins the LSCQ's narrative on how the ruler is to behave in the first month of spring, but it also provides a clear, life-affirmative, organic conception of the art of rulership as the correlative relationship between nature and humans, in particular, the ruler, working together to fulfill the processes of life.

> What initially gives life is nature (*tian*); what nurtures and completes it is mankind. The one who is able to nurture what nature gives life to without interfering is called the Son of Heaven.
>
> When the Son of Heaven acts, he endeavors to keep intact the natural (*quan tian*).[29] This is the reason why court offices were established; offices were established to keep life intact (*quan sheng*).[30] When the confused rulers of this age have many offices but contrarily use them to harm life, then they have lost the reason why offices were established.
>
> The character (*xing*) of water is to be clear, but soil sullies it. So it does not get to be clear. The character (*xing*) of humans is to live long, but things sully it. So they do not get to live long. "Things" are the means to nurture one's character (*yangxing*); "things" are not what is cultivated by one's character (*xing*). Now if among today's people many of the deluded use their character (*xing*) to nurture things, then it is because they do not know their (i.e., the thing's) relative importance.
>
> Therefore, in the sage's attitude toward sounds, colors, and fine flavors, he chooses them, if they benefit his xing. He rejects them, if they harm his *xing*. This is the way (*dao*) to keep one's *xing* intact (*quan xing*).[31]

The organically based social and political root of most pre-Qin, especially *rujia*, and *daojia*, philosophy is represented in this passage. Water has no conscious control over its tendency to be clear. Once soil muddies the water, it cannot take action to clarify itself, and yet by doing nothing, that is, by being natural either flowing downward or stagnating, the dirt will settle out—the water becomes clear again. However, humans have some control over the development of their character by self-cultivation. Even though the various philosophers differ on their respective interpretations of *xing*, those who discuss it focus on the need for self-cultivation, which was understood to be an achievement. Through the ruler's self-cultivation, both the masses and natural world, especially through husbandry, are able to fulfill their respective life processes.

Both social ordering and cosmic ordering begin with the self-cultivation of the Son of Heaven. *Xing* and correlatively the natural environment are achieved, not merely given, and this achievement is consummated through the self-cultivation of the ruler. An important practice of self-cultivation is controlling the sense organs. The early spring chapters of the *shierji* are directed toward practicable approaches for refining the desires to maintain the development of the ruler's *xing* and to promote proper rulership.

The *zhongji* (Emphasis on Oneself) chapter concludes with the position that there is no overriding principle for nurturing character (*yangxing*), but the cultivation of one's character is unique to one's own life.

> The sage kings use the above five [cultural arts: gardens, homes, physical comforts, cuisine, and music] to nurture human character (*yangxing*). They did not do it out of love of frugality, nor out of a dislike of wasting; they did it to adjust the needs of their respective characters (*xing*).[32]

This attitude is typical of the organic Laozhuang teachings, which stress the unique significance of the integration of particular foci forming the field experience of *dao*.

Cultivating One's Desires and Sensual Pleasures to Preserve One's Life and State. Spring is often thought of as the season of sexual, sensual desire. The pre-Qin had traditionally, like many other cultures, associated "the spring" (*chun*) with excessive sexual and sensual craving. The character *chun* is used to mean "lust" or now "erotica" in some contexts. Various chapters of the *shierji* develop a programmatic concern to cultivate and refine basic desires and appetites in a life-affirmative fashion in the spring; to discipline them in the summer; to restrain and coerce unrefined desires in the autumn; and to bury the dead and "take in" virtuous personnel in the winter.

The *qingyu* (Essential Desires) chapter develops the idea of self-cultivation for sagehood by refining the desires (*yu*) and sensual pleasures (*qing*). *Qing* is usually rendered as "passions," "feelings," or "sentiments." I explicate *qing* in terms of the morphological "circumstantial tendencies" or "relational components" in contrast to the genetically "inner" emphasis placed on *xing*.[33] Although the following passage has some similarity with Xunzi, especially the human condition being governed by avarice and desire, nevertheless it shows a marked difference by defining *qing* as the sense organs, rather than Xunzi's analysis of *qing* as the six feelings, namely, love, hate, joy, anger, sorrow, and pleasure. If one understands this natural condition of avarice as an amoral state, then this chapter shows a similarity with a Daoist natural amoral perspective, in addition to Xunzi's natural outlook. The stylistic beauty of the following comes from its unified eclectic format; anyone who can acknowledge avarice in the human character without being pessimistic will want to further acknowledge some means for restraining it by, for instance, education, self-cultivation, or punishment.

> Nature (*tian*, heaven), in generating humans, causes them to have avarice and desire. As for desire, there are the essentials (*qing*, i.e., the relational components, sentience, or sense organ awareness), and as for the essentials, there are appropriate limits (*jie*, moderation). The sage cultivates appropriate limits to contain the desires. Hence, he does not go beyond acting on the essentials (*qing*).
>
> Thus, the ear's desire (*yu*) for the five sounds, the eye's desire for the five colors, and the mouth's desire for the five flavors are the essentials (*qing*, i.e., the relational components, sense awareness). In regard to the above three, the noble and the base, the foolish and the wise, the worthy and the unworthy are one in desiring them.[34] Even Shennong and the Yellow Emperor are the same in this, as are the tyrants Jie and Zhou.
>
> The respect in which the sages differ is that they obtain the essential ones. If one is motivated by valuing life (*guisheng*), he obtains the essentials; if not, he loses the essentials. These two (i.e., venerating and not venerating life) are the basis of life and death, or the preserving or perishing of a state.[35]

The *qingyu* chapter's naturalistic, organic, foci-field perspective, common in pre-Qin philosophy, namely, that human character is correlative with nature, that humans share the same basic desires but are distinguished by their efforts at self-cultivation, and that the fulfillment of life is the root of preserving a state and one's own life are expressed here. Xunzi's *lilunpian* (Chapter on Discussing Ritual) remarks: "Humans are given life, and they have desires. If one has desires but cannot obtain the objects of desire, then one must seek them out." The *qingyu* chapter bears some similarity to Xunzi's notion that human character is composed of natural desires. It should be noted that various pre-Qin philosophers acknowledge that the natural human condition is one of avarice and desire, but they differ in regard to how the desires are to be refined and why they need transforming. Refining the desires is a style of cultivating one's *xing* or one's *qing*.

The above passage contains a sense organ motivation postulate. Throughout the LSCQ one finds discussions on how natural human desires originate in

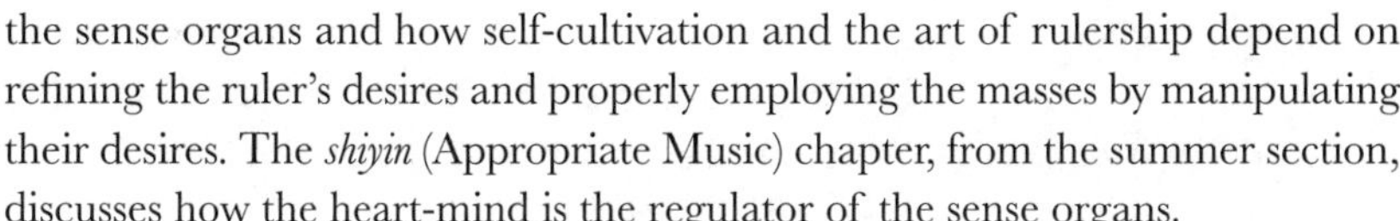

the sense organs and how self-cultivation and the art of rulership depend on refining the ruler's desires and properly employing the masses by manipulating their desires. The *shiyin* (Appropriate Music) chapter, from the summer section, discusses how the heart-mind is the regulator of the sense organs.

> It is essential to the ear (*er zhi qing*, i.e., a relational component of the ear) to desire sounds (*sheng*–music). If the heart and mind (*xin*) do not enjoy it, then even if the five tones are played right in front of a person, one won't listen to them.[36]

Not only is self-cultivation required for one's own development, but also the *guisheng* and *qingyu* chapters draw a political analogy between self-control and ruling. The analogy is strengthened by the character *guan* 官, which means both "court office" and "sense-organ" or "orifice." The *guisheng* chapter opens with an analogy of self-control and controlling the court offices.[37] Through the cultivation of one's character, requiring the mature restraint of sensual pleasure and desire, a ruler likewise cultivates the court officials. These passages display the highly creative, amalgamated eclecticism of the LSCQ in that they take a Yang Zhu notion of venerating life and blend it with a Mengzi-like concern for *yangxing* (nurturing nature), and then in a more administrative (*fajia* or Huanglao) tone they propose an analogy between the body and the state, namely, that just as the heart-mind controls the other organs likewise the ruler needs to restrain the court officers.

Respecting Impartiality and Expelling Self-Centered Attitudes. The character *gong* 公 (rendered here as "impartiality") is important in the *Daodejing*'s understanding of the art of rulership.[38] *Gong* is mentioned toward the end of the *Lunyu* (*Analects*).[39] The "impartial heart" (*gongxin*) and ruling "without partiality" (*wusi*) are discussed in the *Shizi*.[40] The LSCQ, however, contains one of the most elaborate discussions on *gong* in the pre-Qin corpus—second only to the *Hanfeizi*. The *Shuowenjiezi* cites the *Hanfeizi* to define *gong* as "turning one's back on partiality (*si*)." The *fajia*, Han Fei and Shang Yang, and the Huanglao texts such as the *Heguanzi* and the *jingfa* chapter of what is being called the *Huangdi sijing*, discuss the importance of expelling personal biases and being impartial in connection with administering the state according to standards and regulations (*fa*—law).[41]

The discussions of *gong* and *si* in the LSCQ's *guigong* (Venerating Impartiality) and *qusi* (Expelling Partiality) chapters, although decidedly political in focus, display a Laozhuang self-cultivation concern for developing an attitude of impartiality in general rather than *fajia* and Huanglao impartial laws or standards. The Laozhuang, and organically based *rujia* notions of "impartiality" (*gong*), and "getting rid of self-centered attitudes and desires" (*qusi*) ought not to be misconstrued as a kind of self-abnegation. The life-affirmative approach of the organic pre-Qin philosophies does not seek denial of a lower self to attain a higher Self, nor does this understanding of human life deny the ontological priority of the uniqueness of each particular.

The practice of impartiality (*gong*) is a means to maximize self-disclosure in a temporal context. If rulers were to limit the context by coercive governing, then they would restrict their own self-cultivation by not allowing others to develop and influence them. When *gong* is in operation, the context is open and in favor of the full creative disclosure of the particulars, ruler and subject. This is especially true of the LSCQ's *benwei* (Harmonizing Flavors as Basic) chapter, which discusses the art of rulership by appeal to an analogy with culinary arts. The discussion emphasizes the importance of the unique particular. For example, "they each have their particular use . . . each of the ingredients makes its own contribution."[42]

The conception of "honoring impartiality" and "avoiding self-centered desires," contained in the *guigong* and *qusi* chapters, must be balanced against the understanding of the unique integration of each and every particular within the complex processes of change contained in the *benwei* chapter. The *zhongji* chapter stresses the uniqueness of each particular, especially the sage ruler's uniqueness in cultivating *xing*.[43] Emphasis on one's own uniqueness must be understood in light of impartiality—it is not ego-centered selfishness. Each particular is, ontologically speaking, on a parity with every other particular, and each must pursue its own development. Many of the politically orientated passages in the LSCQ maintain that the state operates best under a hierarchical order that is indicative of Mozi, Xunzi, and Huanglao forms of rulership. The sage rulers, in particular, must cultivate their own characters to set the exemplary model for the people to emulate.

The late spring section contains the *xianji* (Priority on Oneself) chapter, which elaborates the need for self-integration, and the ruler's personal integration in particular, to gain and maintain control of the empire. The *xianji* chapter opens with a discussion between King Tang and his famous minister, Yi Yin. King Tang asks Yi Yin about gaining the empire.

> Yi Yin replies, "If you desire to take the empire, then the empire cannot be obtained. To obtain it, you yourself must first be obtained."
>
> The root of all affairs must begin with ordering one's own self. . . . The one who can daily renew his vital-force and life-breath (*jingqi*), completely expel the depraved life-breath in order to live out his natural years is called a *zhenren* (sublime or genuine person).

> Therefore, the one who desires to gain victory over others must gain victory over himself first. The one who wishes to evaluate others must evaluate himself first. The one who intends to know others must know himself first.[44]

"Impartiality" and "avoiding self-centered desires" can be appreciated by understanding the ruler's self-integration. The ruler should not totally deny the personal perspective; rather, the ruler adheres to a unique perspective while maintaining the integrity of each and every other particular in the empire.

The *xuyi* (postscript) chapter of the LSCQ mentions the importance of guarding against selfish desire and adopting an attitude of impartiality in discussing the meaning of the *shierji*:

> Heaven is called "complying"; complying is life. Earth is called "solidity"; solidity is being stable. Human is called "trustworthy"; being trustworthy is being obedient. If all of the above three are fit, then you operate by non-purposeful action. "To operate" means to operate their natural pattern (*li*);[45] to operate their technique (*shu*) is to follow their natural pattern and to even out their partialities.
>
> Looking with partiality (*si*) makes the eye blind; hearing with partiality makes the ear deaf; and thinking (*lü* anxiety) with partiality makes the heart go mad. Once the above three are prepared with partiality in the extreme, then one's wisdom will have no cause to be impartial (*gong*). If one's wisdom is partial, then one's good fortune will decline daily and one's disasters will increase daily.[46]

The ruler must model heaven and earth. One must cultivate the senses and heart-mind, directing both away from excessive biases to establish the wisdom of impartiality. It is the ruler in particular who must cultivate his heart-mind and senses to generate social harmony.

The *guigong* (Venerating Impartiality) chapter highlights the unique conception of the integration of particulars to establish cosmic and political harmony. The *guigong* chapter praises the ancient sage kings who obtained the throne and ruled by being impartial, and it generalizes "Hence, the establishment of any ruler comes from being impartial."[47] The *guigong* chapter cites the Grand Plan (*hongfan*) chapter of the *Book of History* (*Shujing*) to support its authority concerning applying impartiality. Then, the chapter states some of the most egalitarian words of antiquity.

> The empire is not one person's empire; it is the empire of all those in the empire. The harmonious blending of yin and yang does not allow only

> one species to grow. The sweet dew and timely rain never partially favor one thing, and the ruler of the myriad peoples does not personally favor any one person.[48]

One may be tempted to describe the expression that "the empire is not one person's but belongs to the people of the empire" as a democratic tendency. Such temptations should be restrained. Most of the LSCQ, and the *guigong* chapter in particular, advocates a ritualistic monarchy with a worthy prime minister to manage the complex administrative operations, not a democracy. Within this context the ruler, like the cosmic forces of yin and yang, wind and rain, ought to treat the people of the empire with impartiality. The empire is not the ruler's sole possession, nor can the ruler favor individuals.

The *guigong* chapter prefers a *daojia* form of impartiality, placing the myriad things on a parity with each other. This Daoist impartiality is emphasized in the following story:

> There was a man from the state of Jing (Chu) who lost his bow, and he was unwilling to look for it. He said, "A person from the state of Jing lost it, and a person from the state of Jing will find it. So what is there to search for in this case?"
>
> When Kongzi heard this, he said that if the fellow would omit the phrase "from the state of Jing," then his comment would be acceptable.
>
> When Lao Dan (Laozi) heard this, he said that if the fellow would also omit the phrase "a person" from his statement, then it would be acceptable. So, Lao Dan has the utmost in impartiality.[49]

Where Kongzi would like to do away with the distinction of the states and unite all peoples, Lao Dan wishes to move beyond the human realm and unite all things in nature on a parity. The *guigong* chapter paraphrases the *Laozi*, advocating the Daoist paradigm of the ruler emulating the magnanimity of heaven and earth.

> Heaven and Earth are magnanimous;[50] giving birth to the myriad things, but not treating them like children; completing them, but not possessing them.[51] Each of the myriad things receives its favor and obtains its benefit, but none knows from what it begins.[52] This was the virtuous bounty of the Three August Rulers, and the Five Emperors.[53]

The chapter cites a story about Prime Minister Guan Zhong advising Duke Huan of Qi on how to appoint an impartial official.[54] The *guigong* chapter comments on this story by paraphrasing the *Laozi* in describing a Daoist prime minister:

> The prime minister is a high-ranking official. One who dwells in the post of a high-ranking official does not desire to make trite examinations nor to display trivial cleverness. Hence, it is said that
>
> the skilled carpenter does not chop wood;[55]
> the master chef does not chop vegetables;
> the great hero does not squabble,
> and the great army does not maraud.[56]
>
> When Duke Huan practiced impartiality and got rid of his personal dislikes, he appointed Guanzi and became the greatest of the five lord protectors. When he practiced partiality and favored those he loved, he appointed Xu Dao, then the maggots (which grew on his corpse because the burial was delayed due to rebellion) crawled out the door.[57]

The *guigong* chapter contains a unified, composite model of political *daojia*, seeking to establish a prime minister and ruler who will employ impartiality and non-aggressive action (*wuwei*). The chapter is explicit in pointing out that even the impartiality of a worthy prime minister is sufficient to make a lord protector out of an average ruler. A psychological observation is made: in old age, Duke Huan forgot the example of Guan Zhong and ended in disaster.

The chapter concludes with a psychological statement that generally people gain wisdom with age, but even if they remain foolish, they can be successful by ruling with impartiality.

> When one is young, he might be foolish; as one ages, he might become wiser, and so to be clever but employ partiality is not as good as being foolish but employing impartiality. To be drunk daily, and try to issue orders,[58] or to focus on selfish profit, and try to establish oneself as duke, or to be covetous and cruel, and seek to realize the kingly way, even Emperor Shun could not do it.[59]

The competent ruler is one who can rule without allowing personal biases to interfere with political decisions. Impartial judgment in bestowing reward and punishment is the kingly way.

The *qusi* (Expelling Partiality) chapter continues the discussion of avoiding partiality while embracing impartiality. The *qusi* chapter opens with a naturalistic model of impartiality.

> The sky does not cover things with partiality. The earth does not support things with partiality. The sun and moon do not illuminate things with

> partiality. The four seasons do not operate with partiality. They operate their bounty, and the myriad things obtain it and subsequently grow.[60]

This model resounds the Huanglao idea of a hierarchical natural world, where the powers of the universe nourish the myriad things. The chapter claims:

> The Yellow Emperor said: "In music (*sheng*)[61] prohibit excess. In sexual desire forbid indulgence. In clothing prohibit lavishness. Concerning aromas ban overabundance. Concerning flavors forbid excess. In housing prohibit extravagance."[62]

Again we see the importance of properly orienting the natural desires in the spring season to cultivate virtuous people at court and in the empire. The chapter picks up a traditional *rujia* theme of abdicating the throne to the most worthy one instead of passing it onto one's heirs. It relates a story of Qi Huangyang, who could make unbiased recommendations. Then it describes a Mohist master who held such an unbiased, impartial approach toward the Mohist laws that he executes his murderous son, even though the king had granted an acquittal.

The *qusi* chapter presents impartiality as a significant key to maintaining one's office or rulership. One's personal integrity as a unique particular, especially as ruler, is achieved through one's practice of impartiality. The chapter concludes with the following passage:

> The court chef blends the flavors, but does not dare to eat it. For this reason he can be the court chef. Suppose the court chef prepares and eats the food, then he cannot be the court chef.
>
> To rule as a king or lord protector is also like this. Kings and lords execute tyrants but do so without biased partiality in order to enfeoff the worthy ones in the empire. For these reasons they can function as kings or lord protectors. Suppose one rules as a king or lord protector but executes tyrants with biased partiality, then he cannot serve as a king or lord protector.[63]

Interestingly, this passage, like the *benwei* chapter, draws an analogy between the art of cooking and the art of rulership. Here the text emphasizes the need for impartiality on the part of all those involved in ruling from the kings and lord protectors down to the lowest court officials. Just as the lowest court officials, even the chefs, must serve their ruler without bias or self-seeking purposes, so too the kings and lords must serve the empire without personal biases.

Two chapters in the *shendalan* section discuss the importance of the worthy ruler adopting an attitude of and regulating his behavior by displaying *zhigong* (utmost impartiality). The *shenda* (Caution in Major Determinates) chapter discusses *zhigong* in the context of King Tang's ability to treat the conquered Xia people impartially in establishing his own Yin (or Shang) dynasty.

> After King Tang was made the Son of Heaven, the Xia masses were very pleased, as if they had received a merciful parent. The officials at court did not change their posts; the farmers did not leave their fields; the merchants did not move their stores. The people of Xia felt as close to Yin as they had been to the Xia. This is called utmost impartiality; this is called utmost stability; this is called utmost trustworthiness.[64]

The *xiaxian* (To Be Humble to the Virtuous) chapter discusses the role of *zhigong* in the ruler's personal behavior toward knights of the Way.

> Yao was the Son of Heaven, while Shan Quan was merely a commoner. Why did Yao treat him with respect to such an extent? It was due to the fact that Shan Quan was a knight who attained the Way. One who attains the Way cannot be treated arrogantly. Since Yao considered himself to be not as good as Shan Quan, when he graded their conduct and intelligence. Hence, Yao asked for instruction from him while facing North.[65] It is this which is called the utmost in impartiality. If it is not a person of the utmost impartiality, then who else is able to respect excellence?[66]

The ruler ought to be able to embrace impartiality to employ the virtuous and skillful knights. These last two passages appear to be *rujia*-like.

"Impartiality" is shared by many of the traditional sources from which the LSCQ draws, though the various philosophers interpret its scope differently. Treating things or people impartially is framed within a temporal context. It is because oneself and others are constantly changing and adjusting to live in harmony with the environment that humans in general, but the ruler in particular, must treat and promote all life on a parity. The existential parity of the myriad things acts as a benchmark to remind the ruler not to show partiality toward his relatives, friends, or ministers.

Summer: A Literati Paradigm—Cultivation Through Music

In the summer section of the *shierji*, we have a preponderance of materials on typical *rujia* (Literati) concerns, namely ritual/propriety (*li*), music (*yue*), and study (*xue*). Although some scholars claim that the LSCQ's music chapters are an inaccurate source for discussion of traditional pre-Qin music,[67] nevertheless, these chapters comprise some of the scanty, extant, pre-Qin literature on music.

The least that can be said is that the position on music contained in the *shierji* is representative of some trends of *rujia* thought in the state of Qin. Although the music chapters of the LSCQ do not quote the following remark attributed to Kongzi, one can easily surmise that ritual self-cultivation through music was inspired by the following:

> Be stimulated by poetry. Take a stance through ritual. Find maturation in music. (*Analects*, 14/8/8).

Literati Interpretations of *Xing*. Before discussing *xing* in the summer section of the *shierji*, allow me to review briefly the Literati debate on *xing* to highlight what is unique in the LSCQ's passages that adopt a programmatic philosophy concerning human character. It is assumed in much of the literature that most pre-Qin thinkers embrace either Mencius' notion that *xing* is originally good or Xunzi's idea that it is bad—socially deviant. The noted exception is Mengzi's opponent, Gaozi, who proposed that humans are neither good nor bad, but natural. Later, in the Western Han, Wang Chong reviews the earlier theories in his *Lunheng* (*Discussions Balanced*) and adds four more positions.[68] Despite their differences, all these theories, save Gaozi's, are interpreted as proposing that people have a preestablished disposition that enables or constrains their ability to treat others in socially productive ways. Many of the received interpretations of *xing* in Mengzi and Xunzi focus on the one-sided account that it is innate or inborn. These interpretations of the ancient theories tend to be explicit functionalist theories with foundationalist tendencies, assuming a fundamental deep structure or instinct that governs human behavior. This type of metaphysical thinking, with its essentialism or innate structures, cuts against the grain of most classical pre-Qin philosophy which is best described as an organic processes worldview.

This tendency to read the pre-Qin thinkers as harboring some type of innate qualities is exacerbated by Song and Ming dynasty philosopher's "metaphyicalization" of *xing*, which was anachronistically read back into the earlier tradition, especially into Mengzi.[69] One may want to argue that especially Literati and Mohist philosophers had an understanding of a preestablished form of human nature, because the pre-Qin tradition of performing ritual sacrifices for the ancestors implies a persevering "soul" or "spirit" (*shen*). It could be further assumed that this soul or spirit is the essence of human nature. These interpretations support the pre-Qin commoner's interpretation that disembodied spirits are the focus of the rites of ancestor veneration. The belief in disembodied spirits is the commoner's understanding of the royal family's practice and his or her own practice of offering sacrifices to the deceased ancestors, especially the king's ancestors. However, there is almost no discussion of disembodied spirits in the classical literature, and as is evidenced from the *Mozi*'s chapter "On Ghosts" and the *Odes*, where spirits are mentioned, it reflects the commoner's point of view.

Even if one accepts for argument's sake that commoners and scholars alike believed in a spiritual essence, the spirits were not immortal but decayed. Jacques Gernet clearly describes the conceptual differences between rather generalized Chinese and Christian perspectives. He contends that the Chinese did not know of a mind-body dualism; they did not separate feeling from reason: "They amalgamated moral sense and intelligence."[70] Although Gernet may overstate his point, it is well taken—in a world of change, even souls disintegrate. K. E. Brashier clarifies the corporeal character of both the *hun* and *po*, what many misconceived to be two different kinds of souls.[71]

The crux of the issue is whether or not we are justified in interpreting the classical *rujia* philosophers as essentialistic and substantialistic thinkers, or whether coherence demands a process- and achievement-oriented interpretation. Insofar as the thirteen Literati classics have a preponderance of material on history, with a focus on particular contexts or persons, and a strong reliance on argument by analogy and harmonizing with natural change, they must be read as process- and achievement-oriented works. Under this reading, the ancestor, as the focus of ritual sacrifice, continues to "live" not as a disembodied spirit per se but as a part of the continuing processes of family and community life. The notion of an "afterlife" does not necessitate that there be an innate preestablished, and persevering "soul." In a worldview such as the pre-Qin Literati, especially Mengzi's, position, one's personhood is not a given but an achievement that can extend beyond one's physical life span. Under this paradigm, the "afterlife" is not the life of a disembodied spirit but the "life" of contributing to community and cultural meaning.[72]

The LSCQ's *shiwei* (Appropriately Displaying Majesty) chapter implies that the *shen* (spirit) that preserves death is found in the power of one's life to transform later generations by establishing cultural trends:

> This is why the five emperors and the three kings had no match. They themselves had already died, but the later generations were transformed as though by a spirit (—magically—*hua zhi ru shen*). They carefully examined human affairs.[73]

One's "spirit" is not a disembodied substance but one's "creative"ability to transform human life by contributing to or "extending" community and culture.

The correlative relation between nature and humans is found in both Laozhuang and the early *rujia* teachings. Although Kongzi is often subsumed under Mengzi's theory that humans are good, based on two passages in which Kongzi says "All people are born with uprightness . . . " (*Analects*, 6/17), and "In *xing* we are close . . . " (17/2 and 3), nevertheless, the Master is described as being silent on human character (*xing*) and heaven (*tian*) (5/12). These passages do not necessarily imply that humans have a preestablished (innate) nature: "In basic characteristics (*xing*) we are close; practice makes us distant" (17/2). Even if *xing* is taken to mean innate traits or predispositions, it is clear that Kongzi's focus is on the practices of self-cultivation that make us different.

In some of the LSCQ's passages from the summer section concerning *xing*, *rujia* concepts are employed to elaborate a programmatic theme of human character, especially the ruler's character, as an achievement-in-process. Character or person making is creatively and spontaneously developed. Undue emphasis on the notion of a preestablished pattern runs contrary to the respective projects of Kongzi and the Laozhuang teachings. The shared living world and aesthetic paradigm that serves as a common ground of early *rujia* and *daojia* thought do not speculate on a preestablished or a priori nature.[74] Many of the pre-Qin philosophers focus on appropriate present action. For Kongzi, a person primarily contributes to and apportions social and political activities; for the Huanglao and the Laozhuang texts, the ruler primarily contributes to an appropriate cosmic harmony. These natural dynamic and organic perspectives on developing and nurturing one's character (*yangxing*) are incorporated into the LSCQ.

Despite the different conceptions of human character found in pre-Qin philosophy, there is one striking point of commonality among them, namely, that any civilized person, nobility or commoner, has access to the same general possibilities for consummating a realization of social and political achievement or sagehood. This is not to be understood as a mathematical equality of identity, nor general similarities of fixed potentialities, but rather many pre-Qin thinkers recognize the contingent nature of developing a sagely character—one's effort at cultivation and one's socioeconomic status are significant. Some pre-Qin philosophers appear much more impartial, almost egalitarian, in seeing things and people on a parity than other theories of human character that hierarchically stratify people into classes or castes, such as Plato's eugenics plan, Aristotle's natural slavery, Augustine's predestination doctrine, and the caste system of the *Code of Manu*. Although there is a trend of impartiality in pre-Qin philosophy, according to the philosophers, most people will not achieve sagehood. The masses at large are rarely recognized as persons. The basic commonality among humans is shared with the animal world and is not socially and politically significant. The pre-Qin worldview is different from our own, in that humans are classified along with plants and animals.[75] Being "human" is not a privileged category in itself. What is socially and politically important about humans is that they can cultivate themselves through cultural achievement, becoming persons, even sage rulers.

The *qingyu* chapter proposed that all people are of the same type, whatever that "type" might be, such as, good, bad, or neither. For the *qingyu* chapter, this commonality of character is the desire-centered nature of all people.[76] The *weiyu* (Constituting Desires) chapter acknowledges that even the tribal peoples share the same characteristic desires, and that the sage ruler is one who orchestrates the desires under the veneer of social custom.

> The tribal (Man and Yi) states with their different languages, customs, and peculiar habits, their clothes, hats, and belts, their halls and dwellings, their boats, carriages, and instruments, and their music, color arrangements, and tastes are all totally different from ours, but our doings and desires cause them to be one. The three Kings were not able to change their customs, although being able to gain achievement and success without changing their customs is to accord with the natural (*tian*, heaven) in them.[77]

At least some of the contributors to the LSCQ were sensitive to the biological aspects of *xing* as species characteristics. The *yongse* (On Being Obstructed) chapter accepts different morphological characteristics as common sense, and it uses the confusion of such characteristics allegorically to illuminate the madness of improperly applying reward and punishment.

> When climbing a mountain, a cow might appear to be a sheep, or a sheep might appear to be a pig. But in fact the character (*xing*, or *ti* body)[78] of a cow is not like a sheep, and the character of a sheep is not like a pig. This is an error due to the strategic location (*shi*) from which the observation was made. If one subsequently gets angry at the cow's and sheep's small size, this would be the most serious form of being a mad man. To carry out rewards and punishments with such madness, this was why the Dai clan (in Song) was destroyed.[79]

The basic differences among species are presented as a commonsense distinction. In describing the biological and morphological characteristics of humans (*ren zhi xing*), the *shijunlan* (On What a Ruler Relies Upon) chapter presents a rather sophisticated, almost modern, discussion.

> Generally in speaking of human character our nails and teeth are inadequate for self-defense; our flesh and skin are insufficient to protect against cold and heat; our tendons and bones are not sufficient to go after profit and avoid harm. Our courage and daring are not sufficient to turn aside the fierce and to control the cruel.
>
> And yet humans can manage the myriad things, tame birds and beasts, and subjugate reptiles. Cold and heat, droughts and moisture cannot harm them. Is this not because we not only make preparations first, but also is it not because we gather together in masses?!
>
> The fact that the masses can gather together is because they benefit each other. And the fact that benefit issues from their gathering in groups is because the way of the ruler (*jundao*) is established.[80]

The *shijun* chapter describes human deficiencies, and yet it recognizes human mastery due to public planning and a gregarious nature. This proposal is similar to such diverse modern theories as Conrad Lorenz on aggression and Marxism and existentialism, which hold that humans lack instincts or formal structure and that human character develops in social and cultural contexts. For many passages in the LSCQ, there appears to be a hierarchical pattern in the development of character. People are basically the same but differ in their effort and commitment to achieve consummate person-making or sagehood.[81] The *yishang* (Appropriate Rewarding) chapter maintains that the achievements of culture and the contextual influences lasting for a long time occur "as if it were by nature."

> If the trend of being disloyal, dishonest, harmful, rebellious, avaricious, and uncompliant arises for a long time without stopping, then the people will become used to it as if by nature (*xing*). The peoples of the Rong, Yi, Hu, He, Ba, and Yue tribes are examples of this. They cannot be stopped, even with heavy rewards and severe punishments.[82]

The adept ruler is flexible in maintaining order due to the indeterminate and culturally variable aspect of human character. "Proper timing" is the harmonizing procedure that makes the LSCQ's consolidated philosophy on human character a practicable approach to formulating an administrative policy that accords with both cosmic, and social situations. That the very quality of human character is not fixed, and because it varies with time and context, it requires a flexible art of rulership that accommodates and fulfills the interests of the masses. The basis of sound administrative policy for many pre-Qin writers is established in the ruler's self-cultivation as the ultimate authority of the tradition. It is the ruler qua sage that stands as a cultural beacon, drawing the masses and the various levels of society into deferential relationships that encourage the project of personal cultivation. The role of the ruler as an orchestrator of the well-ordered society cannot be underestimated, but this means that the ruler is an authoritative model, not an authoritarian legislator.

The Ruler As Exemplar of Self-Cultivation. The ruler serving as the model of self-cultivation was championed by the *rujia*, but as we have seen the Daoists had a similar theory of exemplar modeling. The Systematizers (*fajia*, usually rendered Legalists) focused on establishing the ruler's majesty and strategic position, generating a mystique around him, but they were not that interested in self-cultivation. The ontological focus of Literati virtue is on person-to-person-care and being appropriate (*ren yi*), while the methodological focus is on filial piety (*xiao*). Filial piety is discussed in the *quanxue* (Encouraging Studies) chapter of the early summer section, which opens by extolling the need for filial piety and loyalty.

> None among the teachings of the former kings is more glorious than being filial; none is more significant than being loyal. Being loyal and filial are what rulers and parents desire the most. Being significant and glorious are what the sons and the ministers want to realize badly.[83]

The chapter points out that loyalty and filial piety require study that necessitates a teacher who can give proper instruction. The sage rulers who were able to order the empire always venerated their teacher (*zun shi*) to guarantee proper learning and self-cultivation. The sage ruler ensures that the people are given proper instruction, and the ruler serves as a model of self-cultivation for them to emulate.

The *xiaoxinglan* (On Practicing Filial Piety) chapter of the LSCQ contains a passage exemplifying the Literati, particularly Zengzi's, model of imperial cultivation through filial piety. This passage comprises the second chapter of the *Xiaojing* (*Classic on Filial Piety*).

> Hence, if the emperor loves his parents, he would not dare to dislike others' parents; if he respects his parents, he would not dare to ignore others' parents. If the emperor's love and respectfulness are exhausted in serving his parents, illumination will be added to the commoners and spread throughout the territory within the four seas. This is the result of the Son of Heaven's filial piety.[84]

Although it does not occur in the *shierji*, it does present a good example of the Literati paradigm of the ruler as the model of self-cultivation. Hu Shi argues that the *xiaoxinglan* provides a model of self-cultivation by filial piety in proposing that one must protect one's body to fulfill filial duty.[85]

When the LSCQ was being compiled during the middle of the third century B.C.E., the teachings of Xunzi and a practicable form of *daojia* were rising in popularity.[86] Mozi's and Xunzi's teachings and those of the different types of practicable political *daojia* in the *Guanzi* and the Huanglao teachings share a common ground in advocating a more systematic and formalized model for the self-cultivation of the ruler.

The first passage of the *guidang* (Venerating Appropriateness) chapter highlights a *rujia* position on the role of *xing* in cultivating the emperor's desires (*yu*) to be a model for the empire to emulate. The *guidang* chapter is complex in its presentation of this concern, drawing from the naturalism of Xunzi and practicable *daojia*.

> Great fame and significant titles cannot be aggressively sought. They must be acquired by according with the right Way (*dao*). The means to put things in order (*zhi*)[87] does not lie in the things, but lies in people. The means to put people in order does not lie in them,[88] but lies in the rulers. The means to put the rulers in order does not lie in them, but lies in the Son of Heaven. The means to put the Son of Heaven in order does not lie in the Son of Heaven, but lies in his desires. The means to put the desires in order does not lie in the desires, but lies in the character (*xing*).
>
> *Xing* is the root of the myriad things. It cannot be lengthened; it cannot be shortened (in degree). Going with what is inherently so, and recognizing it is so, these are the natural degrees (*shu*) from heaven and earth.[89]

The empire, and cosmos for that matter, cannot be set in proper harmony unless the emperor practices self-cultivation that refines the avaricious desires through the achievement of his character. Through cultivation of the ruler's character, the myriad things obtain a model to emulate. The predominant role of proper timing in the *rujia* paradigm is that timing is used in both the self-cultivation process of refining selfish desire and in the timely discharge of social and political action, displaying interpersonal virtues and appropriate policies to maintain the art of rulership.

The *guidang* passage integrates aesthetic *rujia* ideas with a more rigid naturalism indicative of Xunzi or the Huanglao teachings, which advocate that human character is naturally endowed and locked into a pattern. Above, *xing* was described as that which "cannot be lengthened or shortened." The *dayue* (Magnificent Music) chapter contains a similar expression concerning human desire. This emphasis on the constancy of *xing* or desire should not be interpreted as innateness.

The Naturally Endowed Desires and the Employment of Desire in Establishing Order. The *dayue* chapter concisely proposes that human desires and dislikes are a part of our natural constitution which "cannot be changed or replaced" (*bu ke bian*, or *bu ke yi*). These natural dispositions are presented in a decidedly Literati topic concerning the significance of music as a natural desire of humans which, however, can be perverted by excess. The mosaic nature of the text again blends the discussion of the natural desire for music with *daojia* and *yinyangjia* terminology.

> Music is the harmony of heaven and earth. It is the rhythm of yin and yang. That which for the first time generates humans is heaven (i.e., nature *tian*). Humans have no business in this. Heaven causes humans to have desires (*tian shi ren you yu*). Humans cannot choose but to fulfill them.
>
> Heaven causes humans to have dislikes. Humans have no choice but to avoid them. Desires and dislikes are what humans receive from heaven.[90] Humans cannot succeed in getting a share. It cannot be altered; it cannot be replaced (*yi* transformed).[91]

Hu Shi claims that this passage is an example of the LSCQ employing a utilitarian naturalism against the Mohist's utilitarian attack on music. "Saying that music is based on natural characteristics (*tianxing*) which 'cannot be altered and cannot be replaced' to such an extent, this is completely a utilitarian philosophy of naturalism."[92] The *dayue* chapter has generated a hybrid, discriminatingly selective position, drawing off of *daojia* and *yinyangjia* naturalism, *rujia* self-cultivation in music, and Mohist utility. These various philosophies generally advance a type of humane political theory; they respectively propose that the state improve or maintain the benefit of the masses. Where the LSCQ's unified eclecticism breaks new ground is in its integration of *fajia* conceptions of coercive rule by reward and punishment with benefitting the masses by fulfilling their natural desires.[93] This thinking anticipates the *Huainanzi*'s conception of *limin* (benefitting the masses), which draws on both *rujia* and *fajia* perspectives. This syncretic position is advocated in the *yongmin* (Employing the Masses) chapter in the *lisilan*, which contains a concentration of *fajia* material. The *yongmin* chapter integrates the natural characteristics of desire and dislikes to advise the ruler on how to employ the masses.

> What are the draw string and guideline of the masses? They are their likes and dislikes. And what do they like and dislike? They like glory and benefit, and they dislike disgrace and harm. Disgrace and harm are the reason that punishment has come into being, and glory and benefit are the reason that rewards have taken shape. When reward and punishment are in place, then everyone among the masses will be employed.[94]

This passage maintains the composite approach of the LSCQ by proposing that manipulating, through reward and punishment, the natural characteristics of people to desire glory and benefit and to dislike harm and disgrace are the most appropriate means to motivate their employment. The *weiyu* (Constituting Desires) chapter continues this discussion of utilizing the people's desires, proposing to increase the desires to expand the people's employment.

> So those who have many desires can also be employed in many ways. Those who have few desires can only be employed in a few ways. Those who are without desire cannot be employed at all. Even though the people have many desires, if the rulers are without the means to command them, then although the people fulfill their desires, nevertheless they cannot be employed. The way (*dao*) to command the people by fulfilling desire *must* be examined carefully. One who is adept at being a ruler is able to command the people such that they fulfill their desires inexhaustibly. Hence, the people's employment can also be inexhaustible.[95]

This approach provides a complex form of utilitarian thought in that it grounds political order in the natural flesh-and-blood desires of the people, and so the function of political order is to enhance and fulfill those desires. The enhancement and fulfillment of the people's desires will in turn promote their further employment. There is a reciprocal relation between the natural desires serving as the bases for political order and correlatively the political order is strengthened to the extent that it can fulfill and enrich those desires. Within the Literati paradigm, ritual acts (*li*) and court ritual music (*yue*) play an important role in the ruler's self-cultivation.

Maturation through Court Ritual Music. The opening chapters of each lunar month of the *shierji* comprise the Monthly Commands chapter of the *Book of Rites*. The *mengxiaji* (First Month of Summer) chapter contains an important line not found in the Monthly Commands. The passage is of interest because it describes the character (*xing*) of the first month of summer in terms of ritual action (*li*).

> Its tone *zhi* complies with the *zhanglü* pitch pipe. Its number is seven. Its character (*xing*) is to practice rituals (*li*). Its activity is overseeing. Its flavor is bitter.[96]

The *shierji* emphasizes the significance of ritual propriety (*li*) as the emperor's main concern during the summer months discussing ritual music. Most commentators want to delete the above line from the LSCQ because it does not appear in the Monthly Commands, and there is no parallel expression in the other monthly ordinance chapters. Yu Yue argues that the LSCQ's text was the original, and that the compilers of the *Liji* deleted these characters because *li* and *shi* are references to the *wuxing* (five phases) correspondences with the *wuchang* (five constant virtues) and the *wushi* (five activities), respectively. "Its character is to practice rituals" is an important guide for understanding the significance of the extensive discussions concerning rites in honor of the teacher and court ritual music presented in the subsequent chapters.

For many of the pre-Qin Literati, there was a direct correspondence between court ritual, in particular, court ritual music, and successful administration. The *yinlü* (Tones of the Twelve Pipes) chapter furnishes correspondences between the months of the year and the pitch pipes. In concluding the *yinlü* chapter, the ruler is given a guide on what administrative policy to carry out during the months correlated with the respective pipes. For example, the text states:

> In the month corresponding to the *jiazhong* pipe, the second month, the active energy (*yangqi*) tends to be encompassing, plentiful, harmonious, and equally distributed. The ruler should practice being generous of virtue (*de*) and put aside criminal punishments (*quxing*); never initiate affairs to harm any living creature.
>
> In . . . the sixth month, the plant life is thick and flourishing, and the passive [energy] (*yin*[*qi*]) will for the first time begin to push its destruction of life (*xing* lit. punishment).
>
> In the month corresponding to the *yize* pipe, the seventh month, the ruler should organize judicial standards and strengthen criminal punishments; he should select soldiers and sharpen the weapons, preparing for war. During this month he should interrogate and punish those who were unjust so as to appease those who live in the far off corners of the state.[97]

This passage displays extrinsic timing, where policy is altered to correspond with the seasonal changes of the year. In order to harmonize socioeconomic activity with the seasonal cycles, the ruler must understand the co-dependent relations of ritual cultivation and cosmic order.

It is not only a matter of the ruler practicing self-cultivation to harmonize the cosmic forces, but there is also the ruler's co-dependent relationship with the masses. The ruler's self-cultivation is required to harmonize the people so that the style of music the ruler enjoys at court will influence the quality of life and the livelihood of the masses. The good ruler will be sensitive to avoiding bad or excessive music.

The *zhiyue* (The Bad Influence of Extravagant Music) chapter notes the differences between harmonious and extravagant music. The author of this chapter argues that the sounds of nature constitute music in its broadest sense, and that as such music is natural to humans. However, when people become excessive, especially in desires, then "music" becomes exorbitant so that it is no longer "enjoyable music" in the original sense.

> When the state of Chu was declining, its people composed the shaman music (*wuyin*). This was the epitome of extravagance. Were we to examine these cases from the perspective of one who possesses the way (*dao*—tradition), then these declining states lost the essentials of music (*yue zhi qing*). Losing the essentials of music, their music was not enjoyable music.[98] Where the music is not enjoyable, the masses will certainly be resentful; their lives (*sheng*)[99] will certainly be harmed. Their lives[100] toward this type of music are just like the eyes toward the hot sun, rather than benefit, it will bring calamities on oneself. This is due to the ruler[101] not understanding the essentials of music and considering extravagance to be his goal.
>
> Music possesses the essentials just like muscle, skin, form, and the body possesses essentials (*qing* desires) and character (*xing*). Where there are the essentials and character, then there are the processes of nurturing life (*shengyang*).[102]
>
> Too much cold or heat, labor or rest, hunger or satiation, these six are not in tune. In general when nurturing is observed to be out of tune, you guide it to be in tune. If one is able to be settled in tune for a long time, then his life will be long. When one was born, the repose of his body was inherently tranquil; he becomes aware after being stimulated. It is because something caused it. He won't return to the previous state after fulfilling it. Thereby, he would be controlled by craving and desire. If he is controlled by craving and desire, then he would certainly lose what is from nature in him (*tian*). Furthermore, if one's cravings and desires are excessive, then he will certainly be with the mind of avarice and rebelliousness, and undertake affairs of licentiousness and deceit. Therefore, the strong robbing the weak, mobs violating the few, the bold ones oppressing the cowardly, and the elders dominating the young originate from this.[103]

This kind of sophisticated psychological analysis of learning is rarely found in pre-Qin texts. Most importantly though it is the early learning experiences of the ruler that are being discussed. If the court allows the emperor to be raised in a self-centered fashion, this attitude or mind-set will permeate the kingdom, and all forms of abuse will develop, weakening the state severely. This is especially true if the ruler is influenced by extravagant and wild music. Self-cultivation and character building constitute a reciprocal relationship with music.

On Respecting the Court Tutor. The early summer chapters devote a good deal of discussion to the ruler's personal development through study. Some of those chapters discuss the topic of showing proper respect to the teacher or court tutor. This is not too surprising, in that the LSCQ was not only compiled by guest scholars and teachers but it was most likely used by Lü Buwei to instruct the young King Zheng too. The *zunshi* (On Venerating the Teacher) chapter stresses the significance of self-cultivation in learning (*xue* imitation), which can only occur when one is respectful toward one's teacher. The chapter emphasizes the importance of the emperor or king showing respect to the teacher and doing so in a timely fashion.

Bringing out the developmental achievement orientation of human character, discussing how humans must learn to use their natural talents and sense organs in a culturally refined manner, the chapter states:

> Moreover, nature generated humans, and made it possible for their ears to hear. But without study, their hearing is not as good as being deaf. It caused their eyes to see; but without study, their sight is not as good as being blind. It allows their mouths to speak; but without study, their speech is not as good as being dumb. It allows their heart and mind to know; but without learning, their knowing is not as good as being mad.
>
> It is not that study is able to increase (one's talents). It can develop one's natural character (*tian xing*). Being able to keep intact what heaven generates and not spoil it is called being adept at study (*shanxue*).[104]

The concluding sentence is similar to the definition of the Son of Heaven as the one who "completes what nature gave life to, without spoiling it," seen above in the *bensheng* passage. The *zunshi* chapter reveals a Xunzi-like and Mohist concern in its emphasis on the role of study (*xue*) in refining natural endowments that cannot be increased in themselves, but can be culturally refined through education.

The *zunshi* chapter presents a fine example of synthetic literature. It is generally written in a Mohist, and a Xunzi vein in holding that a teacher is necessary for the maintenance of the hierarchical social and political structure of human culture and harmonious social order. The *zunshi* chapter not only extols the significance of the teacher, but it also emphasizes the need for the student (in this case, the ruler) to offer timely sacrifices to the court tutor.

> Generally speaking, in study, one must undertake to advance his career, then his mind will not be confused. One should read loudly with effort. He should be cautious in observing his master, listening for instructions; he should observe when his master is happy, then he can question the meaning of a text. He should make both his ears and eyes work in compliance; he should never oppose his ambition to learn; and he should reconsider and reflect after withdrawing from his master, seeking what he really means.
>
> He should often (*shi*) debate and interpret in order to discuss the way (*dao*). He should never debate casually; in debating he must comply with the standards (*fa*). When he gets it right, he is without arrogance, and when he gets it wrong, he is not embarrassed. He must return to the root.[105]
>
> When the master is alive, then carefully provide nurturing. In the way of careful nurturing, the nurturing of the heart and mind (*yang xin*) is the most venerated. When the master dies, then reverently perform sacrifices. Among the methods (*shu*) of reverent sacrifice, timing is the most important undertaking. These are the means to venerate one's teacher (*zunshi*).[106]

Providing a clear analysis of the mental concentration, activities, and respect for one's teacher, necessary for proper learning, the author assumes that the ruler as disciple will have the quality of character and self-cultivation to be sensitive to the teacher's instruction, and that the disciple will be like a filial son, offering seasonal sacrifices in a timely fashion. If there must be proper timing in ritual, then how much more so in rulership?

Autumn: A Militarist Conception of *Xing*

As the circumstantial and seasonal conditions change, the ruler must appropriate different practices of self-cultivation and administrative policy. With the coming of autumn the forces of yin, the dark, diminishing, and reclining aspects of nature, dominate. In keeping with this and the approaching need to begin storing goods for the forthcoming destruction and hardships of winter, the ruler must turn to harvesting in agriculture. By analogy the ruler must use regulations, punishments, and especially punitive expeditions to weed out and prune off those undesirable elements that arise in the process of ruling the empire. As the monthly command (*mengqiuji*) chapter for the first month of autumn reports:

> The chilly winds come. The white dew falls. The cicada of the cold chirps. Then, hawks sacrifice birds. This is the time to begin the practice of punishments and executions.[107]

The chapter stipulates the ritual implements and the proper days to hold festivals. On the day of the *liqiu* (establishing autumn) festival, the Son of Heaven is directed to lead the feudal lords, dukes, high officials, and ministers in a parade in the western suburb to welcome in the season.

> Upon returning, he is to reward the troops and lead the military officials at court. The Son of Heaven, then, commands the generals and commanders to select knights, sharpen the weapons, and train the gallant and heroic. He should empower and appoint meritorious generals to engage expeditions against those not complying with *yi* (appropriate forms of fairness); he should accuse and execute those who were violent or idle in service to distinguish between the good and the bad, and he should travel far on inspection trips. In this month he should order the proper officials to revise the regulations and statutes, to repair the prisons, to prepare handcuffs and fetters, to restrain and stop depravity, to cautiously investigate crimes and evils, and to undertake making arrests.[108]

Autumn is the season for organizing military and judicial matters. Those who have failed in the lessons of self-cultivation, particularly those rulers who have failed, must now suffer the responses of the virtuous Son of Heaven who will not tolerate criminals nor tyrants.

Character As Majesty and Power Received from *Tian*. The *dangbing* (On Mobilizing the Military) chapter follows the first month of autumn chronicle. It presents an interesting meld of Militarists (*bingjia*), Huanglao, and apparently a *rujia* notion of "just military actions" (*yibing*), which display a *fajia* focus on the interdependency of military and government affairs.[109] In large part, the chapter argues that military actions, in particular, "just military actions" (*yibing*) taken against a tyrant, are inevitable. And the chapter contends that, at the very least, military actions cannot be abolished (*wu you yan bing*).

The *dangbing* chapter employs a twofold argument in its opening passages to justify appropriate military actions: first, it argues by way of historical authority, pointing out the long cultural tradition of just military actions; second, it argues that human character is martial—that it is received from nature and cannot be altered by humans, though as we shall see it can be transformed by fear in battle or, as we have seen above, by cultural refinement.

> The sage Kings of antiquity had just military actions, and they did not abolish the military. Military affairs have come down from high antiquity. They have always existed ever since there were people for the first time.[110]

So there is a strong historical precedence for military actions.

To further strengthen the argument that military affairs have been with the masses from the beginning, the chapter proposes that the masses have a martial character by nature.

> In all cases to be "marital" is to be awe-inspiring; "awesomeness" is strength. That there is awesomeness and strength in the people comes from their character (*xing*). Character is what is *received from nature* (*tian*). It is not something humans themselves can construct. One who is martial cannot alter it, and a capable artisan cannot change it. Military actions have come from antiquity.[111] (emphasis added)

The antiquity of human character must be interpreted as the antiquity of human life itself; the antiquity of life is mentioned in the *shenwei* chapter.[112] The antiquity of human character, however, is not to be taken as an innate structure, but rather, like the filial son who acknowledges that his own body is the gift of the ancestors,[113] one must realize that one's character is the culmination of cultural history. Though many of the paradigm models of human life were established in high antiquity, nevertheless life is an ongoing process in which one must appropriate one's humanity and culture in the present context of living.

In the above we find one of the strongest examples of human *xing* as a basic condition of life that one does not have direct control over. The *chenglian* chapter contains a similar expression that *xing* is received from nature. This is another way of emphasizing that human character is a correlative concept that must always be understood in terms of its relation to nature. To say that humans cannot make or alter their martial character is not to contend that the character is fixed or predetermined; rather, it means that people are limited to working with and cultivating the conditions and circumstances that are co-dependent on nature and cultural history. The point being argued in the *dangbing* chapter is that one's martial character cannot be done away with. In fact, it is an ancient cultural characteristic of humans. Since the martial character cannot be abolished, the ruler must be sure to direct military actions under the guideline of *yi* (rightness, appropriate forms of fairness).

Although people cannot constitute their character by themselves, given the correlative co-dependency on nature, nevertheless, people can influence the character within themselves or others. Most important, for military concerns, the character can be substantially shaken so as to overwhelm the enemy.

Fear and the Breakdown of Character. The second chapter of the second month of autumn, *lunwei* (Discourse on the Majesty of a Commander), introduces further applications of *xing* in a military context. In discussing the five criteria of a majestic commander,[114] the *lunwei* chapter makes note of how a commander overwhelms the enemy troops and drives them into such a state of confusion that their physical form is separated from their character.

> The desired victory will have been already attained before the blades clash. When the enemy is trembling, its shattered morale will be exhausted. They will all be confused and dispirited. Their physical forms and characters will be driven apart. In marching they won't know where to go; in running they won't know which direction they are going.[115]

Human character can be shaken. *Xing* is not a given, fixed potential; it can be disturbed. *Xing* is depicted as alterable in a negative disruptive fashion, so that the majestic commander can instill such fear and trembling in the enemy troops that they will actually lose touch with their sensibilities. They will lose control of their martially trained bodies and characters during the battle. Although the general tendencies of human character cannot be constituted or totally abolished by mankind, it is possible for people to influence their own or another's character both in positive forms of self-cultivation and negative forms of disrupting one's cultural or martial training.

Winter: *Mojia* and *Fajia* Models of *Xing*

According to the monthly ordinance chapters, the early winter season is chiefly devoted to matters of "storage," both of harvest grain and burial of the dead, while the late winter is reserved for fiscal planning. The first two chapters following the early winter ordinance are entitled and concerned with *jiesang* (Frugal Funerals) and *ansi* (Safety in Death). They both present a basically frugal Mohist position tempered with a *rujia* focus on maintaining funerals and mourning practices.[116] The later chapters turn to concerns of administration and personnel, taking a *fajia* orientation.

Death and the Process of Life. The *jiesang* chapter contains an interesting discussion on how the processes of completing life come full circle in death, which require fulfilling the wishes of the deceased and ensuring their safe entombment. The focus of the LSCQ's discussion is primarily directed toward the emperor as sage ruler due to his being a filial son toward his parents and a merciful parent toward his own children. There are significant references to both the cultivation of life and to *xing* and *qing* as the properly refined character and affections required of a worthy person.

> A thorough knowledge of life is what is crucial for the sage; a thorough knowledge of death is what is ultimate for the sage.
>
> As for "knowledge of life," not to let anything interfere with life is what is meant by "*yangsheng*" (nurturing life). As for "knowledge of death," not to let anything interfere with death is what is meant by "*ansi*" (safety in death). These two are things which the sage alone decides. Of everything born between heaven and earth that it necessarily experiences, death is something it will not escape. When a filial son esteems his parents or a compassionate parent loves his son, that he will be pained (by bereavement) in his very flesh and bone is from his human character (*xing*). To cast away the esteemed or loved one in a ditch or gully when he dies, people's basic characteristics (*qing*) cannot tolerate. Therefore, there is the duty of burying the dead.
>
> To "bury" (*zang*) means "to hide away" (*zang*), which the compassionate parent or filial son is careful to do. One careful to do it thinks ahead with the heart of a live man. For thinking ahead on behalf of the dead with the heart of a live man, nothing is as important as they not be moved, not be dug up.[117]

The sage ruler's means of fulfilling life comes to the considerations of death and managing the affairs of the deceased. It is the *xing* (character) and the *qing* (affections, sentiment) that distinguish a person as refined and cultured, that is, an achieved person.

Different Approaches to Cultivation. The *yiyong* (On the Different Uses of Things) chapter, the last of the first winter section, discusses a programmatic approach to the different ways a thing or an activity might be employed. Its discussion is somewhat colored with pragmatic or utilitarian hues in its concern for attaining a desired result by the creative appropriation of events. The *yiyong* chapter displays the far-reaching, creative approaches that the writers of the LSCQ were willing to employ in guiding the ruler's project of orchestrating a well-ordered agrarian society.

> The myriad things are not all the same, and so they are utilized by people in different ways. This is the source of order and disorder, preserving or perishing of a state, and one's life or death. Hence, a state can have an expansive territory, a strong military and wealth, but still not necessarily be stabilized. Or a ruler can be venerated, respected, and highly esteemed, and yet he is not necessarily really significant. They (being stabilized and significant) depend on how one applies them (the resources and respect). The tyrants Jie and Zhou, by using their talents, achieved destruction for

> themselves. Kings Tang and Wu by utilizing their talents achieved the kingship for themselves.[118]

Five examples are given of how skillful people can use some common thing in an extraordinary way to achieve grand results. For example, King Tang prohibited the use of four nets in hunting and thereby won over the empire, or King Wen had an unearthed skeleton reburied with proper funeral rites and thereby won over the empire. Kongzi used a pole to give instructions on the social grades and ranks, and the ancients were noted for esteeming archery because it cultivated the young and nourished the elderly, but now it is esteemed by people because of its use in attacking, fighting, and robbing. Finally, the chapter uses the example of sweet foods that the humane person uses to nurture the sick and support the elderly, but the robber and bandit use them to bribe their way into locked doors. These examples show the wide variety of approaches that one can employ things to unify the empire. The stories in this chapter highlight the creative appropriation of ordinary things to achieve a desired goal. They suggest that the ruler will attempt to emulate the previous sages who employed the appropriation of things in their art of rulership.

The *zhongdongji* (Middle Month of Winter) chapter turns the discussion of the emperor's self-cultivation practices in the direction of a more ascetic mode. This is not overly surprising. given the *shierji*'s concern for temporal seasonal approaches for applying different methods to suit the context.

> In this month there is the solstice when the day is shortest. Yin and yang compete, and all living things are stirred.[119] The *junzi* (moral exemplar) should perform fasts and austerities. In his dwelling he insists on seclusion; for his person he desires tranquility. He gets rid of music and beauties and forbids himself lust, and desires to stabilize (*an*) his physical form and character. In affairs he desires being passive, waiting to see what is settled by yin and yang.[120]

The monthly ordinance chapter directs the ruler to emulate the cosmic model set by *yin* in the winter months and to take a more ascetic and passive approach toward self-cultivation and rulership. By restraining himself in his hobbies, he will settle his body; by restraining his desires, he will stabilize his character. The cultivation of one's desires and pleasures that occurred in the spring and summer seasons has given way to prohibitions.

Foresight in Planning. The late winter is spent in total reserve on the ruler's part, and this provides the opportune time for fiscal and long-range planning.

The *changjian* (Foresight or Forecasting) chapter provides a political historical epistemology based on the assumption that there is a homogeneity that runs through the past, present, and future. This notion that the past and the present are basically the same can also be found in the *chajin* chapter of the LSCQ, the *Xunzi*, and the *Mozi*. Foreknowledge is implied in the *Analects* (2/23). The *changjian* chapter contains an argument that the true mark of a sage is the ability to "see far" both spatially and temporally, but especially historically in order to maintain the reputation of a wise ruler.

> The reason why one person's wisdom surpasses another's depends on whether one has long range vision (*changjian*) or short range vision. The present is to antiquity as antiquity is to future ages. Likewise the present is to future ages as it is to antiquity.[121] Hence if you thoroughly know the present, it is possible to know antiquity. If one knows antiquity, it is possible to know the future. The present and antiquity, the past and the future are one and the same. So the sage rulers know backward one thousand years, and they know forward one thousand years.[122]

The *changjian* perspective has a logical systematic tone with a decidedly *fajia*, *Mojia*, or Xunzi-like perspective in its proposal that the past and the future are the same.

A major criterion in judging a ruler's wisdom and foresight is his ability to select the proper personnel, or *shi*. The *shi* (knights or scholar officials) are a key link in the ruler's ability to set an example for the masses to emulate—the self-cultivating ruler only appoints self-actualizing ministers, generals, attendants, and so on. Since the guest scholars at Lü Buwei's estate contributed to the LSCQ, it is not too surprising to see that they gave their best arguments to justify their own and their patron's position for the proper administration of a state or in unifying the empire.

Managing Personnel. The LSCQ is one of the earliest texts to systematically employ the expression *youdao zhi shi* (scholar-knights who possess the way). Throughout the text there are repeated examples, and even whole chapters, devoted to the importance of selecting and appointing proper personnel who comply with the way (*dao*). The late winter months provide an appropriate time to review one's policy on selecting and appointing personnel.

The *shijie* (A Knight's Disciplined Integrity) chapter describes the type of *shi* a ruler must employ if he plans to settle the empire or a state.[123]

> As for the sort of man a knight (*shi*) is: in coinciding with rationality, he does not shirk the difficulties; in facing calamities, he forgets his own

> benefit. He neglects life to practice rightness, and he looks at death as a return home. If there is one who possesses characteristics like these, then the lord of a state might fail to make him his friend, the Son of Heaven might fail to make him his minister.[124] In the most important case, he will settle the Empire. At the next level he will settle a state—these are the things which necessarily derive from such men. Hence, the ruler who intends to establish achievement and fame on a large scale cannot but undertake to seek out people like them. A worthy ruler labors in seeking personnel, but he is idle in controlling projects.[125]

The rest of the chapter relates a story that climaxes with both Boguo Sao and, then, his friend committing suicide to petition the ruler of Qi to reconsider his accusations that caused the minister, Yanzi, to flee the state. The moral of the story is that if Yanzi had been able to recognize Boguo Sao's integrity as a statesman, then the whole incident could have been avoided.

Besides the *dangbing* chapter, the *chenglian* (Sincerity and Discipline) chapter, concerned with attracting suitable *shi*, contains the other explicit references to *xing* being "received (*shou*) from nature (*tian*)." The notion that human character is correlative with nature is shared by many pre-Qin philosophers, but it was particularly emphasized in the Literati texts (cf. *Mengzi* 50/7 A/1; *Zhongyong*, chapter 1; *Xunzi*, chapters 17, 23). The following occurs in a context that is social and political in nature with a strong Mengzi or Xunzi-like focus, but following the incorporated program, it is applied in a *fajia* context of planning matters of state personnel.

> Stones can be broken, but you cannot take away their hardness. Cinnabar can be ground, but you cannot take away its being red. Being hard and being red is had as their character (*xing*). "Character" is what is received from nature; it is not that one is doing something after making a choice. As for those heroic knights who have a good opinion of self-respect, and cannot be sullied by filth, they are just like this (the characteristics of hard and red).[126]

This highlights the *chenglian* chapter's integration of the interpretations of *xing* as the most basic characteristics that constitute the development of a particular focus. Time and again the LSCQ states that it is nature that provides the context for life, but people must nurture it. Although a person, in particular, the ruler, has the ability to harmonize with nature and assist in the processes of nurturing and cultivation, nevertheless, humans alone cannot constitute the natural conditions by choice.

The *chenglian* chapter goes on to extol the merits of two Literati heros, Bo Yi and Shu Qi, who were of such high moral caliber that they preferred starving to death rather than serving the tyrant Zhou or the young King Wu, who was forming alliances with the tyrant in his early days as king. Bo Yi and Shu Qi not only express their own application of appropriateness and proper timing by their dissatisfaction with both the tyrant Zhou and King Wu, but also in their discourse they make explicit reference to Shennong's use of proper timing in performing sacrifices with utmost reverence.[127] Their story represents the aesthetic and intrinsic Literati paradigm of appropriateness and proper timing, which emphasizes one's personal and unique socio-spiritual integration in the field experience of society.

The *chenglian* chapter concludes with the following description of the essentials (*qing*) to be the *sine qua non* for being identified as a human.

> It is in humans as they essentially are that everyone judges some things more important than others. If you judge something important, you want to keep it intact; if unimportant, you use it to nourish what you judge important. As for the two knights, Bo Yi and Shu Qi, they were willing to take themselves out and abandon their lives to establish their intentions because they had first determined what was to be considered lightly and heavily.[128]

Again we see the significance of having desires, and especially of being able to weigh out and prioritize one's desires as an important part of the self-cultivation processes. Bo Yi and Shu Qi are fine examples of the type of *shi* a good ruler wants to employ, because they recognize that their integrity in service to a worthy king is more important than their own lives.

The *buqin* (The Unintimidatible Character of a Statesman) chapter continues the discussion of employing worthy *shi*. The *buqin* chapter blends in a Daoist attitude of nonattachment for the ruler with the pragmatic concerns of employing proper personnel, and it tempers this with a Literati bias for appointing cultivated statesmen. It opens with the notion that the empire is less significant than one's person, but paradoxically, the ruler needs to find officials who do not have this attitude.

> The empire is less important than one's own person, but the knights use their persons to serve on behalf of others. To use oneself to serve on behalf of another is very important, but if the ruler (*ren* lit. person) does not understand, what chance is there they will find each other?[129] A worthy ruler is sure he understands the knights himself. Then, the knights

will exhaust their strength, drain their knowledge, and they will not avoid personal calamity in a struggle or in giving straightforward advice.[130]

The *buqin* chapter focuses on the superior character of the dedicated knights who willingly die for their principles. The ruler understands that his life is more precious than the empire, but to rule that empire he employs officials who will not avoid personal disaster, let alone seek out personal profit, in the execution of their duties. Thus the chapter proposes that the mark of a ruler's fame is not the size of his state but his ability to attract worthy *shi*.

The chapter describes Yu Rang and Gongsun Hong as statesmen who could not be intimidated in serving their respective rulers. Although Gongsun Hong and especially Yu Rang, a notorious assassin, are not commonly referred to as moral exemplars, there is a prominent Literati and Mohist point of view in the *buqin* chapter. The chapter contends that the rulers of large states could not compete with Kongzi and Mozi, who were just commoners, in attracting scholar-knights. In a discourse with the King of Zhao, Gongsun Hong gives a description of the worthy scholar-knight, asserting that if there were just three such people, they could order a state and be the tutors of great statesmen like Guan Zhong or Shang Yang. The winter season maintains the *shierji*'s programmatic and unified eclectic approach toward human character. It recognizes the inevitability of death, and it strikes a balance between the *rujia* demand for funerals and mourning rites and the *Mojia* criticism demanding frugality in burial. In keeping with the seasonal necessity of staying indoors and conserving energy, the chapters emphasize the importance of long-range planning and the character development of the statesmen and scholar-knights who will administer the state policies and regulations.

Xing, human character, as it is understood in the *shierji* section, is presented as an achievement concept that stands in a correlative relationship with nature. The achievement side of human character is featured because the writers of the text are concerned with establishing and maintaining an imperial rule over a complex network of ethnic groups within a temporal context. With this temporal orientation in mind, it is clear that what the ruler and ministers make of themselves sets an example for the masses, and this provides a model for political order. Many of the passages concerning *xing* in the LSCQ explore the aspects of nature and human life that one can orchestrate to attain harmony in the state. A major concern is to cultivate and refine the ruler's desires to develop his character in both cultural and military arenas. The *shierji* discusses the development of character under a seasonal scheme to attune the emperor's educational ritual practices and his ritualistic co-creation with the cosmos.

For the LSCQ, the practicable program of the ruler's self-cultivation and harmonious political order overrides the theoretical debate on human nature as good, bad, or indifferent. Regardless of the exact quality of the human character, a person must still hold the desires in check, not allowing excess that leads to harm. This is where proper timing and appropriateness come into play. The ruler must be able to apportion the natural desires and fulfill them in a positive, productive manner, that is, without harming or confusing himself.

Those passages from the LSCQ that contain a programmatic position on human character are distinguished by the application of proper timing in the self-cultivation and administrative processes. Regardless of the diverse theoretical conclusions concerning human character, the application of proper timing must be put into practice in at least three areas, namely: (1) State administrative policy must institute precise seasonal, timely practices, for instance, agricultural activities should not be hampered by warfare, or vice versa; (2) The administration must be sensitive to historical and cultural changes, and thereby reform policy in accordance with historical changes; (3) One's self-cultivation and embodiment of virtuous behavior are expressed in one's achievement of proper timing in interpersonal relationships. When the ruler's self-cultivation demonstrates proper timing, then the mutually interdependent, reciprocal interaction of the ruler and the people of the empire is harmonious. Proper timing in social and spiritual cultivation is manifested in the ruler's and the officials' reform of the state's policies and statutes according to historical and cultural timing. The need for proper timing is evident in seasonal policy, which is sensitive to the natural, social, and economic forces of farm labor and the military. For the authors of the LSCQ, proper timing has an important function in the social order, which emerges through human history and the state.

Chapter 3

An Emergent Social Order

When human character is perceived within a temporal setting as an achievement in process, human social order, especially the state, is understood primarily as a historical achievement. Pre-Qin literature concerning the justification and function of civil society focuses on its emergent order. The dominant pre-Qin perspectives do not hold a simple, cyclic view of historical time. The LSCQ treatises describe human society as an emergent order maintained by an enlightened ruler who appoints virtuous ministers and orchestrates, fulfilling the desires of the masses by benefitting them through proper employment.

The twenty-four standard dynastic histories testify to the long-standing historical awareness of the "Chinese" people. Their historical consciousness is rooted in antiquity. By examining some of the major pre-Qin interpretations concerning the origin of the state, one can assess the historical perspectives in the LSCQ. The LSCQ treatises contain sound historical awareness. Zuo Yan's *wuxing* (five phases) interpretation plays an important role in the LSCQ and the subsequent "orthodoxy" or state-sanctioned understanding of history, especially the dynastic cycle. The dynastic cycle should not be understood in the simple sense of a literal cycle, where there is exact repetition. A spiral model of time provides the best heuristic paradigm. A spiral contains both the element of repeating cycles, and it depicts waves of unique ascending "golden ages" and descending periods of decadence, although there are patterns of continuity. Following Zuo Yan's teachings, some of the contributors to the LSCQ recognize that there are patterns of continuity in the "life cycle" of social and political order. They identify the patterns of the five phases and correlate them with past dynasties to discover their own place in the process to institute policies in preparation for the future.

The historical focus found in the LSCQ treatises sustains an "emergent organic instrumental" approach, justifying the function of the state. An organic concept on the origin of the state is grounded in the understanding that people naturally gather in groups for their own protection and fulfillment. An instrumental justification for maintaining the state by manipulating the people's desires through reward and punishment to ensure the fulfillment of those natural desires by competitive employment supplements the organic perspective. The combination of the organic and instrumental positions is what is meant by an "emergent organic instrumental" position. The *daojia*, *rujia*, and *wuxing* elements in the LSCQ support a natural organic social and political point of view. This natural model advocates an art of rulership built on "loving and benefitting the masses by means of employing them so as to fulfill their desires" (*aili yongmin*). For at least some of the contributors to the LSCQ, the lessons of history show that loving and benefitting the masses by properly employing them is crucial in the art of rulership. On the other hand, the LSCQ contains passages influenced by an instrumental perspective derived from such works as the *Mozi*, *Xunzi*, *The Book of Lord Shang* (*Shangjunshu*), and military treatises that feature social order as a human contrivance devised to benefit people. The significance of bringing benefit and employment to the masses by acting in a timely fashion is emphasized in the LSCQ's unified blend of the organic and instrumental positions.

Human Character and Social Order: An Analogy

The state is intimately tied to the achievement of human character, especially the ruler's self-cultivation. Just as one's character must be refined and disciplined to achieve well-rounded maturity, the state must also be developed within the process of natural transformation to achieve its proper function of fulfilling human needs and desires. The myriad things including the state are constantly in flux. The sage ruler appropriates the natural process to fulfill his own desires and those of the masses.

The *bensheng* (Life as Basic) chapter explicitly states that the role of the ruler is to appropriately employ the processes of nature and to establish state offices for the fulfillment of life.

> What initially gives life is nature; what nurtures and completes it is mankind. The one who is able to nurture what nature gives life to without

> interfering is called the Son of Heaven. When the Son of Heaven acts, he endeavors to keep intact the natural.[1] This is the reason why court offices were established; offices were established to keep life intact.[2] When the confused rulers of this age have many offices but contrarily, use them to harm life, then they have lost the reason why offices were established.[3]

Human life can only be fulfilled through political institutions. Through the LSCQ's counsel, a ruler can learn to become an enlightened sage ruler. There is a correlative relation obtaining between human life and the state, and an analogy is drawn between the organization of the state and the organization of the bodily sense organs.

An analogy between controlling state offices and regulating the sense organs is contained in the *guisheng* (Venerating Life) chapter.

> In the sage's profound consideration of the empire, nothing is valued more than life. The eyes, ears, nose, and mouth are the servants of life. Although the ears desire to hear sounds, the eyes to see colors, the nose to smell aromas, and the mouth to taste flavors, nevertheless if they harm life, they must be stopped. If what resides within these four organs (*guan*) does not desire what is beneficial to life, then do not act on it.
>
> Observing it from this perspective, the eyes, ears, nose, and mouth do not get to proceed on their own authority; there must be something they are controlled by (i.e., the heart-mind). By way of illustration, it is like the official functions (*guanzhi*); they do not get to proceed on their own authority; there must be something they are controlled by (i.e., a ruler). This is the art of valuing life (*guisheng*).[4]

The analogy and pun on the sense organs or orifices (*guan*) and the offices of state (*guan*) serve to emphasize the ruler's need to regulate his own person and likewise to regulate the officials. Just as the organs (*guan*) of the body have to be organized and managed to fulfill their function so too the state officials (*guan*) must be regulated to fulfill their proper roles.

The *yuandao* (The Cyclic Way) chapter draws a psychological analogy between the need for the ruler to properly stimulate his officials, just as his own organs and limbs respond best when properly stimulated.

> As for people having a body and four limbs and being able to utilize them, if they are given a stimulus, then one certainly is aware of it. If they are given a stimulus but one is not aware of it, then the body and four limbs cannot be utilized. (In matters of receiving orders) the officials

> are like this (i.e., like the body and limbs being controlled by awareness). If the decrees and edicts are not sensed (by the officials), then they cannot be utilized. Possessing something but not being able to utilize it is not as good as not possessing it at all. A ruler is one who employs what he does not possess. Shun, Yu, Tang, and Wu were all like this. In appointing high officials, the early sage kings were bound to comply with the principle of squareness. If they comply with the principle of squareness, then their designations will be fixed. If their designations are fixed, then the subordinates won't harbor selfish secret desires.[5]

The ruler organizes the officials and issues commands by modeling the principle of earth, squareness, and by establishing fixed and regular patterns of reward and punishment.

The analogy between the human organism and the state is found in different contexts in the LSCQ. The LSCQ accommodates developmental and programmatic conceptions of the state in keeping with some of its views on human character.

A Survey of Pre-Qin Organic and Instrumental Positions and Their Impact on the LSCQ

To fully appreciate their impact on the LSCQ's unified eclectic philosophy, the dominant pre-Qin positions concerning the origin, justification, and subsequent function of the state are examined. There are three explanations concerning the origin of the state: divine creation, natural organic generation, and instrumentalism. Scholars have used these models to interpret pre-Qin political philosophy. The function of the state is usually derived from the suggested origin. Any explanation concerning the origin of the state usually entails the origin of law. Pre-Qin thinkers identify the origin of law in the regulations of culture, rules of the family, the military, and farming. The pre-Qin perspectives are opposed to and cast considerable doubt on Derk Bodde's hypothesis that "Chinese" law, or penal law, had a non-Chinese origin.[6]

First there is the proposal of divine creation, which is not a theory but *mythos*. The divine creation myths describe how the structure and function of human society and law are created by one or more gods. The transcendent model of *creatio ex nihilo* is not a consideration in mainstream pre-Qin thought, given the lack of mythological and supernatural explanation and the notable lack of cosmogony and the concept of transcendence. It has been mistakenly applied to pre-Qin political thought.[7]

The organic theory holds that people are social and political animals by nature. It is popular in theology to unite the philosophical organic model with the divine creation myth, as in Aquinas and Burke. In the case of pre-Qin philosophy, it is best not to do so. From the organic perspective, social political order and law are a consequence of the natural development of culture and custom. In the West, the organic theory was proposed by such thinkers as Plato, Aristotle, Hume, and Whitehead. Because of the impact of Plato and Aristotle, the organic theory is usually assumed to promote the idea that the state follows an ideal (utopian) model or fulfills a teleological potentiality. Because such essentialistic and substantialistic theories do not illuminate an understanding of pre-Qin thought, one might rather reflect on Hume's organic theory of the state and society as a spontaneous order developed out of the habits of humanity and sympathy when considering pre-Qin naturalistic organic concepts of the state.[8] Referring to the organic justification of the state in the pre-Qin context, I intend to summon up the image of a spontaneous, often hierarchical, pattern of particular relationships, that is, the interaction of various foci shaping society in an aesthetic, ritually construed field of experience. The pre-Qin organic conception of the state is not a teleological concept.

The instrumental theory holds that society, government, and law are human contrivances. In Western political philosophy, the instrumental theory is often referred to by a specific form known as the "social contract theory." Although the social contract theorists often begin with "prehistoric" humans devoid of social order, nevertheless, this is rhetorical flair—none of them take the description seriously, nor do they propose that the social contract was a historical event.[9] Pre-Qin versions of instrumentalism provide a historical, social, and economic explanation of the origin of civil society. Not surprisingly, pre-Qin instrumentalism lacks the explicit idea of a "contract."

A fourth proposal on the origin of the state blends the organic and instrumental theories. An "emergent organic instrumental position" advocates that the "reorganization" or "reform" of society, especially its political structure, policies, and laws, is accomplished under the guise of instrumental agreement, but this system is natural to the development of social-moral awareness—organic cultural patterns formulate instrumental agreements or contracts. A critical reading of the instrumental theorists makes it clear that there are few who hold to a pure contract theory.[10] Following the LSCQ's lead, the implications of an "organic contract theory" are elaborated in the final chapter of this book.

Implicit Organic Theories in Some Literati, Daoist, and Agriculturalist Thought

The organic theory on the origin of the state is not as clearly expressed as the instrumental position in the early corpus of pre-Qin philosophy, hence it requires a detailed explication so it can be recognized in the LSCQ.

The Literati Organic Model. The *rujia* position on the origin of the state is implicitly contained in the *Lunyu* (*Analects*), *Mengzi*, Dong Zhongshu's *Chunqiu fanlu*, and other *rujia* texts. The *Xunzi* is the exception, offering a formulation of an instrumental theory. The *rujia* organic postulate proposes that the state is a natural extension of the family. For Kongzi, the political relationships sanctioned by the state are grounded in the natural family relations. *Mengzi* explicitly expands the *Analects*' discussion in terms of the Five Relationships. For the organic *rujia* model, filial piety (*xiao*) is the methodological root for the cultivation of the other virtues, especially for becoming a dedicated and loyal minister.[11] Moral virtues learned from the family are extended to others, contributing to political harmony (*Analects*, 2/21). The family is rooted in the natural and harmonious structure of the world. Except for a few cosmological comments concerning the bipolar process nature of the world, there is no concern for cosmogonic beginnings.

The organic *rujia* thinkers do not elaborate a prehistoric model of humanity. There is no speculation concerning a precivilized "state of nature." From the organic *rujia* perspective, life in a moral community is always historical life. History and morality entail each other, because one achieves person making by emulating traditional moral exemplars. Prehistoric "human" existence proves uninteresting from the organic *rujia* perspective. Cultural history is a necessary condition for the achievement of person making. A prehistoric being could not achieve sufficient personhood, due to a lack of cultural history, to serve as an exemplar.

L. Shih-lien Hsü argues that Kongzi does "not sanction a social contract theory . . ." or "the notion that government was instituted by any one person."[12] For the *rujia* organic position, people naturally construct (patriarchal) families, and the family defines the foundation of the state. The ruler is known as *tianzi* (Son of Heaven), and he holds the *tianming* (mandate of heaven)—family structure is natural, and cosmic order is hierarchical, like the family. The analogy of family and state provides a justification for political authority and obligation. The genealogy of the state is rooted in the family: the nuclear family develops into an extended family, which becomes a clan; out of the extended clan or tribe arises a corporation of "tribes," and the "tribal nation" is born; the tribal nation settles down and the city-state arises. In the *rujia* context, the royal family serves as the exemplar for how other families are to behave, and the royal family acts as the concrete manifestation of the family as state. The "state" is present in germinal form in the cultural authoritativeness of the parents.

In the *Five Classics* and *Four Books*, the state is the natural condition of human life. Though some propose that the pre-Qin cultural attitude reflects a devolutionary view of world history declining after a Utopian past, for Kongzi the historical development of culture and civilization is decidedly cumulative.[13] Kongzi follows the way of Zhou culture because it accumulated Xia and Shang cultures (*Analects*, 3/14).

Although the early corpus of *rujia* texts does not provide an explicit statement on the "origins," there is a clear expression of it in the *Dazhuan*, or *Xicizhuan* (Great Treatise), commentary on the *Yijing* (*Book of Changes*). The *Dazhuan* is consistent with an organic *rujia* description of the origin of culture and civilization, and the *Shiji* (*Records of the Historian*), the Han dynasty attempt at comprehensive history, cites this description for the development of civilization.

The *Dazhuan* addresses the natural organic root of the state beginning in the midst of things with a well-ordered society already in operation with its sage ruler. The section begins: "When Bao Xi (Fu Xi) of old ruled the empire . . . ,"[14] he emulated the patterns of nature and invented the eight trigrams. The natural development of culture and civilization is rooted in the inspiration of Fu Xi to draw *analogies* from nature, creating the system of the eight trigrams, generating the sixty-four hexagrams that serve as the natural/analogical models for the development of culture and civilization.

The *Dazhuan* narrates how Fu Xi was inspired by the "clinging" hexagram to invent nets and baskets; how Shennong's clan arose and was inspired by the hexagram "increase," developing agriculture; and how the clans of the Yellow Emperor, Yao, and Shun were inspired by a number of hexagrams, inventing the various cultural artifacts, tools, and weapons. The *Dazhuan* describes how prehistory developed naturally into civilized life.

> In the earliest antiquity people dwelt in caves or lived in the fields. In later generations the sages replaced these with buildings . . . inspired by the hexagram "power of the great." The funerals of antiquity (were improper because the dead) were covered with brushwood out in the open fields, without a mound or trees, and the mourning period was not fixed. The later sages changed this. . . . In earliest antiquity they ruled by keeping

> records with knots. The sages of later generations changed this; they used written documents to govern the various offices and to supervise the myriad peoples.[15]

The anthropologically respectable tenor of this description further emphasizes the strong historical continuity present in ancient pre-Qin culture and literature. For the *rujia* organic position, mankind is always organized in some political order.

The *rujia* impact on the organic conception of rulership in the LSCQ is most clearly noted in the *xiaoxinglan*, where rule by filial piety is stressed. The important *rujia* influence found in the LSCQ is the *tianming* (heaven's mandate) supposition that originates in the *Shijing* (*Book of Odes*) and *Shujing* (*Book of Documents*). The supposition comes to full expression in the *Mengzi* (1 B/8, 4 A/8, 7 A/1) and impacts on Zuo Yan's theory of the dynastic cycle extant in the LSCQ.

The Daoist Organic Model. Both Kongzi and Laozhuang teachings share a common ground despite their differences.[16] The organic nature of society and the state is one position they share. Following Hu Shi's suggestion, I propose that *daojia* and *nongjia* (Agriculturalist) writers added their own respective early history to the *rujia* understanding. Where the early *rujia* corpus only mentions the sage rulers Yao, Shun, and Yu, the *daojia* writers place the Yellow Emperor before Yao, and the Agriculturalists plant their sage, Shennong, the Divine Husbandman, before the Yellow Emperor. Finally, Fu Xi is placed at the dawn of civilization. Fu Xi is obscure enough to be an acceptable progenitor for either the *rujia* or *daojia*.[17]

The *Laozi* holds an implicit organic theory on the origin of the state, in that the text is written for a ruler, and it assumes that society will always have rulers—the question is: What kind of ruler will there be? Poem Eighty of the *Laozi* describes the ideal *daojia* society that assumes that the society would have a state and a ruler with a simple system of administration and a military.[18] The full consequences of the *daojia* utopia need not be argued here; that the *Laozi*, at least, assumes that a ruler is a natural condition of any human society is all that need be established at this point.[19]

The *Zhuangzi* is a composite text, and so the whole text, like the LSCQ, does not support one consistent point of view. Despite this composite nature, most agree that the "inner chapters" are the extant writings of Zhuangzi. They present an account of personal cultivation, which is chiefly organic in nature. The "inner chapters" are written for the socialized person; chapters 4 and 5 give advice to ministers at court. The text usually assumes that society has a ruler, even though the *real* ruler may not be the person on the throne.[20] It is a misnomer to attribute, as Vitaly Rubin has, a totally antisocial character to Zhuangzi or the other *daojia* thinkers.[21] Zhuangzi is opposed to a contrived, unnatural social order that is imposed on people. Zhuangzi attacks the impositions of *fajia*, and forms of *rujia*. But Zhuangzi does not reject the whole pre-Qin tradition; his worldview is not totally at odds with the Kongzi natural life-affirmative perspective. The *daojia* philosophers, like the *rujia*, embrace change and transformation. However, the Laozhuang perspective concerning nature is, of course, more open ended and indeterminate than the *rujia*.

It is easy to understand why one could argue that the *daojia*, especially the Laozhuang, view of history basically holds a devolutionary theory, where a past golden age of harmony with nature declined with the rise in rigid *rujia* social morals.[22] I argue, however, that this interpretation of historical decline must be reconciled with the *daojia* understanding of nature as a complex field of interpenetrating processes so that the present is not merely a degenerate form of a past golden age. The Laozhuang perspective on nature requires one to *return* directly to nature itself. This return is *not* like the Romantic "return to nature" because, for the writers of the *Laozi* and the inner chapters of the *Zhuangzi*, there is no ideal prehistoric nature or "noble savage" to which one could return. The Laozhuang teachings discern that society is a natural aspect of human life; society is only denaturalized when its customs and interpretations distort one's co-creative harmonization with nature, especially where a person is coerced by custom or law. Returning to nature, from the Laozhuang perspective, is not a simple return to an idealized past; rather, the Laozhuang thinkers acknowledge that everything is changing. Hence it would be impossible to make a simple return to nature. Although chapter 80 of the *Laozi* implies that people should merely return to the old ways, this must be an oversimplified presentation that does not take into consideration the processes of change and transformation. The Laozhuang philosophers are talking about reclaiming the natural attitude. They are not proposing that people actually restore the ancient practice of tying knots to keep records. They were poets and writers. They propose that people keep records with the knot-tying attitude, that is, not attempting to preserve records in order to influence future generations, thereby distorting and denaturalizing other people's creative involvement with nature and culture. The Laozhuang writers seek a return to a naturalizing attitude, developing self-transformation that allows one to mutually integrate with other foci in the field of *dao*.

Huanglao is clearly more political in its orientation than Laozhuang. The excavated silk manuscripts found with copies of the *Laozi*, which are being called the *Huangdi sijing* (*Four Classics of the Yellow Emperor*), are typical of a classical text in their composite and eclectic content. Although their militaristic material supports an instrumental position on the origin of the state, the material that is most "*daojia*-like" implies an organic origin of society in the *dao*. The *jingfa* fascicle claims that *dao* generates *fa* (law or social standards).[23] Jan Yün-hua argues that *fa* must be understood as "law" when applied to the human social level. He cites examples from the silk manuscripts to show that the organic natural development of law arises from the sages' emulating nature.[24] Jan Yün-hua contends that "law" is the manifestation of *dao* in society.[25] Thus both Laozhuang and Huanglao assume an implicit organic origin of the state.

The Agriculturalist Organic Model. The agriculturalist (*nongjia*) literature is also represented in the LSCQ. The Agriculturalists offer another version of the organic origin of society and law. There is a shortage of extant material on the Agriculturalists. Mengzi criticizes them, along with Yang Zhu and Mo Di.

The LSCQ provides us with the primary extant text of the *nongjia*; the *lulun* contains five chapters devoted to agricultural instruments and techniques. Although most of this material concerns the technology of farming, some of their philosophical positions can be drawn out of these chapters.

Three general points can be explicated from this material. First, the organic origin of society and law is generally in keeping with their organic character. Second, they carve a niche in history by appointing Shennong as the spiritual agriculturalist sage ruler. Moreover, just as the *rujia* have Gao Yao as their wise minister who organizes law, the *nongjia* have Hou Ji as their wise minister who develops farming.[26] Third, the unique feature of the *nongjia* organic theory is that it establishes the origin of society on people's natural propensity to farm.

> In antiquity the means by which the early sage kings led their people was to put agriculture before all other affairs. . . . The reason why Hou Ji undertook agriculture was because he considered it to be the *root* of instructing (enculturating/training) the masses.[27]

From this organic model of society, the natural agricultural basis of law is not far away. The LSCQ's *nongjia* material discusses in some detail the rules and standards of field farming—specifications for the size of tools, spaces between plants, the layout of the fields, and so on all imply a systematic ordering and regulating principle for human activity; that is, they imply a kind of "law." The Agriculturalists propose a type of "legal system" or system of mutual accountability based on small groups of families assigned to farm certain fields. These small group "societies" are reminiscent of the *daojia* utopia in *Laozi* poem 80. In their emphasis on warfare and agriculture, the *fajia* thinkers basically organized the commoner's life on the *nongjia* model; that is, the people were gathered around their respective fields.[28] Although the *nongjia* may have instrumentalist tendencies, especially when viewed from a *fajia* perspective, still the *nongjia* hold an organic perspective as their root metaphor.

Instrumentalist Theories in the *Mozi*, *Xunzi*, *Bingjia*, and *Fajia*

It is well documented that societies in general undergo massive change with the innovation of iron. With the appearance of iron in China during the seventh to sixth century B.C.E., Zhou society changed in two important ways, militarily and agriculturally.[29] With agricultural improvements there came a surplus of food that supported a larger population and the birth of a learned scholar-official class, generating the development of philosophy, and legal philosophy in particular. With the military developments and reforms in weaponry, employment of cavalry, strategy, and so forth, Zhou society underwent a drastic overhaul. One should keep in mind that the traditional Zhou system of feudal enfeoffment was built on an instrumental, contract-like model where the feudal lord held half of a broken tally (a jade disk or plaque) as a symbol of authority. With the onset of the iron age, the feudal system began to deteriorate, government administration was altered, the noble class was threatened, and the commoner was allowed an opportunity at social mobility through military prowess, technical skills, accumulation of wealth, or intellectual ability. As a reflection of and a response to these cultural, social, and economic changes, a competitive nonorganic position came into prominence in pre-Qin thought. Early Warring States thinkers such as Mozi, the *bingjia* (Militarist) essayists, and later *fajia* writers such as Shang Yang and Han Fei are strikingly instrumental in their approach. These thinkers are not really contractarians; they do not propose a social contract as the origin of the state. They do, however, propose that the state is a man-made institution. The *fajia* instrumental theories strip away the organic basis of the feudal system, eventually ending the system altogether with Li Si's memorial abolishing it.

Unlike the organic perspectives, the instrumental theories are clearly and explicitly stated. The instrumentalists share some common assumptions with some Western instrumentalists. The pre-Qin instrumentalists advocate a common character shared by all people, sage and commoner alike; human character is regarded as antisocial. The instrumentalists posit a prehistoric, nonsocial, governmentless life that is overcome by instituting a ruler. For the instrumentalists, "law" is positive law—it is human law, made by the ruler or ministers. The various instrumentalists differ as to the circumstances leading up to the establishment of the state: some propose that the state of nature was a state of war, either people against each other (Mozi and the Militarists) or mankind against nature (the LSCQ's *shijun* chapter), or some combination of the two (the LSCQ's *dangbing* chapter and Shang Yang); others (such as the Xunzi and passages in the LSCQ) propose that presocial life was unsettled and that certain sages foresaw the benefits of living in a cooperative society under a ruler.

Instrumentalism in the *Mozi*. The attributed author of the *Mozi* and founder of the Mohist school, Mo Di (fl. 490–403), was a commoner who climbed the social ladder through military achievement and education. Mo Di is one of the most obvious products of Kongzi's motto to educate any person, regardless of class or wealth. Mozi's concept of *jianai* (universal love) can be interpreted as a radical extension of this principle to serve and love all classes and all people equally. Mo Di advances a radical reinterpretation to the *rujia* idea of modeling "superiors." Kung-chuan Hsiao has pointed out: "The principal reason why universal love must (in practice) depend on the agreement with the superior is that man's nature is basically evil."[30] (Evil not in the Judeo-Christian sense, but rather evil in the sense of socially deviant or bad.) Because people are basically desire centered and personally biased by nature, according to the instrumentalists, they are led into strife. Thus a ruler must be enthroned to establish a common standard. The three chapters on *shangtong* (Identification with the Superior Model I, II, and III) display the *Mozi*'s instrumentalist theory for the origin of the state and law:

> Master Mozi said: In antiquity when the masses had come into being, there was not yet penal law or political organization. Now they say that for each person there was a different standard for rightness (*yi*). Such that if there was one person, there was one standard for rightness. . . . If there were ten people, there were ten standards. . . . Such that each person considered his own standard of rightness correct, and the standards of others wrong—thus, mutual disapproval arose. As a consequence, within the family circle fathers and sons, elder and younger brothers became angry and hateful; they were driven apart being unable to harmoniously cohabit. The various families in the world at large all used fire, water, and poisons to harm each other. Surplus energy was not used for mutual aid; surplus goods rot without being shared; good teachings were kept secret without being taught to others.

> The disorder of the world was like that of the birds and beasts. The reason for the world's disorder was that (human) life still lacked a political leader. Therefore, the one who was selected (by heaven or the people)[31] as the worthiest and most capable was established as the Son of Heaven. After the Son of Heaven was established, he felt his strength was insufficient, and so he selected the worthy and capable ones of the world. He established them to be the *sangong* (three leading Dukes). After the Son of Heaven and the *sangong* had been established, they considered the empire to be too vast because they could not clarify and understand the debates concerning right and wrong, and profit and loss of people from distant states and different lands. So they drew up (a map) dividing the various states, establishing the various feudal lords and rulers. After they were established, they felt that their strength was insufficient, and so they selected the worthy and capable ones of their states, and established them as the upright leaders (*zhengzhang*).
>
> After all the upright leaders had been established, the Son of Heaven issued an edict to the various families of the empire which read:
>
> Everything you hear, either good or bad, must be reported to a superior. What the superior takes as right, everyone must take as right; what the superior takes as wrong, everyone must take as wrong. If the superior is at fault, there will be admonishing; if the subordinates are good, there will be recommendations. To identify oneself with the superior and not to take up with the subordinates—this is what the superior should reward, and what the subordinates should praise. On the other hand, . . . [the proclamation warns against the opposite occurring].
>
> The superiors made this the basis of reward and punishment. This deeply clarified investigations and examinations of honesty.[32]

Mozi's instrumentalist theory is a comprehensive one. Politically speaking, he is clearly advocating an instrumentalist position. Legally speaking, his philosophy of law implies a kind of "legal realism" when he says that: "What the superior takes as right, everyone must take as right." Kung-chuan Hsiao reads the *Mozi* in this manner when he quotes it as saying, "Let the clan head issue laws and proclaim . . ."[33] However, Mozi was not a legal realist, in that there is something more to the "law" than merely what the judges or clan heads say. Note that the superior must be admonished when at fault. For Mozi, the ancient sage ruler is the real source of "law." The *Mozi* says in a different context: "In antiquity the sage kings made the (penal law of the) Five Punishments in order to properly govern their people."[34] More in keeping with J. L. Austin's brand of legal positivism, in which law originates with the sovereign, for Mozi, law originates with the sage emperor or the superior model.

The teachings of Mozi definitely have an impact on the LSCQ's instrumental passages. This particular perspective on the establishment of the ruler and the various branches of administration does not occur in the LSCQ. The LSCQ does not contain a description of a time when people differed in their standards of what is right (*yi*); where the LSCQ does contain descriptions of the establishment of a ruler arising out of "differences," it is clearly in a military context. Like the *Mozi* and other texts, the LSCQ makes reference to the "laws of the early sage kings."[35] Every major writer acknowledges that the early kings had their cultural achievements.[36] The LSCQ's discussions of the ruler's use of reward and punishment most often have a humane, *rujia*, and Mohist tone rather than a *fajia* concern for using punishment to maintain control.

Instrumentalism in the *Xunzi*. Although Xunzi (fl. 298–238 B.C.E.) saw himself as a follower of Kongzi and his interpretation of Kongzi was the accepted philosophy through the Han dynasty (206 B.C.E. to 220 C.E.), nevertheless, his perspective is radically different from the aesthetic self-cultivation perspective of Kongzi and Mengzi, which is probably what led the Song and Ming dynasty scholars to not place much emphasis on the *Xunzi*. Examining the *Xunzi*'s views concerning the origin of the state and law, we find that it is strikingly similar to the *Mozi*'s position. Although the *Xunzi* contains a natural organic philosophy and employs many organic metaphors and makes use of *rujia* cosmology and history, nevertheless, its position concerning the origin of the state is decidedly instrumental. Like the *Mozi*, the *Xunzi* held that all people, by their desirous character, are socially deviant, and as such they must be strictly disciplined by a superior, teacher, or ruler to maintain social harmony. Unlike the *Mozi*, the *Xunzi* does not give a clear historical depiction of a state of nature without a ruler—the text apparently infers that there were leaders.[37] The *Xunzi* does imply that a rudimentary form of human society could exist without a "ruler," and a kind of theoretical "state of nature" as a "state of war" is implied in his understanding of the socially deviant character of people, which maintains that desirous humans were at odds with each other. In the *fuguo* (Enriching the State) chapter, Xunzi actually states that humans must live in organized groups, but that without social lots there will be disorder.

> Human life must be lived out in groups. If the people do not have social lots (*fen*) while living in groups, then there will be contention. If there is contention, there will be disorder; if there is disorder, the people will be obstructed. Therefore, living without social lots is the greatest harm to humans. Having social lots is the very root of benefit in the empire.

> Moreover, the one who is the ruler constitutes the very pivot of the social lots of the administrative offices.[38]

So for Xunzi, people must organize themselves in groups. In theory, there could be a primitive social group without lots and without a ruler living in contention, disorder, and in threat of the greatest harm. Clearly, when there is a ruler, then the administrative lots or duties of the officials will be fixed.

The *wangzhi* (Kingly Regulations) chapter indicates that the state begins when a ruler is instituted to manage the people's desires with ritual appropriateness (*liyi*), and there could be some type of social organization without a ruler: "Without the *junzi* (ruler or consummate person) . . . there will be no (appropriate models of) ruler or teacher above (no appropriate models of) father and son below . . ."[39] Unlike Kongzi, Xunzi's society does not naturally order itself; rather, the ruler must establish social order by promulgating ritual appropriateness (*liyi*) and other regulations and laws (*faze*) to control people's selfish desirous character. For Xunzi, people's natural condition is to express their self-centered desires; the ruler imposes social and legal restraints. Law originates, for Xunzi, with the sage rulers of the past, but it is embodied in the present rulers.[40] There is a natural emotional function played out by the rites and laws that was built into the social system of ritual appropriateness by the ancient sage kings.[41] Many passages in the the LSCQ represent the idea that the ancient kings established rites as a natural emotional means to order the empire. As a *rujia* scholar, Xunzi thinks of "law" as part of the system of *li* (ritual action), and so just as *li* expresses the ruler's emotions, so does the law. "The rules governing military expeditions, the gradations of punishments, which assure that no crime shall go unpunished—these originate with the sudden changes of feeling in the *junzi* and are forms expressive of loathing and hatred."[42] Positive law, for Xunzi, not only controls and refines the desire centered emotions, but it also gives civilized expression to them. Xunzi's text or his disciples had an impact on some of the political material in the LSCQ, especially his notion of a precivilized social order.

Instrumentalism in the *Bingjia* and *Fajia*. The Warring states period (403–221 B.C.E.) saw the rise of the "various teachings" (*baijia* or hundred schools), which marks the classical period of pre-Qin philosophy (fifth to second centuries B.C.E.). This was an era of drastic social change that pivoted around developments in agriculture, military arts, and technical skills. Agriculture and military arts came to play such an important role that the teachers and essayists began to focus on agricultural and military topics exclusively. And the major philosophers of that period incorporate one or both of these topics into their teachings or writings, which marks a sharp contrast against Western philosophy. In particular, military arts are incorporated, explicitly, or at least implicitly, in pre-Qin philosophy so that strategy and then even tactical techniques develop out of their respective philosophies. For example, the *fajia* thinkers, Shang Yang and Han Fei, place a great deal of emphasis on both agricultural and military affairs for building a strong state and maintaining the ruler's sovereignty. Basically, both *bingjia* and *fajia* instrumentalism is founded on the assumption that the prehistoric "state of nature" is a "state of war." Some instrumentalist passages in the LSCQ extend this conviction by acknowledging that the ruler not only brings peace to the subdued people but also benefits the masses by organizing them.

The LSCQ gives one of the clearest statements on the origin of the state arising from conflict and war. To some extent the Militarist thinkers challenge the simple distinction between organic and instrumental positions in that the Militarist philosophy generally proposes that humans are drawn together, if for no other reason than to fight, and that social and political order and organization develop in complexity along with martial conflict. The *Sun Bin bingfa* contains one of the rare Militarist conceptions of the transition of dynastic history as one of military conflict. A similar but more complete passage is found in the *Zhanguoce* (*Intrigues of the Warring States*): "In antiquity, Shennong attacked the Fusui tribes; Huang Di fought a battle at Shulu and captured Chi You; Yao attacked Huan Dou; Shun attacked the Three Miao tribes; Yu fought the Gonggong; Tang went against the Xia."[43] This implies that the dynastic cycle is perpetuated by military conflict, but there is no speculation on pre-history.

In the LSCQ, the *bingjia* material is primarily concerned with military strategy and techniques, however, one need not read too far in its treatises to find the basis and structure of military law. Not only is there an internal legal/command structure to the military, but also most military texts refer to the "just war"—that a tyrant or rebel group must be suppressed by "just troops" (*yibing*). Although it is impossible to judge whether or not the LSCQ's *dangbing* (On Mobilizing the Military) chapter is purely a *bingjia* treatise, *fajia*, or basically a unified eclectic treatise, nevertheless, the *dangbing* chapter provides a strictly military "state of war" interpretation on the origin of human society and the state. The chapter develops this instrumentalist perspective as a partial justification of the "just war." The chapter relates that "military affairs have come down from high antiquity," and that military prowess is a basic part of human character that cannot be altered.[44] The pre-Qin instrumental position is grounded in the notion that humans are not social by nature; in this context, people are predisposed to be aggressively antisocial. The *dangbing* chapter corrects the misunderstandings of ancient military history, namely, that Chi You was not the first one to make weapons, because people made clubs and spears before his time.[45]

> Before the time of Chi You (a rebel defeated by the Yellow Emperor), the masses did indeed peel trees from the forest for combat. The one who gained victory became chief. With only a chief, it was still not sufficient to govern them properly. Therefore, they established a lord. In its turn a lord was not sufficient to govern them properly. Hence, they established the Son of Heaven. The establishment of the Son of Heaven comes from the institution of the lord, and the establishment of a lord comes from that of the chief, and the establishment of a chief comes from struggles. The source of conflict and strife is from long ago; it cannot be forbidden; it cannot be stopped. Therefore, the worthy kings of old had just military actions, but they did not abolish military actions.[46]

This military model for the origin of the state implies that "law" also has a military origin. Both the *bingjia* and the *fajia* writers advocate a military arrangement for civil society, thus farming villages are organized and run like military camps. The military order of society not only regulates civil and penal law, but also it is used to sanction other states by the just war. It provides a rudimentary form of international or interstate law, as well as a civil law.

We also find instrumentalist theories for the origin of the state in the *Guanzi*, *The Book of Lord Shang*, and the *Hanfeizi*. Their respective positions are basically in keeping with the military idea that the "state of nature" was a "state of war." The *junchen xia* (Ruler and Ministers, part II) chapter of the *Guanzi* provides the following:

> In ancient times there were no distinctions between prince and minister or superior and inferior, nor did there exist the union of husband and wife, or man and mate. People lived like beasts and dwelt together in herds, using their strength to attack one another. Consequently the clever cheated the stupid, and the strong maltreated the weak. . . . Therefore, the wise took advantage of the strength of the masses to restrain the cruelty of the strong, and violence against people was brought to an end.
>
> As contradictions arose between what people said and what they did, and distinctions emerged between right and wrong, rewards and punishments were implemented, superior and inferior status was instituted, the people came to constitute a political entity, and a national capital was established. Therefore, what makes a state a state is the fact that the body

> of the masses forms a political entity; what makes a ruler a ruler is that he applies rewards and punishments.[47]

The *Guanzi* clearly distinguishes between a pre-political "social" or herd existence and the establishment of a state by the wise one who wanted to prevent the mistreatment of the weak and less fortunate. There is the assumption that early people were gregarious but without political institutions. For at least some of the *Guanzi* treatises, law is basically positive law established by the ruler of a state: "The producer of laws is the ruler."[48] Like the *Mozi* and the *Xunzi*, law, for the *Guanzi*, must not violate the natural desires of mankind, but rather laws control the expression of the natural desires.[49] Many chapters of the *Guanzi* advocate that the worthy ones must be selected to serve in the government as rulers and ministers. Shang Yang and Han Fei reject the idea of rule by the worthies; they simply want everyone to equally abide by the regulations of the state.

The *kaise* chapter of *The Book of Lord Shang* presents its version of the instrumentalist theory—note how the passage attempts to incorporate the *rujia* and Mohist veneration of the worthies as an ancient phase leading to the establishment of a ruler.

> During the time when heaven and earth were first established and humans were produced, people knew their mothers but not their fathers. . . . From loving their relatives came discriminations, and from fondness of what was their own came insecurity. As the people increased and were preoccupied with discrimination and insecurity, they fell into disorder. . . . [Subjugating others by force led to disputes.] If in the disputes there was no justice, no one would be satisfied. Therefore, men of talent established equity and justice and instituted unselfishness, so that people began to talk of moral virtue. . . . [L]oving relatives disappeared, and . . . honoring the worthy arose. . . . [L]ikewise the way of the worthy men came to be to out vie one another. As the people increased and were not restrained, . . . there was again disorder.
>
> Therefore, a sage took over, made distinctions of land and property, and of men and women. Distinctions having been established, it was necessary to have restraining measures; so he instituted prohibitions.[50]

The initial line contains one of the earliest references to one of the few pre-Qin statements that comes close to espousing a type of cosmogonic origin, namely, "when heaven and earth were first established and humans were produced." For Shang Yang, there was a rudimentary prehistoric form of human society loosely organized around a matrilineage, that is, "people knew their mothers but not their fathers." A similar expression appears in the LSCQ's *shijun* chapter. *The Book of Lord Shang* passage develops a sophisticated account of prehistoric life and the development of the state. This passage provides evidence of a *fajia* thinker who is not merely concerned with maintaining political power in the hands of the ruler, as might be expected. Generally speaking, it is commonly understood that a predominant focus of the *fajia*, when it comes to history, is just the bare transformation of changing circumstances and the need to reform law accordingly.[51] In the above quote, one can clearly see *The Book of Lord Shang* advocating historical progress. This conception of history is used as a justification for instituting a ruler who makes laws. This passage depicts the "rule of the worthies" as an early phase in the development of the state, but even the worthy ones fell into strife and political chaos. The state and its regulations did not appear until a sage set himself up as ruler. Even though the *fajia* writers are usually critical of the early sage kings, they do rely on the mythic power of the sage to institute rulership. Implicit in the above quote is the idea that the institution of the ruler and law is the highest form of human organization achieved so far, understood to be the most objective means to bring peace and order to the people. The institution of the ruler and his laws works, bringing about practical results for society.

Because the essays of Han Fei and the text named after that statesman were being compiled during and after the time of the LSCQ, they could only have had a minimal, if any, influence on the LSCQ, so we need only take a brief look at this text. The *wudu* chapter of the *Hanfeizi* proposes an instrumentalist position; it borrows from Shang Yang's and especially Xunzi's theories. For the *Hanfeizi*, it appears that there was some rudimentary form of human society in far antiquity. The people basically lived like other gregarious animals, and because "the people were few and the goods were abundant, . . . they did not quarrel and fight."[52] The *wudu* chapter describes the establishment of a ruler. "In the most ancient times, when men were few and creatures numerous, human beings could not overcome the birds, beasts, insects, and reptiles. Then a sage appeared who fashioned nests of wood to protect men from harm. The people were delighted and made him ruler of the world, calling him the Nest Builder."[53] The people are delighted with the Nest Builder, and they make him ruler of the world. The state of nature is, at least in theory, however, a "state of war" given the desire-centered condition of human life and the conflict with the beasts. Thus systems of order and human inventions need to be established to regulate the flow of goods to satisfy the people and protect them from the forces of nature. For Han Fei, the institution of the ruler is created by the people out of a "state of nature," which is a condition of conflict and is just barely social and certainly without a ruler, a state, and laws. Both Shang Yang and Han Fei deny that the worthy ones should be allowed a place in the administration of the state.

The *Hanfeizi* is one of the earliest texts to exhibit the self-awareness that its writer lives in late antiquity, being preceded by middle and early antiquity. "Men of high antiquity quarreled with moral virtue; men of middle antiquity contended with cleverness and schemes; men of today vie with energy and force."[54] Although *Hanfeizi* refers to its own position in ancient history, it is even more profoundly aware that human life is full of competition. Although there is a strong sense of history, the writer is well aware that the art of rulership is had in adapting to the conditions and circumstances of the different ages. "Circumstances change according to the age, and ways of dealing with them change with the circumstances."[55] For the *Hanfeizi*, the historical examples are not important in themselves as history, but they are significant as examples of rulership adapting to the times and conditions to bring about success. The *wudu* chapter makes it clear that as the population increases and the goods become scarce, the people begin to fight over them. The chapter draws the ruler's attention to the changing conditions of the day, emphasizing that the old forms of rulership cannot be implemented with success any longer.[56] Shang Yang, Xunzi, the LSCQ, and Han Fei all stress the need to "reform the state's regulations" (*bianfa*). The importance of *bianfa* in the LSCQ's *chajin* chapter will be discussed in Chapter 4.

The LSCQ contains two different versions of the instrumentalist justification of the state. The LSCQ's *bingjia* (Militarists) position on the state, namely, that the institution of the ruler emerges from a state of war, was discussed above. The *shijun* (On What a Ruler Relies Upon) chapter offers another instrumentalist perspective.

The *shijun* chapter provides a unified, eclectic exposition on the Mohist, Xunzi, and *fajia* versions of instrumentalism. The *shijun* chapter proposes that the state of nature was inconvenient primarily because of the struggle against nature. The civil state was not formed out of a "state of war," but rather the people were brought together because of mutual benefit, thereby instituting a ruler, and the state arose.

> Generally in speaking of human character, our nails and teeth are inadequate for self-defense; our flesh and skin are insufficient to protect against cold and heat; our tendons and bones are not sufficient to go after profit and avoid harm. Our courage and daring are not sufficient to turn aside the fierce and to control the cruel.

> And yet humans can manage the myriad things, tame birds and beasts, and subjugate reptiles. Cold and heat, droughts and moisture cannot harm them. Is this not because we not only make preparations first, but also is it not because we gather together in masses?!
>
> The fact that the masses can gather together is because they benefit each other. And the fact that benefit issues from their gathering in groups is because the way of the ruler is established. Hence, if the way of the ruler is established, benefit will emerge from gathering in groups and then people's preparations can be complete.
>
> Of old, in high antiquity, there was no ruler. The masses lived and dwelled in groups. They knew their mothers but not their fathers. They did not distinguish between relatives, elders, younger brother, husband and wife, or male and female. They did not have the way between superiors and subordinates, the elder and younger. They did not have the ritual practices of advancing, and withdrawing, bowing and yielding. They did not have the convenience of clothing, footwear, belts, housing, and storage places, and they did not have the provisions of tools, instruments, boats and carriages, inner and outer city walls and strategic places. This is the hardship of being without a ruler.[57]

The *shijun* chapter promotes a unified, eclectic but optimistic conception of prehistoric life. Elements of the organic natural attitude are blended with *Xunzi* and *fajia* instrumentalist ideas. The passage does not dwell upon a state of war, though it may be implied in the line: People's "bravery and daring are not enough to resist the fierce and to prohibit the strong." The fierce and the strong may refer to wild animals though, not exclusively men. Like the *Xunzi* and *The Book of Lord Shang*, the *shijun* chapter implies that there was some type of basic social order in prehistoric antiquity. Although there was no ruler, the people did live in groups, and there was a matrilineage system—"children knew their mothers but not their fathers." That human society is natural to people's livelihood and that the institution of the ruler is to fulfill human natural desires, bringing about greater enjoyment and benefit, are ideas fundamental to the amalgamated eclectic perspectives in the LSCQ.

The *shijun* chapter is definitely instrumentalist in its approach. There was a time in antiquity when there was no ruler. The chapter cites different tribal peoples who lack a ruler.[58] The institution of the ruler arises out of the benefit that this position brings to the masses. The founding of the state fulfills an instrumental function; the function is that the state best fulfills human natural desires, bringing about the greatest benefit. This consolidated, eclectic version of the instrumentalist approach on the origin and function of the state is embedded in an organic framework. First, society in some rudimentary form appears to be natural to the human condition. Second, society brings benefit to people primarily because the individual is weak in confronting nature alone, but in groups people are strong. Third, their strength in groups is due to making preparations and planning ahead. Then the group instrumentally institutes a ruler.

In both cases where the LSCQ presents an instrumentalist perspective, it is steeped in an organic model of fulfilling people's natural characteristics. The institution of the state is organized around fulfilling and properly expressing people's desire to be martial (*dangbing* chapter), or the desire for well-being or benefit (*shijun* chapter). Since there is clearly a blending of both instrumental and organic conceptions of the state and human character, one may want to examine this material as the formation of an amalgamated, hybrid, organic, instrumentalist understanding of the state. But the *dangbing* and *shijun* chapters are heavily influenced by the instrumental perspective. A unique, unified, eclectic, organic, instrumentalist position on the justification and function of the state will be presented later.

Pre-Qin philosophy, as reflected in the consolidated movement represented in the LSCQ, contains different versions of both organic and instrumentalist theories on the nature and origin of the state. As philosophical reflection increased concerning these topics, a legal philosophy developed. From the mainstream perspectives in pre-Qin thought, that is, the insider's observation of his or her own legal philosophies, it is clear that pre-Qin law originated with the ancient sages, and it is maintained by the present ruler. The "sage origin of law" is a common thread shared by both the organic and instrumental positions. Furthermore, it should be clear that the "sage origin of law" was not merely developed on an unreflective acceptance of myth or legend, but for both organic and instrumentalist theories the "sage origin of law" was not only historically evident, but it was also philosophically justifiable based on reasoned judgments concerning the nature of human life—that the state, like the family, will have to discipline and punish deviant members. Both organic and instrumental theories generally share the common consideration that social laws must somehow complement human character in particular and the natural environment at large—this is the cosmic harmony component of pre-Qin law that is so often celebrated. It should be noted that, from the perspective of the above pre-Qin philosophies of law, Derk Bodde's hypothesis concerning the non-Chinese origin of law, or even penal law, in ancient China must be seriously called into question.[59]

The LSCQ's Unified Eclectic Conception on the Origin and Role of the State: An Organic Instrumental Position

The LSCQ's Philosophy of History

The historical consciousness of the contributors and the editor of the LSCQ is revealed in a number of passages. The text contains evidence that, at least, some of the contributors and the editor were well aware of the textual significance that the LSCQ held for its era.

It is important to recall that the LSCQ is one of the few pre-Qin texts that dates itself. The *xuyi* (postscript) at the end of the *shierji* begins with the expression *Wei Qin banian* ("In the eighth year of Qin . . .").[60] Although it is an imprecise date, because we are not sure whether it means eight years from 249, when Lü Buwei took office, or eight years from 247, the year the previous king died, or 246, when King Zheng "officially" came to the throne, that is 241, 239, or 238, nevertheless, the important point is that the authors want to inform the reader of the text's temporal situation. The opening sentence of the postscript continues, reporting that "Jupiter (*sui*) is in the *tuntan* . . ." and that auspiciously it is the "first day of the first month of autumn and a *jiazi* year" (i.e., the first day of the new year, according to the old Qin calendar, and the first year in the sixty-year cycle).[61]

The postscript goes on to relate that Lü Buwei studied the ancient teaching of the Yellow Emperor, and that the *shierji* deals with some of the perennial concerns of the ruler and statesman, namely, the guiding principles of order or disorder, the perishing or preserving of a state, and one's own life span and fortune.[62] Implicit within this conception of receiving the transmission of an ancient teaching is the notion of historical continuity—with the "proper" teachings from the past, one's cultural experience can be cumulative.

To assert its credibility as a political handbook compiled while the state of Qin was gaining power, the contributors to the LSCQ present a thoroughgoing understanding of the history of rulership. The LSCQ states that: "The royal house of Zhou has been vanquished, and the Son of Heaven has been cut off."[63] Of course, a Qin text should report the historically significant victories of its own state. And as a *chunqiu* (seasonal annals of a state), one expects the LSCQ to relate the exploits of other states where appropriate, and it does, noting that various states "Qi, Jing, Wu, and Yue tried to gain victory, but they all failed."[64]

The contributors to the LSCQ are aware of the significance of the Zhou house having been destroyed, namely, that Qin may be able to usurp the throne, unifying the empire. They are able to make this conjecture about the future based on their comprehensive view of ancient history and the *wuxing* (Five Phases) philosophy of history.

It should be noted that Kung-chuan Hsiao holds a different opinion. The LSCQ was written almost twenty years before the Qin unification, and shortly after its publication, Lü Buwei fell out of favor with the court, and his guests were scattered. On this basis, Hsiao argues that: "The authors of the book (the LSCQ) could never have anticipated such a thing."[65] I believe that Hsiao has overlooked the foresightedness of its authors, editor, and patron. The context of his argument will help clarify why he takes this view. Hsiao contends that the LSCQ was an anti-Qin text, but this does not follow, given that Qin will not become an oppressive legalist state for some twenty years after the completion of the LSCQ, and that its patron was the prime minister of Qin. Moreover, when the *Shiji* (Records of the Historian) chapters, "The Basic Annals of Qin Shihuangdi" and the "Treatise on the Feng and Shan Sacrifices," relate the story regarding the Qin right to rule because of the black dragon omen, in fact, Qin Shihuangdi was actually appropriating the idea from the *yingtong* (Responding and Identifying) chapter of the LSCQ.

I start with the following assumptions. The LSCQ was prepared as a handbook for the child king, Zheng. The text presents a complex vista of history and even a philosophy of history that justifies dynastic succession. Once King Zheng had unified the central states, he harks back to the LSCQ's *wuxing* justification to support his unification of the empire. Although the LSCQ is a synthetic text, nevertheless, it contains a fairly consistent examination of history, especially the dynastic cycle, and it contains the earliest extant passages advancing a *wuxing* philosophy of history.

The LSCQ treatises present their own understanding of two millenniums of ancient history. It is safe to say that a core of at least the last thousand years (1300–300 B.C.E.) of that ancient history was passed down in some written and oral form, constituting some of the basic history of the Shang and Zhou dynasties. Sima Qian's record of the names of the Shang rulers, preserved on the oracle bones excavated from the Shang capital, stands as evidence of the transmission of a core of written history. It was believed by many pre-Qin writers that the core of the oral tradition of the first thousand years (2300–1300) or more of highest antiquity had also been passed down, including the reigns of Yao and Shun, and the founding of the Xia and Shang dynasties. The scholars contributing to the LSCQ were well aware that "The ancient states of Yu, Xia, Yin, and Zhou are no longer preserved."[66] The authors have a comprehensive scope of history that enables them to make broad historical generalizations, such as, "There were many who possessed the empire in the past, but they have all perished."[67]

The LSCQ contains the seminal passages for the theory of dynastic cycles, the theory that Edwin O. Reischauer and John K. Fairbank used in their well-known history, *East Asia: The Great Tradition.* The LSCQ includes passages describing the exploits of the establishment and the destruction of the prior dynasties. Different chapters of the LSCQ tell us that Shennong's clan ruled the empire for seventy generations.[68] The Yellow Emperor governed the empire next and had to suppress the rebel Chi You.[69] He was followed by Emperor Quan Xu and Emperor Ku.[70] Emperor Yao abdicated the throne to Shun.[71] Shun passed the throne to Yu.[72] Yu established the golden age of the Xia dynasty. The last ruler of the Xia was the tyrant Jie; Tang, the founder of the Shang, destroyed Jie.[73] The golden age of the Shang falters when the dynasty changes its name to Yin, and its last ruler was the tyrant Zhou, who was destroyed by King Wu, who established the Zhou dynasty.[74] The tyrants Jie and Zhou and other poor rulers, such as King Li, are often cited in the LSCQ as inferior rulers and examples of what not to do when ruling a state.[75] The LSCQ contains various incidents concerning poor rulership and inappropriate personality traits and behavior on the ruler's part that led to ruin. The *guanshi* (Examining the Era) chapter details five factors that destroy a state: (1) to exhaust credibility (*xin*); (2) to exhaust reputation; (3) to exhaust affectionate relations; (4) to exhaust property; (5) to exhaust achievement through unemployment.[76] The ruler must be able to take advice[77] and cannot be arrogant.[78] With this wealth of historical information on the art of rulership, a contributor to the LSCQ is willing to conjecture that "The ages of order are short, while the ages of disorder are long."[79]

The wealth of historical data, especially the history of the dynastic changes, puts the authors of the LSCQ in a position to reflect back on the patterns of ancient history and to formulate a philosophical interpretation of history. The philosophy of history that emerges from the LSCQ is both dependent on the recognition of the dynastic cycle and the awareness that the art of rulership perseveres through historical change. The *shijun* (On What a Ruler Relies Upon) chapter states that: "From ancient times on, although many states in the empire have perished, nevertheless, that the way of the ruler (*jundao*) has not been abolished is because of the benefit it brings to the empire."[80] States come and go, but the position of the ruler perseveres. Great dynasties degenerate; their tyrants are overthrown by worthy rulers who establish new dynasties, and the process goes on.

Because of the composite amalgamated nature of the LSCQ, there are always opposing views found in the text. In Chapter 4 of this book, we will examine the suspicions voiced in the *chajin* chapter, that the received historical tradition may not be accurate. Or when the more mechanistic approach is appealed to, then, the LSCQ generates a view of natural historical change that is not dependent on the worthy or ill character of the ruler. For example, the *yongzhong* (Employing the Multitude) chapter proposes that the plight of the state goes beyond the ruler's own control.[81] The environmental restrictions on one's life may control one's lot more than any cultivation of one's character, or even one's birth rights. Kung-chuan Hsiao claims that, for the LSCQ, "success and failure [in the state] always develop from unplanned circumstances."[82] He cites the *changgong* (Long Term Order) chapter:

> All instances of order and disorder, of survival and downfall, of safety and peril, of strength and weakness, necessarily depend on a chance [combination of circumstances] and only in consequence of that, then take their shape. If the combination is the same on each [of two opposing sides], then the situation [favoring one side over the other] would not present itself.
>
> It can be illustrated with the example of the good farmer. He may be able to ascertain the most suitable conditions of the soil and apply himself arduously to the plowing and the harrowing, but it is not certain that he will harvest a crop. If one does harvest, however, it begins with such a man. After that it is the chance of encountering timely rains. Encountering timely rains is a matter of heaven and earth (*tiandi*, the natural world); it is not something the good farmer can bring about.[83]

One's position as ruler is not totally dependent on factors under one's control. However, Kung-chuan Hsiao has misinterpreted the LSCQ when he overgeneralizes from the above passage that the LSCQ "inclines toward the view that rise and decline of governments exhibits a random convergence of cosmic forces."[84] The LSCQ is not totally pessimistic, even in the passages that express a mechanistic point of view, because the LSCQ contains a complex, naturalistic conception of the dynastic cycle that follows the pattern of the destructive cycle of the five phases (*wuxing*). The ruler who harmonizes with the cosmic changes could unify the empire, and such a king would be the kind of sage ruler Mengzi expects.

The teachings of Zuo Yan (305–240 B.C.E.) explicate the natural processes of change in nature and society by the alteration of yin and yang and the five phases.[85] Zuo Yan's proposal on the alterations of the five phases may be primarily due to his observations of the dynastic cycles and historical change rather than observations of nature. In this regard, the *wuxing* have greater application in the social and political realm than the natural. However, this did not prohibit the use of the five phases in the development of Han science, technology, and medicine. The *yinyang wuxing* paradigm plays an important role in the LSCQ's incorporated eclectic program of integrating the various pre-Qin teachings into a comprehensive social and political philosophy.[86] In Chapter 2 of this book, it was shown that the seasonal orientation of the *shierji* corresponded to the *wuxing* model. The *wuxing* processes of the conquest cycle form the basis of a major part of an important philosophy of history found in the LSCQ: earth obstructs water, wood grows out of earth, metal cuts wood, fire melts metal, and water extinguishes fire. The *yingtong* (Responding and Identifying) chapter, from the first *lan*,[87] actually presents a *wuxing* interpretation of ancient history and the dynastic cycle.

> Generally when an emperor or king was about to arise, heaven above (*tian*) would surely first reveal a good omen to the people. In the time of the Yellow Emperor, the heavens first revealed giant earth worms and giant mole crickets. The Yellow Emperor said, "The energy (*qi*) of the earth is dominant. Since the energy of earth is dominant, its color yellow is superior and administrative affairs are to model (the virtue of) earth."[88]
>
> Then in the time of Yu, the heavens first revealed grass and trees which did not wither in autumn and winter. King Yu said, "The energy of wood is dominant. Since the energy of wood is dominant, its color indigo is superior and affairs are to model wood."
>
> Then in the time of King Tang, the heavens first revealed metal blades being produced in the rivers. King Tang said, "The energy of metal is dominant. Since the energy of metal is dominant, its color white is superior and affairs are to model metal."
>
> Then, in the time of King Wen, the heavens first revealed a fire-red bird holding a red-cinnabar document (*danshu*) in its mouth, perching at the *she* (earth) alter of Zhou. King Wen said, "The energy of fire is dominant. Since the energy of fire is dominant, its color red is superior and affairs are to model fire."
>
> That which will replace the energy of fire will be water. Moreover the heavens will first reveal that the energy of water is dominant; when the energy of water is dominant, its color will be black and affairs are to model water.[89] When the energy of water arrives, and the people do not know that the calculated course of water has already been completed, then it is about to shift to the power of earth. Heaven produces the seasons (*shi*); yet it does not assist in agriculture.[90]

> Things of the same category will attract each other.[91] If things have the same energy, they will be united. Tones that are close will respond to each other. When we play a *gong* tone, another *gong* tone will vibrate; when we play a *jue* tone, another *jue* tone will vibrate. Pouring water on a level surface, the water will move toward the moisture. Lighting a fire with even pieces of wood, the fire will spread to the dry ones.[92]

The passage does not say that water is the dominant energy, but only speculates that water will replace the fire of Zhou, and earth will replace water, completing the cycle. The passage suggests that the next one to rule the empire will do so by acknowledging and instituting in his government the cosmic changes. The passage sounds mechanistic. "Heaven produces the season . . ." or "nature produces time . . ."; one must accord with it to be summoned as ruler. The natural transformations of yin and yang and the five phases can be anticipated; nature will run its course. It is not fated which person will master the cosmic transformation and become emperor. A person can master an art of rulership. This ability of the ruler to harmonize with the cosmic operations exemplifies the LSCQ's optimistic side. The *yingtong* chapter states:

> The Yellow Emperor said: "So subtle and abstruse, it is responsive to heaven's majesty and shares the same energy as the origin." Hence it is said that sharing the same energy is superior to sharing the same standard of right. Sharing the same standard of right is superior to sharing the same strength. Sharing the same strength is superior to sharing the same accommodations; and sharing the same accommodations is superior to sharing the same reputation.[93]

This advice is given to a ruler who must attempt to gain harmony with nature. Sharing the cosmic energy, one can establish oneself. The chapter describes people controlling their good and bad fortune, but the point of the story is that one's good fortune preserves the state. Kung-chuan Hsiao's claim that the LSCQ "takes the view that although good and bad fortune are called forth by man himself, success and failure [in the state] always develop from unplanned circumstances"[94] is oversimplified and does not consider other ideas in the text that are inconsistent with his claim. He does not consider the passages that support an optimistic attempt on the ruler's part to establish harmony with nature and the masses. He overlooked the syncretic perspective that proposes that benefitting the masses by fulfilling desires through employment is essential to the art of rulership.

A Justification of and Role for the State from the LSCQ.

A good portion of the LSCQ's unified eclectic perspective advocates an organic, naturalistic view of the cosmos as a series of processes of interacting bipolar similarities and opposites. Humanity is a part of the natural world process, and the state is rooted in it. The state is the cumulative depository of tradition, of humanity's self-awareness through cultural history. Hu Shi, interested in pragmatism and utilitarianism, first noted both the apparent "individualism" (*gerenzhuyi*) and the "utilitarianism" (*ailizhuyi*) in the LSCQ.

> The political thought of the LSCQ is based on a natural point of view of "modeling heaven and earth." It fully developed the thought of venerating the process of life; it emphasized the essential desires in order to establish a type of utilitarian political philosophy.[95]

The LSCQ's Natural Point of View. The *dayue* (Magnificent Music) chapter provides a natural, organic perspective on the origin of music. The chapter's interpretation of music is, like many of the LSCQ treatises, highly composite in that it unites *rujia*, *daojia*, Mohist, and *Yinyang* ideas.

> The origins of the tones and music go far back into antiquity. They are produced from the measurements of length and weight; their root is in the Supreme One (*taiyi*). The Supreme One produced the Two Exemplars (*liangyi*—heaven and earth). The Two Exemplars produced yin and yang. Yin and yang change and transform—one ascends, the other descends—and coalescing, they take on shapes. Mixing and blending (*hunhun dundun*), they separate out, only to coalesce again. They coalesce only to separate out again. This is called the regularity of heaven.
>
> The operations of heaven and earth are like a chariot wheel. As soon as it reaches its end, it begins again. As soon as it reaches its extremity, it returns again. Every thing has its complement. The sun and moon, stars and constellations some move quickly, others slowly. The sun and moon are not the same which enables them to complete their operations. The four seasons succeed each other—sometimes hot and sometimes cold, sometimes short and sometimes long, sometimes mild and sometimes severe.[96]
>
> The means by which the myriad things are produced is that they are made by the Supreme One, and they are transformed by the interaction of yin and yang.[97] The processes of germinating and sprouting begin; condensing and freezing into form. Any form or body occupies a position; all of them make a sound. Sounds are produced from harmony. Harmony

comes out of what is fitting. It was by this model of harmony and what is fitting that the early kings composed music; it developed from this.

With the empire in great peace (*taiping*), the myriad things secure and stabilized, and all transforming in attunement,[98] music could then be developed. The development of music has its conditions—one must be measured in one's preferences and desires.

> It is only when one is not indulgent in preferences and
> desires that one can devote oneself to music.
> There is a certain way to devote oneself to music; it is
> necessary to produce it from tranquility (*ping*).
> Tranquility comes from impartiality; impartiality comes
> from the *dao* (the moral way).

Hence it is that one can only discuss music with one who has attained the *dao*![99]

The *dayue* chapter generates a hybrid eclectic position drawing off of *daojia* and *yinyangjia* natural points of view, *rujia* self-cultivation through music, and Mohist utility. The consolidated nature of the text blends the *rujia* discussion of the natural desire for music with *daojia* and yinyang cosmological terminology. This passage reveals an interest in the "Supreme One" (*taiyi*). The conception of the "Supreme One" is found in other composite texts, such as the Mawangdui Yellow Emperor texts, the *Heguanzi*, the *Huainanzi*, and so forth. The "Supreme One" is the unifying field in which the world emerges. The operations of nature function on the *daojia* pattern of reversal and the yinyang patterns of interacting, complementary opposites. Sounds emerge as the natural vibrations of objects. The early sage kings discovered how to compose music by observing the harmony between sounds. The text forewarns its readers that those who undertake to compose music must control their desires. The *dayue* chapter's justification for the state is rooted in this natural point of view, which acknowledges a close relationship between the natural ground of music and human desires.

> Music is the harmony of heaven and earth. It is the rhythm of yin and yang. That which for the first time generates humans is heaven (nature, *tian*). Humans have no business in this. Heaven causes humans to have desires. Humans cannot choose but to fulfill them. Heaven causes humans to have dislikes. Humans have no choice but to avoid them. Desires and dislikes are what humans receive from heaven.[100] Humans cannot succeed in getting a share. It cannot be altered; it cannot be replaced (*yi* transformed).[101]

Human desire has a natural origin. Although the natural desires cannot be altered in kind, humans, especially the Son of Heaven, can and must direct and refine the natural inclinations. Without self-cultivation there can be no harmony in music, society, or the world. The *dayue* chapter presents a unified point of view, revealing a basic concern for the correlativity obtaining between nature and humanity. This basic focus typifies the concern for "cosmic harmony," characteristic of pre-Qin thought.

The LSCQ on Loving and Benefitting the Masses Some of the passages containing the expression *aili* (loving and benefitting the masses) emphasize that the art of rulership depends on the ruler's ability to show affection for and to bring benefit to the masses. Loving and benefitting the masses is indicative of a virtuous ruler or minister. In some chapters, the concept *aili* is linked to the notion of *yongmin* (employing the masses). The *lisilan* stresses the importance of loving and benefitting the masses in a timely fashion.

Hu Shi uses the above quote from the *dayue* chapter as an example of the LSCQ employing its own utilitarian natural point of view against the Mohist's attack on music. The Mohists attack music, because they perceive it to be an extravagant use of funds that could be better used to strengthen the state or benefit the masses. Hu Shi comments:

> Saying that music is based on natural characteristics (*tianxing*) which "cannot be altered and cannot be replaced" to such an extent, this was completely a utilitarian (*aili*) philosophy of naturalism.[102]

Hu Shi coins different Chinese expressions for "utilitarianism." In reference to the LSCQ, he uses the expression *ailizhuyi* ("love and benefit-ism"); discussing Mozi, he uses the expression *lelizhuyi* ("joy and benefit-ism"). However, the usual translation of Jeremy Bentham's and J. S. Mill's "utilitarianism" is *gonglizhuyi* ("public benefit-ism"). The amalgamated approach of the LSCQ allows it access to all of the progressive and advantageous teachings of the various schools. The followers of Kongzi's and Mengzi's teachings on moral cultivation, focusing on *ren* and *yi*, usually interpret *li* (benefit) negatively to mean "personal or selfish advantage." The *Shizi*, *Mozi*, and *Guanzi* advocate *li* as a positive moral value when understood to mean "benefitting the masses." Kung-chuan Hsiao argues that the opposition between Mengzi and Mozi is oversimplified. In fact, their views are markedly close.[103] Mengzi certainly wants to bring benefit to the masses, and the Mohists certainly want to avoid partiality (*bie*). The real intellectual opponents against benefitting the masses are the *fajia* thinkers.[104] Even the *daojia* writers are in favor of benefitting the masses. "Drop wisdom and abandon cleverness, and the masses will be benefitted (*minli*) a hundred fold."[105]

The *li* (benefit) plays an important role in the political and moral thought in many of the LSCQ's chapters; the character *li* is used over 150 times throughout the text. The concept *li* ("to bring benefit to") defines the programmatic or utility perspective of the LSCQ's "government for the people." The *zunshi* chapter in a hybrid eclectic fashion even defines *li* (benefit) in terms of *yi* (rightness). "Among great acts of rightness, none is greater than benefitting others and in benefitting others, nothing is greater than instructing them."[106] Education is highly valued among the *rujia* and Mohists and a morally appropriate means to benefit others.

The *ailei* (Showing Affection to One's Species) chapter is devoted to the theme of bringing benefit to the masses. The chapter presents *limin* (benefitting the masses) as both the moral expression of *ren* (human love) and the key to governing the empire.

> One who is loving (*ren*) with respect to other things and yet not loving with respect to other people cannot be considered loving. One who is not loving with respect to other things but is only loving with respect to other people can still be considered loving. Being loving means to act with love toward those of one's own species (*lei*). Hence, the attitude of the loving person with respect to the masses is that he will do anything that brings benefit to them.[107]

In defining human love (*ren*) as showing *ren* to those of one's own species (*lei*), we have an extreme anthropocentric, rather Xunzi-like, approach toward *ren*.

The *ailei* chapter relates the story of Shennong farming and his wife weaving cloth, concluding that these "were the means by which they showed others how to benefit the masses."[108] The chapter proposes that the worthy ones who travel everywhere within the four seas "frequently coming and going to the courts of kings and dukes do not seek their own personal profit (*li*), but they do it because they consider the benefit of the masses to be their undertaking."[109] The chapter weaves into the discussion the importance of benefitting the people in uniting the empire.

> If there was a ruler who was able to devote himself to the well-being of the masses, then all in the empire would flock to him. As for what it means to be "the King," it necessarily is not a matter of strengthening the armor, sharpening the weapons, selecting crack soldiers, training knights, nor does it mean destroying the fortifications of other cities or

> massacring their inhabitants. Those who realized the kingly way in antiquity were numerous, and their particular circumstances were all different. However, when it comes to confronting the trials of their respective ages, concerning themselves about the masses' benefit, and clearing away obstacles to it, they were all the same.[110]

Bringing benefit to the masses is the determining factor in realizing the kingly way. The ancient rulers worried about bringing benefit to their subjects, and anyone among the present rulers could win over the empire by acting accordingly. The moral argument for realizing the kingly way, which is accomplished by benefitting the masses, not by military maneuvers, and the emphasis on responding to the unique context of one's situation, that is, everyone's achievement is different, but the general guideline is the same, namely, benefitting the masses, are of particular interest.

The *ailei* chapter relates the famous story of Mozi making a special trip at risk to his own life to persuade the King of Jing to stop Gongshu Ban's attack on the state of Song. In summary of Mozi's valor for saving the underdog, the chapter states that: "Concerning the sage king's understanding (*tong*) of the outstanding knights (*shi*), there won't be one case which has not come from benefitting the masses."[111] The chapter cites the case of King Yu draining the floods in ancient times and thereby saving the lives of the people of the numerous states. It praises Yu: "Being diligent and laboring for the sake of the masses, no one was more earnest than King Yu."[112]

The chapter presents a discussion between Huizi and Kuang Zhang, which presents a *mingjia*-type paradox where Huizi defends his serving a king while holding the general principle of not venerating positions. Huizi proposes that just as a father would prefer that a stone receive a blow meant for his beloved son's head, so he, Huizi, would rather benefit the masses by serving the king. The master of language, Huizi, in acting as a statesman, was motivated by the humanistic value of benefitting the masses, just as one would benefit one's children.

The chapter discusses the natural desires of the masses and the way to stabilize them.

> When the masses are cold, they desire heat; when they are hot, they desire ice; when it is dry, they desire moisture; when it is too moist, they wish it were dry. Cold and heat, or dry and moist mutually oppose each other, but they are the same (*yi* one) in benefitting the masses. How could there be only one way to benefit the masses? It is only a matter of matching the times (*dang qi shi*).[113]

Here we see the unified, eclectic perspective of the LSCQ in full bloom. Human desire is rooted in the yinyang natural perspective; the world is a dynamic interplay of mutually opposing opposites, and human desire pursues the opposite of what nature imposes. The way to establish and maintain a humane and moral state is that its ruler must utilize these natural phenomena and their correlative human desires to benefit the masses. This benefit can only be had in harmonizing things by "matching the times." The state must be attuned to carrying out its affairs in such a manner that it benefits the masses by fulfilling their desires. In the agrarian lifestyle, human desire corresponds to cosmic seasonal changes. The execution of state affairs in a timely fashion provides the means to harmonizc human desire and the natural environment. The ruler who harmonizes human relations with the environment is closer to an orchestra conductor "keeping time" than to the helmsman steering a ship.

The *ailei* chapter presents a sustained argument for the social advantage achieved by political institutions benefitting the masses. Throughout the treatises of the LSCQ, there are numerous references to the importance of *aili*, that is, both showing affection toward (*ai*) and bringing benefit to (*li*) the masses. *Aili* is consistently presented as either a quality of the ancient sage kings or as a means to become the Son of Heaven. The references to *aili* congeal within the *lisi*, *shiwei*, and *yongmin* chapters of the *lisilan*.

The *lisi* (Distinguishing Customs) chapter uses the expression *aili* (love and benefit) to describe the root of social and political order that the early sage kings employed.

> If one is like Shun or Tang, then he is all encompassing and accommodating; he takes action only when he has no other choice. In whatever he does he acts in a timely way. He takes loving and benefitting the people to be his root, and takes the masses as his standard of right.[114]

Like the *ailei* chapter, here we see the association between the sage ruler acting in a timely fashion and expressing love for and bringing benefit to the masses.

The *shiwei* (Appropriately Displaying Majesty) chapter emphasizes the use of *aili* in ruling the empire in antiquity. The chapter blends some of the standard *rujia* virtues with *aili*.

> The ruler cannot but be totally aware of how to win the hearts and minds of the people. It was because Kings Tang and Wu were conversant with this principle (*lun*) that they were able to be both accomplished and renown. Those who ruled the masses in antiquity governed them by human kindness and rightness, brought peace to them with love and benefit, and led them

> with loyalty and trustworthiness. They devoted themselves to eliminating misfortune and thought constantly about how to bring about prosperity.[115]

The moral basis of orchestrating the state and bringing order to the masses marks a recurring theme running through many of the LSCQ's treatises.

The *qingtong* (Essential Communication) chapter, from the late autumn section, defines the key to the art of rulership as having the intention to love and benefit the masses.

> When the sage is on the throne facing south and concerns himself about loving and benefitting the masses, before his edicts and orders have even been issued, the people of the empire are all craning their necks and standing on tiptoes expecting to hear it. This is because he is one in spirit with the masses. Now when one is cruel and injurious to others, they will respond in kind.[116]

The mind of loving and benefitting the masses must be cultivated and achieved by the sage ruler. If the ruler is not aware of public opinion, he cannot successfully fulfill people's desires. Maintaining the position of ruler requires one to win over the masses by loving and benefitting them. If one has the intention to harm the people, they will recognize this just as quickly as they would their benefit, and rebellion follows.

The *tingyan* (Taking Advice) chapter presents *aili* as the very art (*dao*) of rulership.

> The *Zhou documents* (*Zhoushu*) say "The one who those who follow cannot catch and those who have arrived can no longer wait for, and who makes his age worthy and enlightened is called the Son of Heaven." Hence, in the present age for one who is able to distinguish between good and bad, it is not difficult for him to be a true king. The distinction between good and bad is rooted in benefit and love.[117] Love and benefit as a way of rulership (*dao*) is great indeed.[118]

The one who unifies the empire and becomes the Son of Heaven can do it without difficulty if he can discriminate between what is good and not good, and the key to the distinction is found in expressing love and benefit to the masses. The moral art of rulership or *dao* is defined in terms of *aili*. Emphasizing the moral basis of rulership may well be directed against the strong arm of imperial law.

There is an interesting discussion on the art of rhetoric in the *shunshuo* (Persuasion by Compliance) chapter. Part of the discussion sets forth the example of Hui Ang's use of rhetoric in his attempt to persuade King Kang of Song to take up the moral way in governing. Hui Ang seeks an audience with King Kang. The king says that he does not want to hear about *ren* and *yi* but bravery and strength. Hui Ang tells the king that he knows the principle that will cause the brave and strong not to have the intention to stab or strike another. The king is interested in such a principle.

> Hui Ang said, "Even though people might not be of a mind to inflict injury, they are not necessarily of a mind to love and benefit. I have this principle to make all of the men and women in the empire love and benefit you gladly. This is better than having courage and might on our side and lifts you above the four kinds of injurious conduct. With this you could dwell above the people. Does your majesty alone have no interest in this?"
>
> The King said, "This is exactly what I desire to attain."
>
> Hui Ang replied, "The caliber of Kongzi and Mo Di was precisely of this kind. Kongzi and Mo Di were kingdomless rulers and officeless leaders. None among the men and women of the empire do not crane their necks and stand on the tips of their toes wishing to gain stability and benefit from them."[119]

Hui Ang tricks the king of Song into listening about the moral art of rulership advocated by Kongzi and Mozi. The moral of the story is clear: When the masses are stabilized by love and benefit, then they are willing to fight and die to protect their lifestyle. Manipulation of the people's desires is crucial in the justification of the state as the institution that regulates and fulfills desire by employing the masses.

The *yongmin* (Employing the Masses) chapter considers the relationship between the ruler's intention to show love and bring benefit to the masses and his own ability to display majesty.

> Hence, majesty cannot be done away with, but it is inadequate to be relied upon solely. This is the same as the use of salt in flavoring. Generally in the use of salt, there is certainly that on which it depends. Where the amount used is not appropriate, then it spoils that which it depends on and makes it inedible. Majesty is certainly of the same kind. It is only when we ascertain what it depends on that it can be displayed. What does majesty depend on? It depends on love and benefit. It is only when the people understand that the ruler is acting with a heart of love and benefit (*aili zhi xin*) that the ruler's majesty can be displayed. When majesty is excessive, then the heart of loving and benefitting the people is lost. The

> heart of loving and benefitting the people having been lost, if the ruler is keen to display majesty, calamity is sure to befall his person. This was the reason the Xia and Yin dynasties perished. The benefit and political purchase of the ruler is the basis on which he ranks his officials.[120]

The ruler cannot expect to control the situational factors or political purchase if he does not show affection toward and bring benefit to the masses. The people's desires must be fulfilled. The *yongmin* chapter makes it clear that the people's desires cannot be fulfilled unless they are properly employed.

The LSCQ on Employing the Masses. The ruler's affection for and ability to bring benefit to the masses is expressed by proficiently employing the masses (*yongmin*). There is a connection between employing the masses and the art of virtuous rulership, which is linked to the pragmatic concerns of reward and punishment. Various passages propose that the way to employ the masses is to manipulate their natural desires. Some passages note the significance of "employing" the masses in military affairs where they are deployed against a tyrant. The *weiyu* (Constituting Desires) chapter contains a discussion on the benefits of employing the people with a high degree of competition, and the *yuanluan* (Tracing the Sources of Disorder) chapter stresses the importance of making timely use of the people.

The various proposals concerning the function of rulership in the LSCQ make use of the concept of "employing the masses" (*yongmin*); sometimes different expressions are used, for example, *yongzhong* (employing the multitude), *shizhong*, and *shimin* (utilizing the multitude). The *yongmin* chapter portrays a vital connection between *aili* and moral rulership. The *yongmin* and *shiwei* chapters and the *tingyan* chapter discuss both loving and benefitting and employing the masses.

The *yongmin* (Employing the Masses) chapter, the fourth in the generally *fajia*-sounding *lisilan*, opens with a composite approach to employing the masses, where the *rujia* moral use of *yi* (rightness) is ranked above the use of reward and punishment.

> Generally in employing the masses the most superior ruler does it with rightness (*yi*); the next best does it with rewards and punishments. There has never been the case, past or present, in which one who was able to employ the masses with rightness was not sufficient to have people die for him, or whose use of reward and punishment was not sufficient for the people to trade evil for good.[121] It is not that the masses can never be employed. It is only when one has the right way that they can be employed.[122]

The moral way in ruling the masses is preferred, but the chapter is generally concerned with making proper use of the people for political and military power. It describes a moral kingdom that properly employs reward and punishment. The chapter cites He Lu, who became king of Wu, and Wu Ji, who became a general in Chu, as examples of what a great leader can achieve with only 30,000 to 50,000 troops. It critiques contemporary states with hundreds of thousands of troops who cannot successfully oppose an enemy or defend their homelands, proposing that the root of the problem is managerial.

> It is not that his people cannot be employed, but that he did not obtain the means to employ them. If the ruler does not obtain the means to employ them, then even if his state is large, his political purchase (*shi*) fitting, and his troops numerous what good is it to him? The fact that there were many in ancient times who had the empire and lost it was because they could not employ the people. The discussions for employing the masses must be thoroughly understood.[123]

The organic, instrumental justification of the state is explicated here. The ancient lesson of rulership has immediate application in properly ordering one's own state and unifying the empire—one must understand how to properly employ the masses. Organically, the state is rooted in the fulfillment of people's natural desires. Historically, states or rulers vary in their ability to fulfill the people's desires by properly employing them. Therefore, the present rulers must take it upon themselves to meet the challenges of the age and to instrumentally reform political order, especially the people's employment.

The *guixin* (Venerating Credibility) chapter, in the *lisilan*, bears some similarity to the *yongmin* material in its concept of employing the masses. Both chapters emphasize the need for the ruler to examine the *lun* (theory/discussion) of employing the masses. The adept ruler is able to control and employ all things, and thus possesses the empire.

> If trustworthiness is established, then even empty, insincere words can bring reward.[124] If empty words can bring reward, then all in the six directions will be one's treasury. Wherever his trustworthiness reaches, he will completely control it. Controlling something but not employing it, this is another's possession. It is only when one controls and employs something that it is really one's own. If it is really one's own, then everything between heaven and earth will be completely employed by him. Those rulers who see the point of this discussion (*lun*), their achieving the kingly way will not take long. Those officials who understand this discussion can minister to a true king.[125]

Various chapters of the LSCQ discuss loving and benefitting the masses (*aili*) in connection with gaining the empire; now the concept of employing the masses is advanced in the LSCQ's art of rulership. This passage challenges rulers and officials to employ the masses as the instrumental means to reform the art of rulership and establish kingly rule. The *yongmin* chapter proposes that one must first be able to employ the oppressed people over whom one does not hold sway to establish one's position as emperor.

Kings Tang and Wu and Prime Ministers Guan Zhong and Shang Yang are cited, in the *yongmin* chapter, as significant historical examples of rulers and leaders who succeeded in the art of rulership "because they realized the means to employ the masses."[126] Referring to other noteworthy leaders, He Lu again, Gou Jian, Shennong, and King Wen, who were able to employ the people of other rulers to attain their respective positions, it concludes:

> Kings Tang and Wu were not only able to employ their own people, but they were also able to employ those who were not their own. Being able to employ the people who were not their own, although their states were small and their soldiers few, still they were able to establish fame and achievement. That in ancient times there were many who were able to go from being commoners (lit. wearing cotton clothes) to bring peace to their age was because they were all able to employ what was not their own. The attitude of employing what is not one's own is a basic principle which must be examined.[127]

A virtuous leader employs all of the people in the empire, especially those of the tyrant, whose own people assist in his overthrow. The adept ruler is established by using the enemy's people. The *yongzhong* (Employing the Multitude)[128] chapter echoes the idea that it is the adept ruler who employs the masses to secure his own position.

> Inherently none among the myriad things do not have their strong points; none do not have their shortcomings. People are also like this. Hence, one who is adept at learning avails himself of other people's strong points to make up for his own shortcomings. Hence, one who avails himself of others will come to possess the empire.[129]

The instrumental effect of properly using others is possessing the empire. The *yongzhong* chapter has a positive, optimistic side: one can have political achievements by utilizing others and their skills. The chapter holds the conviction that a worthy ruler might rule a state that is doomed to perish. One's environmental situation plays an important role in determining matters of rulership, but this discussion does not lead to fatalism; rather, it challenges one to examine the situation.

> (It is just because) the environment in which he was born and raised was not fitting. Hence, the environment where one is born and raised must be examined carefully.[130]

In examining the environmental conditions, the wise ruler makes appropriate use of others. There is a program one can follow to better one's lot—*aili yongmin.*

The *yongzhong* chapter supports this claim to rulership through employment of the masses by drawing an analogy with producing pure white fur—by relying on the strong points, one can make up for shortcomings. It describes how the cumulative organization of the masses can be a greater benefit than the talents and achievements of just one person.

> That there is no such thing as a pure white fox in the world, but that there are pure white fox fur garments is because the white fur for the garment is taken from many foxes. To take (the strong points) from the many was the way in which the Three August Rulers and the Five Emperors established their great achievement and fame.
>
> Generally speaking the reason why the ruler takes the throne is because he emerges out of the multitude. Once the position of the ruler is established, for him to then abandon the multitude is to obtain the twig but lose the trunk. I have never heard of a stable government when the ruler obtains the twig and loses the trunk. Hence, with the bravery of the multitude, one need not fear a Meng Ben. With the strength of the multitude one need not fear a Wu Huo. With the vision of the multitude, one need not stand in awe of a Li Lou. With the wisdom of the masses, one need not stand in awe of a Yao or a Shun. Using the multitude is the greatest treasure in ruling the people.[131]

The *yongzhong* chapter is generally in agreement with the *yongmin* chapter in that both hold that it is natural for the masses to be employed and that the great achievements of individuals are either overcome by employing the masses or, in the final analysis, what is called the achievement of one ruler is really attributable to the masses the ruler was able to employ and command. Both chapters connect one's employment of the people and one's ability to establish and maintain one's position as minister, ruler, or even the Son of Heaven. It is the *yongmin* chapter that proposes that a ruler masters employing the masses of another state to establish an empire. Where the *yongzhong* chapter hinted at a soft, environmental fatalism, the *yongmin* chapter takes a more optimistic programmatic stance, advocating that the ruler is in the proper social position to manage the people and thereby to maintain order.

The *yongmin* chapter appeals to allegory to drive its point home: "A sword will not cut by itself; a carriage will not drive by itself; someone has to cause (*shi*) them to do it."[132] Likewise, someone must command the masses. The causal image gives way to an agricultural one. The people feel nothing strange in harvesting wheat after planting wheat, and the employment of the masses is the same. "There is also a 'seed' to employing the masses. There is no greater confusion than seeking to employ the people without thoroughly investigating this 'seed'."[133] The "seed" is the proper use of, what the opening passage of the *yongmin* chapter called the second best model of rulership, reward and punishment.

> At the time (*shi*) of King Yu, there were a myriad states in the empire. By the time of King Tang, there were over three thousand states. That none of these states still survive is because they were not able to employ their people. That the people were not properly employed was due to the ineffective use of reward and punishment.[134]

The use of reward and punishment is this chapter's contribution to the state's function of fulfilling the desires of the people.

The *yongmin* chapter integrates the natural characteristics of the desires and dislikes as the basis for employing the masses.

> So the employment of the masses has its rational, and when one obtains this rational, there is no where the masses cannot be employed. In employing the masses, there is the draw string and the guideline. One tug on the draw string, and the myriad net eyes close up; one tug on the guideline, and the myriad net eyes open up. What are the draw string and guideline of the masses? They are their likes and dislikes. And what do they like and dislike? They like glory and benefit, and they dislike disgrace and harm.
>
> Disgrace and harm is the reason that punishment has come into being, and glory and benefit are the reason that rewards have taken shape. When reward and punishment are in place, then everyone in the masses will be employed.[135]

A unified, eclectic understanding emerges. Using reward and punishment to manipulate the natural characteristics of people to desire glory and benefit and to dislike harm and disgrace is the most appropriate means to motivate them to seek employment. After securing the position of ruler through the proper employment of the masses, the ruler must continue to properly employ them to fulfill their desires. The ruler fulfills their natural desires, their likes and dislikes, in an instrumentalist fashion by arranging their employment. The application of reward and punishment and the analogy with the draw string and guideline of a net have a Mohist and *fajia* instrumentalist ring to them. The state has its natural roots in the desires of the masses, but the state maintains itself by fulfilling the desires of the masses by facilitating their employment.

The *shiwei* (Appropriately Displaying Majesty) chapter supports the notion of *aili* in keeping with the *lisilan*'s syncretism. The *shiwei* chapter integrates *aili* with the notion of utilizing the masses (*shimin*) expressed with dynamic images of properly employing the masses.

> The way in which the early kings utilized their people was like driving fine horses. With a light burden and a new whip, you cannot stop them from running, and thus it was that they would travel one thousand *li* (333 miles). The one who is adept at employing his people is like this also. Day and night the people seeking to be employed are unsuccessful. If they could gain employment from the superiors, the people would flood to them like the surging of pent up water through a gorge eight thousand feet deep. Who could hold them back?[136]

The images of the energetic horse and the flood washing down a gorge affirm the dynamic and powerful forces at work in the proper employment of the masses. The function of a well-ordered society is to skillfully employ the masses. The chapter cites a passage from the *Zhou documents* (*Zhoushu*), which is no longer extant in that text, to lend historical authority to the claim that the ruler must maintain a harmonious relationship with the people. "The *Zhou documents* say: 'If the masses consider him good (*shan*), then they prefer him. If they consider him to be no good (*bu shan*), then they oppose him.' It is better to have no admirers than to have many enemies."[137] It supports this quote with the example of the tyrant King Li (r. 877–826) of Zhou, who almost lost the dynastic line because he ruled with cruelty and made the people his enemy. The chapter critiques the contemporary rulers who, like King Li, do not understand the proper way to employ the masses.

> King Li of Zhou was the Son of Heaven, and his enemies were numerous. So he was expelled to Zhi and calamity fell on his descendants. If it was not for Zhaogong Hu, Duke Shao's [son of King Li] lineage would have been severed, and he would be without descendants. Most rulers in the present age desire the population of their people to increase, but they do not know how to treat them well. This only increases one's enemies. If he does not treat them well, then he cannot win them over.[138]

> Winning them over necessarily including their hearts and minds is what is called love. To simply hold sway over their bodies cannot be called winning them over. It is for this reason that Shun as only a commoner (lit. cotton clothes) won over the empire, but Jie as the Son of Heaven found no rest in it. It is from this his enemies were produced.[139]

A sophisticated understanding of political authority is expressed in this passage. One does not hold sway over people by controlling their bodies alone; rather, the ruler must hold a certain attitude toward the people. If the ruler does not show personal concern for and commitment to love and benefit the masses, then they will not be his people in spirit, and the ruler's downfall is inevitable. Emphasizing the transitory and uncertain nature of rulership, pointing out that commoners such as Shun come to possess the empire, but tyrants such as Jie lose the empire, the *shiwei* chapter promotes the skills needed to rule effectively.

The *shiwei* chapter describes the story of Marquis Wu of Wei, who wants to know the reason the state of Wu fell, offering another negative example of how improperly employing the masses to fulfill one's own selfish desire leads to ruin.

> Li Ke said, "Wu fell because it had many battles and many victories."
>
> Marquis Wu replied, "But many victories in many battles is good fortune for a state; so what is the reason that it brought Wu's downfall?"
>
> Li Ke replied, "If a state engages in war frequently, then its masses will be fatigued. If a state gains victory frequently, then its ruler will be arrogant. To have an arrogant ruler employing fatigued people and yet for the state not to perish would be a rare event in the world."[140]

The people were organized into military units, and part of their obligation to the state was to provide labor and military service. So the proper employment of the masses entails their proper use or deployment as troops, especially in the overthrow of their tyrannical ruler. The *tingyan* (Taking Advice) chapter uses the character *yong* (use) in the sense of military deployment of troops, offering another negative example of abusing the people to fulfill the ruler's selfish desire. The chapter describes bad rulers who rob the people to support their own luxurious lifestyle, so that "the masses die from casual deployment (*yong*) to satisfy the ruler's anger."[141] Employing the masses entails deploying them as troops. The key is to fulfill the masses' desires through a just war. To improperly deploy the masses for one's own selfish gain will not preserve one's state or life in the long run.

The sixth chapter in the *lisilan*, the *weiyu* (Constituting Desires), continues the discussion of utilizing the people's desires to employ them. "If the people have no desires, then even where you have a worthy ruler, he would not be able to employ them."[142] Although other chapters in the LSCQ recommend guarding against the ruler's excessive desires, especially when he begins to show partiality, nevertheless, the text does not advocate becoming entirely desireless. The masses must have certain desires, or else even a worthy ruler will not be able to employ them properly. The *weiyu* chapter promotes a workable model of rulership, and so it advocates a practicable Laozhuang philosophy. The problematic of Laozhuang thought is that a ruler must not obstruct one's own life with affairs of state. The ruler must employ ministers who are willing to give their lives in service to the state. In a sense, it is only the person who possesses everything, that is, the ruler, who can afford to practice *daojia* nonattachment to property.

The *weiyu* chapter describes the highly competitive (*zheng*, literally meaning "to contend") spirit with which the people are to be employed, if the society is to remain well ordered.

> Generally well-ordered states cause their people to compete (*zheng*) in doing what is right (*yi*). Disordered states cause their people to compete in doing what is not right. The strong states cause their people to compete for the enjoyment of employment; weak states cause their people to compete in not being employed. The balance between fortune and misfortune lies in the difference between competing to do what is right and enjoying to be employed on the one hand, and competing to do what is not right and competing not to be employed on the other.[143]

This optimistic, competitive outlook is notable. It clearly fosters an optimistic expectation that the fruits of fortune are had, at least in part, through the competitive employment of the masses. Well-ordered, strong states, encouraging their people to competitively engage in practicing what is right and seeking employment, provide an example to be emulated in establishing and maintaining one's own position as ruler. The notion of "competitively employing" the masses yields a profound insight into human social character; this notion has an almost modern, capitalistic resound to it. The "competitive employment" of the masses is certainly a hallmark for the LSCQ's utilitarian perspective. For the well-being of the state, which fulfills the needs and desires of its people, the masses must be encouraged to compete in seeking employment. This competitive edge has the reciprocal influence of motivating the people to desire more. In working harder to attain their desires, they stimulate the state's economy. Without a competitive spirit among the people, a state will wither and perish. The *weiyu* chapter's type of utility requires the competitive spirit to strengthen the people's desires.

The *weiyu* chapter proposes increasing the desires of the masses to expand the people's employment.

> So those who have many desires can also be employed in many ways. Those who have few desires can only be employed in a few ways. Those who are without desire cannot be employed at all. Even though the people have many desires, if the rulers are without the means to command them, then although the people fulfill their desires, nevertheless they cannot be employed. The way to command the people by fulfilling desire *must* be examined carefully. One who is adept at being a ruler is able to command the people such that they fulfill their desires inexhaustibly. Hence, the people's employment can also be inexhaustible.[144]

Providing a complex style of utilitarian thought, grounding political order in the natural desires of the people, the function of political order is to enhance and fulfill those desires. The enhancement and fulfillment of the people's desires will in turn promote their further employment and the growth of the state. There is a reciprocal relation between the natural desires serving as the bases for political order and, correlatively, political order is strengthened to the extent that it can fulfill and enrich those desires. The LSCQ's principle of loving and benefitting the masses by properly employing them is succinctly summarized in the expression: "With the inexhaustible fulfillment of the people's desires, they can be employed inexhaustibly." The state is constantly renewed through the dynastic cycle in which the people are abused and misused under a tyrant, and become "employed" by a virtuous ruler who stimulates their desires with rewards and punishments, motivating the people to work and fight for the state.

The importance of properly employing the masses cannot be overstated in examining the unified, eclectic thought of the LSCQ. The *guanshi* (Examining the Era) chapter notes that one aspect of rulership is: "If one cannot employ others and he cannot employ himself, then he has exhausted his achievements."[145] Such a ruler is certainly in dire straights. The *fenzhi* (Dividing up Offices) chapter details the type of ruler who can successfully employ the masses. The *yuanluan* (Tracing the Sources of Disorder) chapter deliberates "the timely use of the masses."

The *fenzhi* chapter opens with a *daojia* description of the ruler who uses what he does not possess, who is empty and simple, without wisdom (*wuzhi*), without capabilities (*wuneng*), and without action (*wuwei*). This kind of *daojia* ruler utilizes the masses and his assistants to establish his name and reputation, and the people's achievements become his.

> The early kings who employed what was not theirs as if it was theirs understood the way of proper rulership. As for a ruler, he should dwell in vacuity, grasp simplicity, and seem as though he is without wisdom. Thus, he is able to take advantage of the wisdom of the multitude. It is because his wisdom is based on his inability that he is able to take advantage of the capabilities of the multitude. It is because he is able to hold fast to non-purposeful action that he is able to take advantage of the actions of the multitude. To be without wisdom, without capability, and without action are what a true ruler holds fast to.[146]

The LSCQ's amalgamated approach develops a practicable Daoist political philosophy, borrowing heavily from the *Laozi* but clearly defining the political context; the key to the art of rulership that the early sage kings mastered was employing what they did not possess. The ruler creatively, by no apparent effort of his own, has the people spontaneously and simultaneously fulfill their own desires and his. This is part of the beauty and harmony of *daojia* political thought.

The *fenzhi* chapter criticizes the confused rulers of the present day who exert their own energy and yet botch things up.

> Those among rulers who are confused will not be like this. They force wisdom with wisdom; they force ability with ability; they force action with action. This is to take on the duties of one's ministers. To take on the duties of one's ministers and yet to expect to be without obstruction—even a person like Shun will not be able to do it.[147]

It is the confused ruler who does not properly employ the personnel and masses to operate the state's endeavors. The chapter directly addresses the responsibilities of the ruler as opposed to those of the official. It is only the ruler who can afford to practice the *daojia* principles of detachment and *wuwei*. The office and position of leadership that the ruler holds require a unique response and lifestyle that a *daojia* attitude fosters.

The *fenzhi* chapter draws upon the common, organic root of *daojia* and *rujia* thought; to illustrate the *daojia* idea of using what one does not possess, it appeals to the *rujia* hero, King Wu. The chapter describes how King Wu utilized the skills of other people to establish himself as ruler.[148] The art of rulership is had in employing what one does not possess as if one possessed it.

How does the ruler benefit from the knowledge and abilities of others? The *fenzhi* chapter offers two examples: it describes how one gains the benefit of riding horses well trained by skilled horsemen, and it mentions the custom of praising the host after a grand occasion and not the entertainers to illustrate how a ruler gains benefit without personally taking action. "The early kings in achieving fame and accomplishment are similar to this. Employing all of the able and the worthy, such that the great accomplishments and reputation of the age is not credited to the assistants but is given to the ruler is because the ruler employed them."[149] The art of rulership and establishing oneself as a historical precedent is found in utilizing the abilities and virtues of others. The role of the ruler is compared to that of the master draftsman in constructing a building; he does not even understand how to use the carpenter's tools, but without his organization the carpenter cannot work.

The *fenzhi* chapter's discourse of utilizing the multitude entails a dynamic conception of history in which rulers establish themselves based on their understanding that the art of rulership entails not exerting one's own strength or virtue but employing the masses and ministers to this end. The *yongmin* and *yongzhong* chapters stress the importance of establishing and maintaining the position of ruler by employing the skills of others and the masses at large. The ruler achieves this "ability of being without any particular ability" by adopting *daojia* practices of detachment and acting beyond action. In addition to this *daojia* approach to rulership, there is another important aspect of "employing the masses in a timely manner" in achieving a well-ordered society.

The *yuanluan* (Tracing the Sources of Disorder) chapter delineates how successful rulership depends on the timely employment of the masses. The chapter narrates Duke Wen of Jin's (r. 635–628) reforms as one of the Five Lord Protectors; one important measure was to employ the masses according to the right time.

> Duke Mu of Qin was angry at his (Duke Huai) having fled; so he assisted prince Chong Er to attack Duke Huai; killed him at Gaoling, and enthroned Chong Er as the ruler. He became Duke Wen. Duke Wen was generous in his dispensation; he employed those who had been set aside and those denied mobility; he rescued people from the dire straights of poverty; he saved people from disaster and calamity; he prohibited licentiousness and depravity; he lightened taxes; he pardoned criminals and wrongdoers; he economized the use of tools. He employed the masses according to the right time (*yongmin yi shi*). As a result he defeated the Jing (i.e., Chu) army at Chengpu, brought stability to the throne of King Xiang of Zhou, broke the siege on Song, and forced the occupying Chu garrison out of Gu [the capital of Qi]; both those within and outside the state were submissive, and after this, all disorder in the state of Jin ceased.[150]

By employing the masses according to the seasons, one can strengthen the state. The dynamic process of political history teaches any wise ruler that a good ruler can reform the state and strengthen one's position by employing the masses.

The organic base of human society and the state is rooted in the natural desires, and likes and dislikes of the masses. Human life in the state is grounded in the cosmic forces of heaven and earth. The state, especially the ruler, occupies the choice position in the world to balance the fluctuations of nature and the desires of the masses. By employing the masses in a seasonal and timely fashion, the ruler can fulfill their desires by showing his love for and bringing benefit to the people. Without the proper moral attitude of loving and benefitting the masses, a ruler cannot hope to fulfill their desires. The ruler must not only fulfill the desires of the masses, he must enhance and increase their desires to increase their employability. Although the role of rulership is rooted in the focus-field understanding of the natural desires and employability of the masses, nevertheless, there are the dynamic fluctuations of nature and the decay of states and the corruption of rulers, so that the state no longer makes proper use of its people, and the way of loving and benefitting the masses is perverted into loving and benefitting oneself. Thus the virtuous ruler can establish himself as the Son of Heaven by deploying the masses against the tyrant. By instrumentally manipulating the desires of the masses through rewards and punishments, an adept ruler can preserve the state.

The best philosophical and literary material available was contributed in compiling the LSCQ. That material was selected out of the various teachings and documents available during the Warring States period. The historical significance of the LSCQ is that it contains what was considered "the best" of the earlier teachings and traditions, and it transmits the unified, eclectic (*za*) material as a nexus for establishing a new dynasty and a new tradition or state-sanctioned orthodoxy emerging out of the Warring States diversity. Particularly the positions on the origin, justification, and role of the state provide a powerful image of "the best of the past" being used to inform the establishment of a new era. The LSCQ embodies a centripetal harmony that blends the different into patterns of continuity. In this regard, it is like the *Laozi*, in that it provides a basis for orthodoxy out of apparently different perspectives.[151] The unified, eclectic (*za*) orientation of the LSCQ is approaching orthodoxy in the text's concern for unification of the empire. By drawing from the various complex positions on the state and developing them into a coherent "organic instrumental" understanding of the state, the LSCQ serves as a guideline for both Qin and Han literature and their social and political institutions. At least this is true to the extent that later Qin and Han rulers and scholars justified their own states by appealing to the idea of the dynastic cycle, based on the five-phases theory contained in the LSCQ.

The LSCQ champions a comprehensive perspective on pre-Qin history; it depicts a vital history. This dynamic conception of history is tied up with the LSCQ's composite blend of nature philosophies from Laozhuang, Huanglao, and Zuo Yan. Whereas the *daojia* and *fajia* thinkers focus merely on change, both natural and historical, many of the LSCQ's chapters advocate a progressive or developmental view toward history, such as Kongzi, Mengzi, and Zuo Yan. For the *wuxing* material in the LSCQ, there is a definite pattern to historical change—the dynastic cycle prompted by the conquest order of the five phases. The dynastic cycle has both natural and moral underpinnings; the moral exemplar is the one who harmonizes with the natural patterns of transformation. Although the disposition of the state is rooted in the focus-field arrangement of the environment, nevertheless, any particular state is in jeopardy of being destroyed if its ruler cannot integrate with nature and especially the natural desires of the masses.

Thus we saw that various passages in the LSCQ advocate a type of naturalistic utilitarianism of *aili yongmin*. This focus-field arrangement of society, which requires the instrumental renewal of dynasties and the manipulation of the desires of the masses for their employment, is a hybrid "organic instrumental" position. The "organic instrumental" position that emerges from the LSCQ leaves it open for its readers, the ruler, and ministers to take advantage of its interpretation of history, its conception of integrating with nature, fulfilling the people's desires and employing them everywhere to ultimately unify the empire. Qin shihuangdi employed the LSCQ's *wuxing* paradigm to justify his unification of the empire. The founder of the Han did likewise, and Han scholars debated the question of where exactly the Han dynasty stood in the *wuxing* succession. The LSCQ provides direction on how the ruler is to employ proper timing to integrate with cosmic, cultural-historical, and interpersonal realms.

Chapter 4

Proper Timing in the Cosmic, Historical, and Moral Realms

When the ruler employs proper timing in public and private endeavors, the officials and governing policy will utilize a timely reform of regulations, promulgate seasonal policy, and perform ritual actions in a seasonal manner. If the ruler, officials, and governing policy are flexible enough to respond to situations in a timely and appropriate fashion, then the state will be well ordered in the spirit of harmony rather than a strict "rule of law" or coercive government. This is not to say that there should be no "rule of law" at all, but rather that law and the rule of law would always be subordinate to the aesthetic values of proper timing, appropriate seasonal policy, virtue, and ritual action. The LSCQ's unified, eclectic, political philosophy exemplifies both paradigms—a qualified "rule of law" mitigated by an aesthetic harmony derived from and creative of proper timing.

Because the LSCQ is a handbook concerning the arts of rulership, the authors of the text are especially concerned with how the ruler manages public and private interests, exercising both intrinsic timing and the extrinsic appropriation of nature's seasons. The ruler's articulation of time ensues within three realms. First is the environmental realm, where the ruler and the state must integrate with the forces of nature, especially heaven and earth, *yinyang*, the five phases, and the four seasons. Second is the historical political domain, requiring the reform of statutes and regulations. Third is the interpersonal sphere, where the ruler must articulate proper timing in meeting and maintaining appropriate relations with the ministers and the events at hand.

Because of the organic network of interrelatedness that harmonizes the LSCQ's pluralistic and diverse perspectives, the claim that the text is inconsistent is unwarranted. The three realms—cosmic, political, and interpersonal—which require the ruler's application of proper timing are fully interpenetrating, forming an organic foci-field unity in which no one part or aspect has more value or weight than another. When the ruler performs an action, it reverberates throughout the court, nation, cultural history, and cosmos. The proper timing of the ruler's gesture is just as important as the timely reform of law or the performance of seasonal ritual, because the ruler holds that pivotal position and performs those portentous ritual actions that create and maintain *time*—cosmic, historical, and interpersonal.

Cosmic and Seasonal Proper Timing

At first glance, the notion of acting in a timely fashion by behaving in a certain manner because a particular season is manifest may appear to be the most menial type of extrinsic timing. One may feel that there is no intrinsic timing in this kind of behavior at all, since it does not allow one to act spontaneously and creatively but controls one's behavior according to the season. Although there is a certain restraint placed on the potentials of human life by dictating seasonal activities, nevertheless, there are certain factors which, when considered from the perspective of mutual interpenetration of the people and the environment, require such stipulated seasonal policy to direct the masses, generating a well-ordered, agrarian state.

Despite the fact that the concept of the "hundred schools" was an attribution designed during the Han dynasty by royal bibliographers Sima Tan, his son, Sima Qian, Liu Xiang, and his son, Liu Xin, and later by Ban Gu, many Warring States writers themselves did distinguish between the teachings of different masters who established lineages of practice and instruction. In the pre-Qin tradition of ancestor veneration, these teacher-father figures, with the passage of time, were credited with founding *jia* (households or schools). The differences between the teachings may be difficult to distinguish because of the strong similarity of cultural practice, common language, and overlapping heritages. Certain abstractions can be made to highlight, for heuristic purposes, a major distinction among the different teachers of the Warring States period, which has relevance for the LSCQ's various discussions of proper timing.

The major distinction to be drawn is a paradigm shift. The two major paradigms are undoubtedly quite archaic, but they are clearly represented in the contrast between Kongzi and Mozi—even though Mozi was educated as a Literati. There are differences between their teachings, especially as seen by a later writer such as Mengzi. The distinguishing characteristic between the two teachers was Kongzi's flexibility in the appropriation of values verses Mozi's strict "rule of law" model. For Kongzi, values of rightness (*yi*) are cultivated through one's timely execution of ritual-propriety (*li*) in order to manifest appropriate human relationships (*ren*). For Mozi, values (*yi* standards of judgment) are fixed by the will of Heaven (*tianzhi*) for the indiscriminate benefit of all. Kongzi acknowledges a model of "parity on balance" or "equal consideration of interests," which requires treating people differently. Mozi adheres to a strict standard of "formal equality," or the one-per-one equality of the rule of law. Hence Kongzi is willing to make exceptions, that is, appropriations of social norms, to treat a father or ruler properly, and thereby differently. Mozi wants to treat all people, regardless of relation or office, with the same all-encompassing love (*jianai*). Mozi's position may appear to have contextual application as an expression of unconditional love (*agape*), but it actually follows a strict adherence to a rule of law model, accepting an absolute standard imposed on unique situations. To draw the contrast in modern terms, in comparison, Mozi appears to be similar to an absolutist rule utilitarian and Kongzi to an ethical contextualist. As we saw in the previous chapter, Mozi's political thought advocates a form of instrumentalism, while Kongzi's is natural or organic political philosophy. The paradigm shift is accentuated in contrasting Kongzi's clan values with Shang Yang's or Han Fei's rule of law.

Because followers of Kongzi, Mozi, and Shang Yang were among the writers of the LSCQ, these two models may in part account for the different conceptions of time and proper timing in the LSCQ. The "rule of law" model demands a strict adherence to seasonal or daily performance of acts to ensure, in a judicial sense, precision, and similar verdicts for identical cases (formal equality). The organic model, based on Kongzi's teachings, requires an appropriation of proper timing, regardless of the season, in the performance of virtuous acts.

Given the diversity of positions found in the LSCQ and its composite, amalgamated character, it is not surprising that two disparate perspectives on proper timing impact on its social and political philosophies. Moreover, the complex content of the LSCQ actually makes it difficult to distinguish the strict, extrinsic, seasonal model of proper timing from the intrinsic appropriation of proper timing in one's personal conduct, because the two positions meld together as one in the person of the ruler. It is the ruler's responsibility as the exemplar of humanity to appropriate the seasonal changes into his own personal and public behavior.

This full interpenetration of the emperor's timely ritual actions and the promulgation of edicts in accordance with the seasonal transformations are clearly stated in the twelve "monthly ordinance" chapters opening the twelve subdivisions of the *shierji* volume. For example, in the spring, the emperor must wear green clothes. He rides in a green spring chariot and performs rites in the east (i.e., spring) section of the Bright Hall (*mingtang*) temple. The ruler must perform ritual plowing with the ministers and encourage the masses to begin plowing and planting. By performing ritual action and promulgating military and agricultural policy in tempo with the natural environment, the ruler orchestrates both cosmic and social factors. If the ruler does not perform the proper rituals, he is responsible for the imbalance. The *mengchunji* (The First Month of Spring) chapter warns the emperor: "If the summer ordinances are carried out in the early spring, then the winds and rains will not be timely; the plants will wither early, and then there will be apprehensiveness in the capital (*guo*)."[1] All of the monthly chapters conclude with similar warnings of the disasters that follow from performing the rites out of season.

This kind of thinking may sound trivial, or even absurd, until one begins to think in an agricultural frame of reference. The central plains of northern China are situated between the fortieth and thirty-fifth degrees north latitude, parallel to Iowa and Kansas. With the full seasonal changes, it is crucial that planting in the spring be completed early enough to allow for maturity of the crop and a full harvest each year. This focus on the seasonal changes led the Han Chinese to develop a sophisticated lunar calendar[2] and an early form of astronomy and astrology that bears some resemblance to the Greek concern, voiced in Plato, to be in accordance with the cosmic harmonies. Thus the need to control the environment was and is a major concern. The ritually ordered world of the LSCQ's *shierji*, controlled as it is by the court scholar officials, justified the hierarchical structure of the social and political order through this ritual magical mystique of the ruler both activating and appropriating seasonal weather conditions.

Cosmic Timing in Agriculture

From the modern, technological perspective, one may imagine that the agricultural metaphor represents the organic paradigm. One can easily argue, as Martin Heidegger has, that man's dominance of nature in agriculture lies at the root of technology. The "rule of law" model fits the agricultural material in the LSCQ. In the *lulun* (Six Discussions) volume, the last four chapters are solely dedicated to Agriculturalist philosophy, technique, instruments, and other technological concerns. Timing is, as expected, a major concept in these Agriculturalist chapters. The character *shi* (season/time) appears forty-five times in these chapters alone. The final chapter, *shenshi* (On Examining the Time), makes use of the character *shi* twenty-three times itself. The focus of the chapter is "to obtain the proper time" (*deshi*) in planting, weeding, and harvesting the best crop; "to obtain the right time" is not a passive affair; one must articulate time in waiting and acting. The chapter describes the advantages of obtaining the right season and the disadvantages of waiting too long or acting out of time. The *shenshi* chapter shows that the focus is not merely on grain production, but also that the grain grown in accordance with proper timing is good for one's health and the cultivation of one's character.

> In measuring out equal amounts of both types of grain (timely and untimely) for eating, the grain planted in accordance with the right season defends against hunger. Therefore, grain planted in accordance with the right season has a fragrant smell, a sweet taste, and a strong *qi* (life-power). Eating it for one-hundred days, one's eyes and ears will perceive clearly. One's heart-mind and intentions will be enlightened and intelligent. One's four limbs will be strong. Bad *qi* won't enter, and one's body will be without disease. The Yellow Emperor said, "The incorrectness of the four seasons is just a matter of correcting the five grains."[3]

Eating grain is contrary to the *daojia* hygiene practices for long life, as mentioned in the *Zhuangzi*. The traditional Agriculturalist perspective, of course, advocates grain consumption, and the Agriculturalists lay the foundation for Chinese exoteric dietary practices for maintaining health and self-cultivation. Thus the rigid, seasonal interpretation of proper timing in accordance with the seasonal changes is not so mundane and trivial when considered from within the perspective of the organic, focus-field interpenetration of humans and their environment. In ancient China, the state-managed agricultural labor and thus its policy had to be especially sensitive to the seasons. Without the seasonal administration of labor, an agrarian culture could not thrive. Thus the state, as the ruling family, especially the emperor, and the masses are dependent on the harvest of nourishing crops for their mutual health and well-being.

The crucial questions in assessing the various strands of thought in the LSCQ are whether or not humans can control the natural environment, and if they can, to what extent? The monthly commands and the *shenshi* chapters are clear in their proposal that humans, especially the ruler, can affect some control over the environment by performing rituals and undertaking timely action in planting, weeding, and harvesting. Other LSCQ chapters strongly imply that humans cannot control the environment.

The *changgong* chapter in particular presents a type of fatalistic thinking. Based on this chapter, Kung-chuan Hsiao proposed that the LSCQ's account of nature's role in the dynastic cycle is a variety of fatalism that humans cannot control, just like the farmer who is not able to control timely rains.[4] The *changgong* chapter describes the plight of the ruler as analogous to that of the adept farmer.

> It can be illustrated with the example of the good farmer. He may be able to ascertain the most suitable conditions of the soil and apply himself arduously to the plowing and the harrowing, but it is not certain that he will harvest a crop. If one does harvest, however, it begins with such a man. After that it is the chance of encountering timely rains. Encountering timely rains is a matter of heaven and earth [*tiandi*, the natural world]. It is not something the good farmer can bring about.[5]

The ruler is instructed to make preparations for "harvesting the masses," and like the good farmer, the good ruler must await the timely transformations of nature to gain benefit. This is not a hard determinism where farmer and nature are totally controlled. It is a form of soft fatalism where humans are limited in what they can do. The extrinsic and soft, fatalistic thought of the *changgong* chapter appears to be an extremist position found within the LSCQ anthology.

This soft, fatalistic naturalism advocates that although humans cannot regulate the seasons and natural changes, nevertheless, they can appropriate the natural cycles to their advantage. The *guixin* (Venerating Trustworthiness) chapter proposes an appropriation of the seasons. It discusses the *sishi* (four seasons) and *xinde* (credible bounty, or accretion) of the seasons, which can be achieved through human policy.[6] The *guixin* chapter offers an interesting anthropomorphic description of the regularity of a season as nature's trustworthiness (*xin*). Agricultural and civil engineering projects can be accomplished, because one can trust in the climate and weather conditions. Accommodating and appropriating the natural seasons, humans can complete agricultural, social, and political affairs.

> If trustworthiness is set up, then even empty, insincere words can bring reward. If empty words can bring reward, then all in the six directions will be one's treasury. Wherever his trustworthiness reaches, he will completely control it. Controlling something but not employing it, this is another's possession. It is only when one can control and employ something that it is really one's own. If it is really one's own, then everything between heaven and earth will be completely employed by him. Those rulers who see the point of this discussion, in achieving the kingly way, will not take long. Those officials who understand this discussion can minister to a true king.

If heaven operates without trustworthiness, it could not complete a year. If the earth operates without trustworthiness, the grasses and trees cannot grow large. The power (*de*) of the spring is wind. If the wind does not blow with trustworthiness, the flowers cannot grow abundantly. If the flowers are not abundant, the fruit cannot be produced. The power of summer is heat. If the heat does not come with trustworthiness, the soil won't be fertile. If the soil is not fertile, the growing of the plants won't be essential. The power of autumn is rain. If the rain does not fall with trustworthiness, then the grain won't grow solid. If the grain does not grow solid, then the five seeds won't mature. The power of winter is coldness. If the cold does not come with trustworthiness, then the earth won't be frozen firmly. If the earth is not frozen firmly, then the ice won't melt (in time). Even with the greatness of heaven and earth, and the transformations of the four seasons, still they cannot complete things without trustworthiness. So how much less can human actions do it?![7]

The *guixin* chapter implies that the regularity of the climatic conditions of the seasons provides a model of credibility that humans can trust in and of which they can avail themselves. People can benefit by following the changes of the four seasons. The concluding rhetorical question tells us that humans must emulate the regularity and "honesty" (*xin*) of nature to accomplish political policy.

The idea that people may acquire benefit from the seasonal changes without actually controlling those changes allows for the possibility that such an advantage could only be achieved through a state-run agricultural system. The *rendi* (Employing the Earth's Benefits) chapter outlines an agricultural, extrinsic approach toward the appropriation of seasonal change.

[Farmers should plant according to the] growing and withering of the various grasses.

According to the five periods of a year (every 73 days), we should sow living plants when we see life, and we should harvest the dead (i.e., ripe) ones when we see the period of dying. Heaven bestows the seasons, and earth produces wealth without planning with the people. [People should] sacrifice to the god of earth in years with crops. They should sacrifice to the god of earth in years without crops. Never [allow] people to lose the proper time [for tilling and ritual], and do not allow them to govern the inferior. Know the tools (i.e., methods) of poverty and wealth. In all of these start off with the season, and stop with the end of the season. This is why even the strength of the old and young could be mobilized completely. In such cases the effort is "half," while the achievement is "twofold." One who does not understand affairs, he might start

> planting before the season has come, or he might wish for the right season when it has already gone, or he might consider it lightly when the right time comes. If the ruler lets his people farm with neglect, then since they were negligent, they reminisce about the right time.[8]

The planning undertaken by the masses plays no role in nature's seasons and earth's bounty. Although the people cannot cause the season to change, the ruler can order the people to take advantage of the natural changes. Despite the soft fatalism of the *changgong* and *rendi* chapters' extrinsic approach to appropriating natural seasonal conditions for agricultural benefit, the dominant tendency in the *shierji* and other passages with a *daojia* or *rujia* aesthetic approach is that humans, especially the self-integrating ruler, can effectively control the natural environment.

The *dayue* (Magnificent Music) chapter blends *daojia* and *yinyang* naturalistic cosmology with a *rujia* use of music for moral cultivation and a *fajia* agenda to strengthen the ruler's authority. The timely fulfillment of the people's desires according to the seasonal demands is the focus of the programmatic approach of the LSCQ's eclectic syncretism in the *dayue* chapter.

> The *dao* is the utmost subtlety. It cannot be formed. It cannot be named.[9] If compelled to, then call it the Superior One (*taiyi*). Therefore, the One regulates orders. The two comply and obey. The early sage kings put aside the two and took the One as standard. This is why they could know the essentials of the myriad things. Therefore, the one who is able to use the One in administering affairs of state brings enjoyment to the lords and ministers. He brings harmony to those near and far, pleasure to the masses (lit. dark heads), and unifies the clans and families. The person who is able to use the One in governing himself will avoid calamity. He will complete a long life span, and keep intact his natural relations (*tian*).[10] The person who is able to use the One in ruling his state will cause the depraved and licentious to depart, causing the virtuous ones to arrive, accomplishing the great cultural transformation. The person who is able to use the One in ruling the empire will cause the proper distribution of hot and cold weather, causing the timely operation of wind and rain. He himself will become a sage.[11]

The ruler of the empire becomes a sage ruler by developing the efficacious abilities to influence the climatic weather conditions. Therefore, despite some of the more objective extrinsic passages in which people are described as not being able to affect the course of nature, a reappearing motif in the LSCQ is the sage ruler who can bring about appropriate, timely weather conditions.

The *yishang* (Appropriate Rewarding) chapter, which precedes the *changgong*, presents a possible explanation as to how humans can gain control over the natural environment. The *yishang* chapter, with a strong anti-spontaneity position, proposes that there are determinate "causes." This implies that people may be able to activate those "causes" and thereby alter nature. The *yishang* chapter discusses the means by which things occur in the natural world and links this to the political arena.

> When the spring life-forces (*qi*) arrive, the grasses and trees grow. When the autumn life-forces arrive, the grasses and trees wither. Flourishing and withering have something cause them; it is not that they are so of themselves (*fei ziran*). So if the causal conditions arrive, there is nothing which does not come about. If the causal conditions do not arrive, nothing can be produced. The ancients examined carefully that which caused things. So all things were put to use. The control levers of reward and punishment are the means by which the ruler causes things to be done. If his application of them is right, then the way of being dedicated, trustworthy, intimate, and loving will be made known. Being made known for a long time and growing more and more, the people will be content with them as if it were their natural characteristic (*xing*). This is called the accomplishment of moral instruction. If there is accomplishment of moral instruction, then it cannot be prohibited, even if one offers heavy rewards and severe punishments. Hence, the one who is adept at moral instruction, his instruction is completed without employing reward and punishment. Once instruction is completed, reward and punishment cannot prohibit it. Applying reward and punishment inappropriately is also like this.[12]

Starting with a type of positivist, causal approach toward nature, this passage quickly moves to a moral one, proposing that just as the seasons change, so too the ruler can transform the people. Once the people have been cultivated with moral instruction, they cannot be reshaped by reward and punishment.

In contrast to the *yishang* chapter's anti-*ziran*, causal naturalism, the *lunren* (Discussing Personnel), and the *shenfen* (Distinguishing Lots) chapters contain affirmative expressions of *ziran*. Both of these contexts confine *ziran* to the manner in which the *daojia* ruler conducts his personal life. For example, the *lunren* chapter gives a description of the superior ruler who, in a Laozhuang style, is able to rule appropriately because he "seeks it in himself." The chapter explains that "to seek it in one's self" entails properly using one's senses, physical and emotional desires, and one's attitudes, and "to get rid of tricks and cheating to allow your intention to meander in the unlimited and establish your heart-mind on the path of spontaneity."[13] The *shenfen* chapter likewise describes a *daojia* ruler who appropriates the natural conditions to rule properly. The means by which such a ruler integrates with the natural conditions is by allowing "his intentions and will to meander at ease under the eaves of quiet solitude, and to allow his shape and character to settle into a place of spontaneity."[14] The LSCQ contains two opposing and yet not incommensurate positions on the role of *ziran*.

These two positions concerning *ziran* draw attention to the two foci of proper timing within the LSCQ—the extrinsic, timely action of the Agriculturalist and the intrinsic timing of the aesthetic (Kongmeng and Laozhuang) philosophers. From the Agriculturalist perspective, humans must act in accordance with the seasonal transformations; planting and harvesting cannot be performed on a whim. In the context of extrinsic timing, it is important that things not occur in a spontaneous manner; humans must be able to count on the seasons and be prepared to act accordingly. It is the ruler and his court who observe the seasonal transformations and set the ritual example for society to follow. If rulers are going to realize fully their personal integration with the cosmic forces, then they must attain a certain meditative state of mind. Their personal life experience must be orientated toward creative and spontaneous action. The LSCQ presents two very different approaches toward proper timing on the cosmic level.

Daoist Cosmic Timing

Although the opening chapters of the *shierji* integrate a Yang Zhu, *daojia*-type approach, and the *xuyi* (postscript) describes the *shierji* as expressing the teachings of the Yellow Emperor, the Laozhuang paradigm is not easily found in the LSCQ. Some of the references to Lao Dan, Zhuangzi, and Liezi do not always accompany the kind of nature images one expects to find associated with these figures. For example, the story of Liezi practicing archery, found both in the *shenji* (Examining Yourself) chapter and in the *Liezi* itself, is decidedly not *daojia*.[15] On the other hand, many of the passages shared by the LSCQ and the works the *Laozi*, *Zhuangzi*, and *Liezi* describe a *daojia* type of limited anarchy. However, to the extent that the authors of the LSCQ were concerned with depicting a centralized state ruling the empire, it is not too surprising that the full thrust of Laozi's and Zhuangzi's philosophy is rarely seen, and the limited anarchy is used as a check against the ruler's extravagance.

One must look carefully through the LSCQ's pastiche of unified, eclectic positions to extract its Laozhuang perspective on cosmic harmony and intrinsic timing. The naturalism of the LSCQ is heavily tempered with Huanglao and *yinyang wuxing* assumptions that more precisely fit both the centralizing government concerns and the agricultural paradigm, requiring a type of causal, almost mechanical, operation—planting wheat to harvest wheat, spring blossoms arising after the winter frost and before the autumn harvest. The LSCQ contains a Laozhuang idea of spontaneous nature.

Zhuangzi's comment on time, in the *dazongshi* chapter, captures the *daojia* intrinsic attitude: "He who operates by the natural seasons (*tianshi*) is not versatile."[16] The *Laozi*, in chapter 8, noted for its natural image of modeling water, highlights some courses of action for ruling naturally:

> In speaking, be adept at trustworthiness.
> In social and political attunement, be adept at harmony.
> In projects, be adept at choosing the capable.
> In taking action, be adept at choosing the right time.[17]

The Laozhuang perspective on proper timing holds that time is dependent on one's integrative actions. Proper timing, for Zhuangzi, is not acting in accordance with external affairs, such as the Agricultural model of timely planting. Proper timing from the Laozhuang account is dependent on the quality of one's action to develop cosmic integration.

Some of the stories concerning Laozi (Lao Dan), Zhuangzi, and Liezi display how these masters interpret and practice proper timing in their own lives. Excerpts from the LSCQ give an interesting description of Lao Dan. They tell us that he had the highest form of impartiality.[18] The *dangrang* (Appropriate Influences) chapter claims that Kongzi studied with Lao Dan.[19] The *buer* (Not Two) chapter describes Lao Dan as venerating *rou* (being supple).[20] Lao Dan is described as one of three sages who could hear the soundless and perceive the formless.[21] The concluding line of the *quzhi* (Expelling Restrictions) chapter praises Lao Dan. "As for Lao Dan, he got it (the way of no restrictions). He was like planting a tree that stands alone. If you insist on not complying with custom, then how could one's way be broadened?"[22] The LSCQ contains some unifying themes, such as the concern to promote a programmatic approach for achieving and maintaining political success. The LSCQ's social and political passages are somewhat wary of the Laozhuang teachings, since they usually advance ideas that appear impractical, if not antithetical, to managing a multi-ethnic empire. And yet the LSCQ's eclectic syncretism has a place and time for the intrinsic, cosmic timing of the Laozhuang masters.

The *biji*[23] (Self Certainty) chapter contains a story from the *Zhuangzi*'s *shanmu* (Mountain Tree) chapter concerning Zhuangzi's understanding of the "utility of the useless," in which, as we shall see, "timing" plays a role.

When Zhuangzi was traveling in the mountains, he saw a tree that was very beautiful and tall; its branches and leaves were thick and lush.[24] A woodcutter did not take it after having stopped by its side. When asked the reason why, he replied, "There's no way to use it." Zhuangzi said, "Because of its uselessness, this tree could fulfill its natural life span."

When Zhuangzi came out of the mountains and arrived in town, he stopped at the home of an old friend. Delighted, the old friend prepared food and wine. He ordered his servant to butcher a goose to prepare dinner. His servant asked, "One of our geese is able to squawk, another cannot; please, tell me which one to butcher?" The host said,[25] "You should butcher the one that cannot squawk."

The next day a disciple asked Zhuangzi, "Yesterday that tree in the mountains was able to fulfill its natural life span because it was useless; but the host's goose was butchered because it was useless. Master, what is your position?"

Zhuangzi smiled and said, "My position is between the useful and the useless. Between the useful and the useless appears to be it, but it really isn't. So one has not yet avoided entanglement in external things. As for *dao* and *de*, they are not like this. They are beyond praise and criticism.[26] [Availing oneself of the spontaneous way of *dao* and *de*,] once a dragon, once a snake, everything transforms according to appropriate proper timing, never willing to hold to one course only. One rising, one falling, take harmony as your standard, and drift and roam in the ancestor of the myriad things. If you can treat things as things and never be treated as a thing by things, then how could you become entangled in anything you do? This is what Shennong and the Yellow Emperor took as their standard.

"But the actual state of the myriad things and the transmitting of moral interpersonal relationships are not like this. Once something is complete, it will fall into ruin; once it attains size, it starts to decline; once something is sharp, it will start to become dull; once a person has achieved a venerated position, others will try to detract from him; once something is straight, it will begin to be twisted; once things are joined, they begin to separate; once love is given, rejection comes. The wise will be plotted against; the unworthy will be duped. How could anything be supposed to be certain?![27] [Alas! remember this my disciples, only one thing can be relied upon the realm of *daode*!]"[28]

This passage contains a number of key concepts and expressions that mark *daojia* Laozhuang discussions of "timing" within the LSCQ. Two ideas are integral to the Laozhuang perspective on timing: first, each particular must play its own role in cosmic timing; second, timing is integrated throughout the field of interrelated processes, so that it extends out of the particular action of the focus into the field and back again. This integrative and co-arising manifestation of timing as the creative and spontaneous relation obtaining between field and focus accounts for the indeterminacy and world of flux and transformation typical of the Laozhuang perspective. The passage describes a world of indeterminacy and flux with the expression: "Once a dragon, once a snake, everything transforms according to appropriate proper timing, never willing to hold to one course only. One rising, one falling, take harmony as your standard . . ." The complex changes and flip-flop transformations between opposites occur "according to appropriate proper timing," and this is accomplished pluralistically, "never holding to one course only." The sage ruler or enlightened ministers operating under the aesthetic paradigm of the Laozhuang teachings would be the people who could enhance both their own personal lives (the foci) and the social and environmental (field) condition in and through their personal actions, which allow for the free expression of all other particulars.

It takes a great deal of self-cultivation to develop the kind of self-control required to behave with timing that integrates focus and field, self and other. The *quzhi* (Expelling Restrictions) chapter cites a passage from the *Zhuangzi* that gives a description of the self-control needed:

> In the *Zhuangzi* it says that the one who bets for tiles in an archery contest will be skillful. One who bets for expensive buckles will tremble. One who bets for solid gold will be a nervous wreck. One's skill is the same—but that he becomes a nervous wreck is because he has weighted heavily external considerations. One who weights heavily the external will bet clumsily internally.[29]

Self-cultivation balances consideration of both the internal and external, and it is this kind of emotional and physical control that is required of the enlightened ruler and ministers who "gamble" with the lives of the masses and the destiny of the empire.

The LSCQ contains references to Liezi, who is frequently referred to as Zi Liezi (our Master Liezi)—possibly indicating that the stories were recorded by Liezi's disciples. The *buer* (Not Two) chapter states that: "Master Liezi venerated *xu* (vacuity)."[30] The *guanshi* (Observing the Age) chapter discusses the story of master Liezi and his family living in poverty, and yet he rejects food presented from the corrupt ruler of Cheng who was later overthrown.[31]

> Was not master Liezi's rejection of what is improper and avoidance of non-compliance penetrating? Moreover, when one is suffering the calamities of cold and starvation, and yet one does not take things improperly, this is to foresee transformation. To take action already foreseeing the transformation coming is to be fully penetrative with the reality of one's character and natural relations.[32]

Master Liezi serves as a model of one who is able to behave with proper timing because of his self-cultivation and self-control. Liezi is described as a knight of the *dao* (*youdao zhi shi*) who has fully realized "the reality of his character and natural relations," and an integral aspect of his realization is his ability to exercise timing in self-control under adverse conditions.

The LSCQ contains *daojia* descriptions of "cosmic timing" from the ontological perspective of the natural environment. The *yuandao* (The Cyclic Way) chapter describes cosmic harmony:

> Heaven's way (*tiandao*) is cyclic fluidity. The earth's way is square fixedness. The sage kings take them as a standard (*fa*), whereby they establish the *superior* and *inferior*.[33] How are we to explain that heaven's way is cyclic? The vital essence and life force (*jing qi*) [operate in succession];[34] one *rising*, the other *falling*—in cyclic revolution, repeatedly in rotation—without halting or pausing anywhere. Hence it is said that heaven's way is cyclic. How are we to explain that the earth's way is square? The myriad things are different in kind and shape. All of them have their allotment and office.[35] They cannot fill each other's positions.[36] Hence it is said that the earth's way is square (fixed).
>
> The ruler holds fast to the cyclic process. The ministers abide by the square fixedness. When the square and the cyclic do not switch, then their state flourishes.[37]

The *yuandao* chapter presents a model of integrative cosmic harmony. Granted, it has a Huanglao tone in prioritizing superior and inferior, but it generally presents the image of a complex web of interrelated processes. Like the *Zhuangzi*, it mentions the cyclic process: "one rising, the other falling—in cyclic revolution, repeatedly in rotation—without halting or pausing anywhere." Political order can be established by imitating the operations of heaven and earth in court administration and policy. The idea of the human modeling the natural, instead of acknowledging the mutual dependency of both, is again in keeping with the Huanglao and Agriculturalist extrinsic approaches.

The *yuandao* chapter discusses "cosmic time" in terms of environmental processes, celestial orbits, and geographic cycles of wind and water:

> Day and night constitute a complete cycle; this is the cyclic way. The moon's orbit through the twenty-eight mansions (constellations), and Zhen and Jue (the first and last constellations) connecting up; this is the cyclic way. The vital essence (*jing*)[38] operates[39] in the four seasons; one rising (*shang*), the other falling (*xia*)—each participating in what they meet (*yu*); this is the cyclic way. Things when stirred, sprout; when sprouting, generate; when generated, grow; when growing, enlarge; when enlarging, mature; when matured, decay; when decayed, diminish; when diminished, it goes into hiding (stored);[40] this is the cyclic way. The clouds' vapor (*qi*—life forces) moves westward on and on through winter and summer without stopping; the rivers and streams flow out eastward; day and night they do not rest; the source above never drains empty, and the destination below never floods full. The small (streams) becoming large, and the heavy (evaporates) becoming light. This is the cyclic way.
>
> The Yellow Emperor said: "The Emperor is without a constant place. To have a constant place is, on the contrary, to have no place." This is to say that he is not obstructed by any fixed form; this is the cyclic way.[41]

A developed ecological perspective is presented, revealing an understanding of the celestial, the atmospheric, the terrestrial, and biological growth and decay. But most importantly, the *yuandao* chapter brings the discussion of the cyclic pattern of cosmic harmony back around to its application in social and political order as a model for the emperor to follow, and it does this in the words of the Yellow Emperor. The chapter contains other interesting ideas, such as a *rujia* and Mohist conviction of giving the throne to the most worthy ruler instead of passing it onto one's descendants, implying that the timely succession of the throne might entail a *daojia*-like abdication.

The social and political focus of the LSCQ's eclectic content draws on the Laozhuang creative and spontaneous use of intrinsic timing as a model for harmonizing the empire. The *benwei* chapter provides a *daojia* analogy between cooking and governing and describes the articulated use of timing.

> Among the fundamentals (*ben*) of the various flavors, water is the most primary. With the five flavors—[sweet, sour, bitter, hot, and salty]—and with the three basic powers—[*sancai* water, fire, and wood]—multiple cookings will produce various changes in flavor, and temperature (lit. fire) serves as the regulating principle. To control the duration of the cooking process (lit. quickly or slowly—timing) is the key to eliminating the fishy, putrid, and rancid smells. To be certain of success one must not lose sight of the principle (*li*) of using heat. In the process of achieving a harmonious flavor, one must rely on the sweet, sour, bitter, hot, and salty

> spices, but the proper order (lit. first and last) and amount (lit. more and less) in the combining of ingredients makes their proportions a subtle affair, wherein each of the ingredients makes its own contribution. The changes which occur in the caldron (*ding*, tripod) are subtle and delicate; it cannot be expressed in words or conceptualized. It is just as subtle as the arts of archery and chariot driving, the transformations of *yin* and *yang*, and the calculable course of the four seasons.[42]

The *benwei* chapter has a Laozhuang flavor, and its analogy of creative cooking as a model of proper administration is compelling. Two important ideas are contained in this passage: it stresses the role of timing, and it emphasizes the significance of each particular contributing to the achievement of a well-integrated dish or state. Since the *ding* was a symbol of state sovereignty, the metaphor of creating a harmony in cooking fits the problem of maintaining an emergent social and political order. The expression "each of the ingredients makes its own contribution" is indicative of the Laozhuang perspective, which emphasizes the significance of each particular, and it is similar to the expression found in the *Huainanzi*, "each element achieving what is appropriate to it" (*ge de qi yi*).[43]

The LSCQ's descriptions of cosmic proper timing entail at least two predominant themes of extrinsic and intrinsic timing. The distinction is drawn for heuristic purposes because, in fact, as we saw above, the extrinsic timely action of according with the proper time is first a matter of state policy to ensure that the planting and harvesting occur in the right season, second, that it is the masses or farmers who must be employed properly within the season, and third, the season or time is not entirely objective but dependent on the ruler's performance of ritual action. The extrinsic, timely action of the farmer must await both the credibility of the season and the ruler's auspicious and timely performance of seasonal ritual. The ruler, holding the pivotal position between heaven, with its seasons and weather, and earth, with its productivity and people, must perform ritual action, in fact, any action, in such a way that it is in timely sequence with the extrinsic environment. Simultaneously, imperial action must articulate and create an intrinsic timing that generates a whole atmosphere, both social and climatic. Not only must the ruler's ritual action be performed in time with the seasons, but in return, his action conditions the environment and the masses. The ruler's ritual action has its own intrinsic timing appropriate to itself, but it also has a cultivating influence on the people and the climate.

The LSCQ contains descriptions of both Laozhuang and Huanglao intrinsic proper timing, and again, the extrinsic and intrinsic images overlap. The ruler, at least, allows his intentionality and consciousness to meander at ease on the path of spontaneity (*ziran*). He lives the creative and spontaneous life, if each is to come into its own. The ruler's creative self-transformation opens up the field of experience in which each and every other particular can make its creative contribution to the emergent harmony of both the cosmic environment and the social atmosphere. It is the Huanglao tendency to prioritize and hierarchicalize the world into superior/inferior and ruler/subject that blends the intrinsic creativity of the ruler's actions with the extrinsic model it sets for the rest of the world. The synthetic content of the LSCQ finds coherence in its persistent use of proper timing in orchestrating social harmony. There is a strong pragmatic and progressive voice in the programmatic conception of social order found in the LSCQ's treatises, which is again indicative of a meld of the ruler articulating historical timing in the reform of statutes and regulations, and that legal reform in turn sets an extrinsic model for the empire to follow.

Historical Proper Timing

The LSCQ contains a *fajia* approach to the timely reform of state regulations (*bianfa*). The role of proper timing in successfully managing the state, and its role in agricultural and military ventures, is a recurring theme. The *fajia* elements in the LSCQ draw from the agricultural and military models, advocating timely reform of regulations.

The ruler must exercise the use of proper timing in the timely reform of statutes, regulations, and laws to comply with historical and cultural changes. This type of proper timing is closely related to the "rule of law" paradigm, and it was advocated in its most radical form by the *fajia* writers in their motto *bu fa xian wang* ("Don't model the early sage kings").

Most pre-Qin political philosophy accepts the use of proper timing in the reform of government policy, and this is particularly true of the unified, eclectic positions in the LSCQ that describe legal reform in establishing and maintaining order. For example, the *yuanluan* (On Tracing the Origin of Disorder) chapter relates Duke Wen's use of proper timing in reforming the state of Jin.

> Duke Wen was generous in his dispensation; he employed those who had been set aside and those denied mobility; he rescued people from the dire straights of poverty; he saved people from disaster and calamity; he prohibited licentiousness and depravity; he lightened taxes; he pardoned criminals and wrongdoers; he economized the use of tools. He employed the masses according to the right time. As a result, he defeated the Jing

> army at Chengpu, brought stability to the throne of King Xiang of Zhou, broke the siege on Song, and forced the occupying Chu garrison out of Gu [the capital of Qi]; both those within and outside the state were submissive, and after this, all disorder in the state of Jin ceased.[44]

The *buguang* (Not Neglecting [Proper Timing]) chapter describes the enlightened ruler's application of proper timing. "A wise one's endeavors must accord with the right time. If his timing cannot be certain to succeed, then his people and affairs won't be far reaching."[45] The commonsense approach toward proper timing in government affairs grew out of its successful use in economic, agricultural, and military arts. Ancient political administration was chiefly concerned with agriculture and military affairs. The backbone of pre-Qin civilization was its success at producing a surplus crop and being able to defend it against other states or tribal peoples.

The Systematizers (*fajia*) draw heavily from the practicality of the Militarists (*bingjia*) and the Agriculturalists (*nongjia*), reinforcing the idea that farming and warfare are the main functions of the state. There is an Agriculturalist concern in the works attributed to Shang Yang and Han Fei. The *Hanfeizi* describes proper timing in farming. "Without the proper timing of the seasons, even the Yaos cannot grow a single ear of grain in the winter."[46]

Timing is of crucial importance in warfare. The LSCQ's *juesheng* (What Decides Victory) chapter, from the autumn section, defines military wisdom in terms of timing.

> Military affairs have their roots and trunk. They must be appropriate, wise, as well as brave. . . . *If you are wise, then you will know the transformation of the proper time.* If one knows the transformations of the proper time, then you understand how to utilize the changes between the weak and strong points, or flourishing and declining, and you would understand the measures of before and after, far and near, following and leading.[47] (emphasis added)

This kind of military flexibility in articulating time in tactics has relevance for the *fajia* writers and their vehement cry for reform in governing techniques, statutes, and policy. This culminates in their motto, "Do not model the early sage kings," because government, like military tactics, must be reformed to meet the needs of contemporary circumstances.

Although the social and political philosophers of ancient China were generally sensitive to the problem of contemporizing traditional government policy, nevertheless, it is Shang Yang's, Han Fei's, and some *fajia* writers', possibly Li

Si's, contribution to the LSCQ that champions a radical reform of policy and regulations to account for historical changes and be in accordance with contemporary conditions. Underlying the need for timely reform of statutes is a theory of historical transformation. Hu Shi called it a "theory of historical evolution." The *rujia* and *Mojia* philosophers recognized the need to practice proper timing in reforming traditional policy. The *rujia* methodology is not a simple conservativism of reclaiming the past. Even Kongzi acknowledged the importance of remolding the past to suit the present. The *Analects* says: "One who can infer the new by reanimating the past can be considered a teacher."[48] When the *Mozi* (chs. 35–37) argues against fatalism, it holds that the acceptance of a belief is based on three criteria, and the third is the applicability of an old belief in the present, which implies not blindly accepting the past as one's model. The process ontology so familiar in pre-Qin philosophy favors the interpretation of change as a constant. However, the *fajia* writers make the most out of historical transformation.

Hu Shi collects evidence to show that Li Si authored the *chajin* (On Investigating Present Necessities) chapter. Whether or not the *chajin* chapter was written by Li Si remains a mystery. Even though statements in his memorial for burning the private libraries bear a close resemblance to passages in that chapter, nevertheless, there is always the possibility that Li Si paraphrased the LSCQ material or similar *Hanfeizi* material in writing the memorial. We know that Han Fei's ideas preceded him to Qin, and given the similarity between some of the LSCQ material, such as the *chajin* chapter and the *Hanfeizi*, Han Fei's ideas or very similar ones may have influenced LSCQ contributors, Li Si, or others.

The core of Hu Shi's discussion of *bufa xian wang* focuses on the origin of the theory of historical evolution (*lishijinhua*), or what I prefer to call "historical transformation," because the pre-Qin theories of history accept change or transformation as integral to the processes of history but, generally speaking, they do not have a Hegelian, Marxian, Judeo-Christian, or social Darwinism conception of the historical process evolving toward a higher state. There is no goal (*telos*) nor any stages of development in the *fajia* conception of historical change. The *fajia* thinkers are concerned about the dynamics of social change, because such dynamics challenge the ruler's security. They do not advocate evolution. The aesthetic elements in *rujia* and *daojia* philosophy focus on the "locality" and particularity of temporal change; they do not discuss evolution. Although contemporary scientists struggle to free scientific theory from teleological assumptions, nevertheless, microbiologist René Dubos notes that evolutionary theory has not escaped the concept of "purpose."[49] Where Christian theology and even political theory, like Marxism, operate under the assumption of teleological development, the aesthetic paradigm of *rujia* and *daojia* thought perceives a spontaneous order generated out of particulars. At first, Hu Shi attributes both Li Si's and Han Fei's respective positions on "historical evolution" to their teacher, Xunzi, who advocates "modeling the later sage kings" (*fahouwang*).[50] Hu Shi is quick to point out that this cannot be the origin of the idea of "historical evolution" since Xunzi's position is not evolutionary. Xunzi accepts the unity of the past and the present and merely recommends modeling the later generations' sage kings because the most ancient material and records are lost. Thus Hu Shi concludes that the theory of historical evolution received influence from the theory of natural evolution from one of the schools of thought represented in the *Zhuangzi*.[51] Hu Shi's conclusion is perplexing, because the Laozhuang writers were not evolutionary—their world is in transformation and indeterminate flux, not progressive evolution.

Moreover, Li Si and Han Fei were preceded by Shang Yang and King Wuling of Zhao in the call for reform of regulations and statutes. What Hu Shi did not recognize was that Shang Yang, or at least his work *Shangjunshu* (*The Book of Lord Shang*), and possibly the fragments of Shen Buhai, both mid-fourth-century B.C.E. writers, had a theory of historical transformation—what Hu Shi calls historical evolution. Hu Shi's oversight here may be due to the early-twentieth-century theory that most of the Warring States material, like *Shangjunshu*, was not authentic. Hu Shi believes that Shang Yang and King Wuling called for the reform of regulations (*bianfa*) and had a theory of "natural evolution," but the theory of historical evolution, he proposes, developed later. However, the following quote from *The Book of Lord Shang* shows that it does contain the idea of historical transformation:

> A ruler won't model antiquity when he can strengthen his state.
>
> There is more than one way to govern the world, and there is no necessity to imitate antiquity. . . . Yet their (Yao, Shun, Tang, and Wu) methods cannot be applied to later times.[52]

The key to Shang Yang's call for reform was a theory of historical change. A similar position is associated with Shen Buhai. A passage associated with Shen Buhai describes an understanding of historical transformation.[53]

> In the past, seventy-nine generations of rulers did not use the same methods and regulations; their pronouncements and decrees were not the same, and yet they all ruled the empire as kings. How was this possible? It must be that the state was rich and grain was plentiful.[54]

Although there is some doubt that this passage was written by Shen Buhai, it is an example of historical transformation, and it appears to be prior to the LSCQ and the *Hanfeizi*. Moreover, the basic concept of "historical transformation" is contained in the Zhou dynasty idea of *tianming* (Heaven's mandate), which accounts for dynastic change. Whether the throne is willingly abdicated or usurped from a tyrant, that dynasties change, that well-ordered societies degenerate, are overthrown, and are established in succession, provides pre-Qin writers with experiences of transformation in addition to environmental changes. These experiences allow them to not only develop a processes worldview of natural transformations but also help them articulate an operational understanding of human society and political order.

Not only is Hu Shi's interpretation incomplete in not recognizing a theory of historical transformation in Shang Yang and the *tianming* theory, but also he misrepresents the *fajia* position by calling it a "theory of historical evolution." This is an inappropriate name for the theory, because "evolution" implies a sense of development. Strictly speaking, "historical evolution" indicates a theory that advances the continuous development and adaptation of society in history—Marx's dialectical materialism can be described as a theory of "historical evolution." However, the *fajia* concept of history does not imply development in history. For the Systematizers, there is constant historical change, and regulations need to be reformed in order to keep up with these changes to ensure the sovereignty of the ruler.[55] I refer to their position as "historical transformation" to avoid the implications of "evolution." Hu Shi wanted to use the most scientifically sophisticated terminology available when he wrote his article in 1930.

What concerns us here is that the *chajin* chapter presents historical transformation and the call for reforming regulations (*bianfa*) in association with proper historical timing. In this context, "proper timing" does not refer to one's self-cultivation per se, nor does it reference proper seasonal timing in agriculture or cosmic harmony—it refers to the state making historical changes. The *chajin* chapter begins with a concern that led Xunzi to advocate "modeling the later sage kings," namely, that the records of the early sage kings are lost or corrupt, and thus the chapter proposes that one must reform regulations in a timely fashion.

> Why don't the rulers take as a standard (*fa*) the regulations (*fa*) of the early kings?[56] It is not because they are not worthy; it is because they cannot be obtained and taken as a standard. The regulations (*fa*) of the early kings have come down from the previous generations. In some cases, people might have added to them; others might have deleted things from

> them. So how could they be obtained and taken as a standard? And even in cases where they have not been tampered with, still they cannot be obtained and taken as a standard.[57]

The passage ends with the comment that even if the records were preserved, the ancient ways could not be followed. The reason is made clear.

> How could the regulations of the early kings be obtained and taken as a standard. Even if they were obtainable, still they cannot be taken as a standard. All of the regulations of the early kings owe their importance to their respective times (*shi*). Those times, however, have not come down together with the regulations. So even if their regulations had come down to the present, still they could not be taken as a standard.[58]

The *chajin* chapter presents a number of analogies to draw out the significance of historical transformation and the need to reform regulations. One such analogy describes how the scout of an attacking army measured the depth of a river for fording before the water rose, and so when they followed the old mark, they were devastated. The passage ends with a warning:

> The rulers of the present generation, taking as standard the regulations of the early kings, bear a resemblance to this (i.e., crossing a flooded river by an old mark). Their time is already unfit for the regulations of the early kings, but they say: "these are the regulations of the early kings," and thereby take them as a standard. How could it not be a pity to govern like this?![59]

The chapter relates the well-known story regarding the person from Chu who dropped his sword overboard while fording a river. So he notched the side of the boat where the sword fell in, and after docking he used the notch on the boat to look for the sword in the river! This analogy ends with another warning. "To govern one's state with those ancient standards is the same as the above story. The times have moved on, but the old standards have not followed. Won't it be difficult to govern with them?!"[60] The *chajin* chapter advocates a reform of regulations due to the historical transformations that have left the ancient ways outdated. The chapter discusses the significance of changing regulations because of cultural differences.[61] It emphasizes the need to reform law due to historical changes: "Since generations change, and *time moves on*, it is appropriate to reform regulations."[62] With time having moved on, and regulations needing reform, the chapter emphasizes that the proper means of reforming regulations is to do so "in accordance with the right time"(*yinshi*).[63]

> Hence, in initiating affairs, one must act according to some standard. In reforming regulations, they should be transformed in accordance with the requirements of the time. If one behaves as this theory proposes, then he will not have erroneous endeavors. Those who do not dare judge the regulations are the common masses. Those who hold fast to the regulations till their death are the officials. The one who reforms the regulations according to the requirements of the time (*yinshi bianfa*) is a worthy ruler.[64] Thus, there were seventy-one[65] sages who ruled the empire. All of their regulations differed. It was not because their missions opposed each other; rather, it was due to the different situational factors of the times.[66]

Since the *fajia* writers are heavily influenced by military arts and Agriculturalist skills, it is not too surprising that they explicitly call for reforming regulations in accordance with proper timing. The articulation of proper timing is not a social, spiritual integration of one's behavior within an ethical situation. Rather, the *fajia* writers are concerned with commandeering the historical and cultural transformations in order to institute reform in regulations and government policy to ensure political control.

Proper Timing in Moral and Interpersonal Relations

The third and ethically most interesting style of proper timing examines the significance of articulating "proper timing" in one's personal behavior and interpersonal relations. For many passages in the LSCQ, the cultivation of proper timing in the ruler's behavior is crucial to impact social and political order. The emperor's behavior must be fully integrated with cosmic and historical proper timing. On a day-to-day and moment-to-moment basis, the emperor must articulate time in and through his personal conduct to ensure safety for his person and state. The *yuhe* and *shoushi* chapters devote attention to this type of proper timing.

Timely Encounters

The *yuhe* (The Rare Opportunity of Meeting) chapter discusses the significance of individuals, especially rulers and ministers, meeting each other or "meeting" their generation. It describes how these "encounters" influence the state. The ruler's choice of friends and ministers does not merely affect his own person but also has ramifications for everybody: "It is not the case that the calamity falls upon oneself only."[67] Meeting others is a basic aspect of proper timing. If one meets up with others at the inappropriate time, then disaster is sure to follow. Meeting others need not be inappropriate. Proper meeting is in harmony with proper timing: "Opportunity (*yu*), in general, is a matter of fitting (*he*). If one does not fit (*he*) with the times (*shi*),[68] one must wait to fit, and only afterward can things be done."[69] Proper timing plays an important role when people meet each other, especially a ruler and his ministers. "Waiting to fit" is not necessarily a passive affair of merely aligning one's behavior in a timely fashion with extrinsic conditions. Given the dynamic focus-field paradigm, waiting should be understood as an activity in which time is articulated as well as appropriated.

Avoiding untimely and inappropriate encounters are a concern.

> If there is the case where friends meet by chance when it is inappropriate to meet by chance, or if they do not meet by chance when it is appropriate for them to meet by chance, then there will certainly be destruction.[70] These are the reasons why a state falls into disorder and a generation perishes. The bitterness, grief, and laborious affairs of the people in the empire are produced from this.[71]

The ruler is warned that inappropriate encounters will lead to the destruction of the state, and the people's hardship. Gao You's commentary to the line "These are the reasons why a state falls into disorder and a generation perishes" is worthy of our attention, because he draws out the importance of proper timing in this passage.

> The worthy ones consummate the way-of-governing. With just one chance meeting (with a worthy one), a generation can be enlightened; he can assist with *the timely patterning* of things and affairs. If he is not encountered by chance, a state cannot be well-ordered, which leads to chaos, and the generation cannot distinguish between the worthy and the unworthy, which causes them to perish.[72]

Although there could be a timely meeting of friends, or ruler and minister, which could probably pacify the world, the *yuhe* chapter focuses on the destruction of states due to an inappropriate encounter, or rulers and ministers not meeting. The first example concerning Kongzi sets the theme for the rest of the chapter.

> Kongzi traveled around the empire, introducing himself to the rulers of that age. He went to Qi and he went to Wei, he met over eighty rulers. . . .

With all of his traveling, Kongzi just barely got the office of Sike (criminal judge) of Lu. This is why the Son of Heaven is constantly (*shi*) cut off, and why there is such serious disorder among the feudal lords.[73]

The royal house of Zhou lost its opportunity by not meeting Kongzi. The chapter points out that one must be on guard against inappropriate relationships being formed in one's state. If there are numerous inappropriate relationships, some individuals will make a fortune but ruin the state.

If there is such disorder, the foolish will have a windfall of luck. If there is such luck, people certainly cannot live up to their responsibilities. If the responsibilities have not been lived up to for a long time, this kind of luck on the contrary becomes a calamity. The greater the luck, the greater too the calamity. And it is not the case that the calamity falls upon oneself alone. Hence, a *junzi* does not put trust in luck, nor does he behave expediently. He takes employment only after carefully examining it in himself. He acts only after he is employed. Whoever is able to listen to advice is a man who understands judgments. But only a few of today's rulers are able to understand judgments. So how could what they encounter not be done expediently?[74]

The *yuhe* chapter presents some examples of how confused people mismanage affairs and misunderstand things. For example, understanding debates is compared to understanding music. People who do not understand the five tones cannot make proper judgments about music. When they hear the tones played properly, they do not enjoy it. Contrarily, they enjoy wild compositions. The chapter goes on to relate a peculiar divorce story about a newly wed woman who decides to store some wealth outside of her home as insurance against being expelled for not bearing a son. When her in-laws discover this, they expel her. But the young lady and her parents never realize exactly what happened. The author comments: "The destruction of an ancestral altar and the perishing of the empire have similar causes."[75]

The *yuhe* chapter compares the appropriateness of meeting others to developing a deep meaningful relationship or to finding rare delicacies.

Hence, it is said that the fitting opportunity is never constant, and giving advice is a matter of occasion too. For example, consider people toward the opposite sex, they all know how to be pleased, yet beauty is not necessarily happened upon. Thus, Muo Mu was obedient to the Yellow Emperor. The Yellow Emperor said, "You never forgot when I encouraged you with virtue; you never failed when I gave you uprightness. Even though

> you are ugly, what harm will it be?" Or it is like people toward delicacies, they are all fond of the sweet and the crispy, yet the sweet and the crispy are not always received. King Wen liked to chew calamus (a peppermint). Kongzi took some after hearing this; he ate it and wrinkled his brow. It took three years before he overcame his dislike of it.[76]

The chapter describes a man who had such a terrible body odor that his family could not live with him, but after moving to the seaside, the people there were obsessed with his odor. The story of Dunxia (or Dunqia) Choumi and the marquis of Chen is told. Dunxia was an ugly fellow. He had a forehead pointed like an awl and a broad face with a reddish-brown lacquer color, drooping eyes, nostrils pointing upward, and long, twisted eyebrows.[77] But the marquis of Chen befriended him, enjoying his company. When the marquis fell ill, he sent Dunxia to meet the king of Chu. The king was so insulted by Dunxia's appearance and inability to speak well that he attacked the state of Chen. Even though the state of Chen was destroyed, the marquis and Dunxia remained friends.

After pointing out that the masses suffer because of inappropriate relationships, the author concludes with the following advice about appointing personnel and avoiding disaster:

> In general, the roots of appointing personnel are as follows: the most superior ruler does it according to their (the appointees') intention;[78] the next do it according to their job performance, and the next do it according to their achievement. If the above three cannot be put into practice, the state will certainly be ruined and perish. Various calamities will arrive in large scale, and the ruler (lit. your body) will die in disaster. It is only by luck that a life span can last seventy or ninety years. Even the descendants of a worthy minister or sage ruler can turn around and bring calamity on the masses. This is how he harms himself, but how could he be the only one to suffer?[79]

For the *yuhe* chapter, if the ruler cannot secure intimate relationships with excellent ministers, then he will meet with calamities inevitably leading to his death. The calamity will not only fall upon the ruler, but others will suffer.

The *yuhe* chapter argues that the ruler must actively engage himself in "making the time" to encounter proper ministers of state. The ruler and minister must build an intimate relationship so that they work together as one person. The ruler must develop deep relationships with his ministers so he can discover their innermost intentions, thereby securing his life and state. The types of personal relationships the ruler builds have historical consequences. If the ruler creates proper relationships with his ministers by articulating time and by awaiting the right time, then he articulates the social order and generates a cultural history for his people.

Priority on Timing

The positive expression of proper timing in conducting one's self-cultivation for establishing social and political order is explicitly addressed in the *shoushi* or *xushi* (Awaiting the Right Time) chapter.[80] Although proper timing is a concept shared by the various Warring States philosophers, nevertheless, they do not provide us with any extended discussion of it, so the *shoushi* chapter is a unique piece of pre-Qin literature entirely devoted to a discussion of proper timing.

The *shoushi* chapter depicts the application of timing in managing government affairs. "The sage ruler's administration of state affairs appears to be idle, but in fact is quick; he appears dilatory, but is prompt, and thereby awaits the right time (*daishi*)."[81] Gao You suggests reading the expression "appears idle" to mean *wuwei*, "nonaction," and "prompt" to mean "to complete merit." He cites the story of King Wu to illuminate the meaning of the "apparent slowness but timely action of a king." He tells us:

> King Wu organized the meeting of eight hundred lords at Mengjin, and all agreed that the tyrant Zhou could be attacked (the time had come). King Wu said that they did not yet understand the Mandate of Heaven. He went home for two years—which was like delaying. But on the *jiazi* day he defeated Zhou at Muye. Therefore, it says "await the (right) time."[82]

Gao You's commentary on the above passage helps elucidate the meaning of the subsequent story in the *shoushi* chapter concerning King Wu serving the tyrant Zhou while he avails himself of the *jiazi* day at Muye when he finally defeats Zhou. This took a great deal of patience on King Wu's part, which imparts his level of self-cultivation in behaving in a timely fashion for the benefit of the empire. The story of King Wu concludes with the comment that "The (right) time is indeed not easy to find."[83]

The *shoushi* chapter gives three examples of worthy ministers who practiced self-cultivation and articulated timing in service to a ruler, or who sought revenge by waiting for the right time. It mentions Lü Wang fishing and waiting to serve King Wen. The drama of Wu Zixu's life is related to show how he articulated proper timing in taking years to finally attack Chu to avenge his father.[84] The aesthetic or creative model of articulating the proper time is metaphorized in the story of the Mohist, Tian Rui, who wanted to meet the king of Qin, but he could not do so until he was sent there by the king of Chu. This paradox of having "to go to Chu to arrive at Qin" displays an aesthetic appropriation of time. The paradox is highlighted with the following comment: "Certainly there are situations when one is 'far away' when near to it, but near when far away. Time is also like this."[85] The aesthetic approach acknowledges a complete indeterminacy of any given situation, allowing that the timely, sagacious act may appear paradoxical, yet it creates and maintains the proper time. The fullest development of this approach to the social and spiritual arrogation of proper timing in self-cultivation and achieving social and political order is found in the *Mengzi* (*Mencius*, II/A/2, V/B/1), the *Zhongyong* (*Commonality and Centrality*, ch. 25), and commentary appendixes of the *Yijing* (*I ching* or *Book of Changes*). These *rujia* texts prefer to use the binome *shizhong*, literally, "timely equilibrium."[86]

The *shoushi* chapter employs the expression *shizhong* in its discussion of creating and maintaining intrinsic proper timing in self-cultivation, and in some passages it lapses into the more rigid "rule of law" paradigm of meeting extrinsic timing by interpreting the appropriation of time in a fixed, causal order. This may not be readily apparent, but compare the following passage from the *shoushi* chapter with a related discussion from the *Mengzi*.

> Even if you have the worth of Kings Tang and Wu, but the times are without tyrants like Jie and Zhou, then one cannot complete the kingly way, or even if the times provide tyrants like Jie and Zhou, but one is not as worthy as Tang and Wu, then again one cannot complete the kingly way. The sage ruler's perception of the right time is like the inseparability of taking a step and reflecting a shadow.[87] Hence, a knight who possesses the *dao* who has not yet happened on the proper time will go into retirement or hiding, *awaiting the right time*. When the time arrives, there are those who could be a commoner (lit. plain clothes) who could become the Son of Heaven (e.g., Shun), or there could be a ruler with one-thousand chariots who might come to possess the empire (e.g., Tang and Wu), or a humble person of low rank might become an assistant to one of the three sage Kings (e.g., Lü Wang or Yi Yin), or a commoner (e.g., Yu Ran) might be able to seek revenge against one who possesses ten-thousand chariots (i.e., a powerful ruler). *Therefore, it is only timing which a sage ruler values.*[88] (emphasis added)

Although this interpretation of timing is somewhat rigid and formalistic and appears to follow an extrinsic model of aligning oneself with an external time, nevertheless, one must keep in mind that "awaiting the proper time" is an activity that creates and maintains intrinsic timing. The above passage appears to follow what Mengzi considers the way of Bo Yi, rather than the way of Kongzi. Fung Yu-lan has made note of the fixed rigidity of Bo Yi's appropriation of proper timing and Mengzi's preference for Kongzi's way of fitting the "exigencies of circumstances."[89] The *Mengzi* passage states the following:

> "How about Bo Yi and Yi Yin?"
>
> "They followed paths different from that of Kongzi. Bo Yi was such that he would only serve the right prince and rule over the right people, took office when order prevailed, and relinquished it when there was disorder. Yi Yin was such that he would serve any prince and rule over any people, would take office whether order prevailed or not. Kongzi was such that he would take office, or would remain in a state, would delay his departure or hasten it, all according to circumstances. All three were sages of old. I have not been able to emulate any of them, but it is my hope and wish to follow the example of Kongzi."[90]

The *shoushi* chapter of the LSCQ advocates a Bo Yi-like withdrawal from a disordered society, describing an abstract, generalized, and extrinsic notion of proper timing rather than the intrinsic, timely appropriation of circumstances that Mengzi believed Kongzi had.

The *shoushi* chapter shares similarities with the *Zhuangzi*'s *rangwang* chapter, advocating retirement in bad times. This withdrawal is not passive. It is a return to the roots of order in the immediate context: "If they encountered a period of order, they did not run away from public office; but if they encountered an age of disorder, they did not try to hold on to an office at any cost."[91] This notion of withdrawing in a time of disorder is so basic to pre-Qin eclectic thought that it is voiced in the *Analects*:

> The Master said, "Make an earnest commitment to the love of learning and abide to the death in service to the efficacious way. Do not enter a state that is in peril; do not stay in a state that is in danger. Show yourself when the Way prevails in the empire, but hide yourself when it does not. It is a disgrace to be poor and humble when the Way prevails in the state. Equally, it is a disgrace to be rich and noble when the Way falls into disuse in the state."[92]

The idea of withdrawing from a disordered state then may not be entirely out of step with Kongzi's intrinsic timing. Everyone, but especially the minister, must be able to recognize when one cannot influence a dangerous situation, and then withdraw. The *shoushi* chapter emphasizes the need to correlate one's self-cultivation with proper timing in opposing the tyrant, implying that a person can create and maintain time.

In some places, the *shoushi* chapter is more extrinsic and almost mechanistic in approach, which is not too surprising since many passages in the LSCQ appear to have been influenced by the paradigm shift, replacing the aesthetic model of early *rujia* and *daojia* teachings with the less creative, uncompromising "rule of law" model, and culminating in the *fajia* writers and in the state of Qin finally uniting the empire—of course, many of the LSCQ's chapters promote unification under one ruler. The LSCQ's descriptions of history and its *wuxing* (Five Phases) philosophy of dynastic history both propose that one can harmonize with the natural cycles of change and establish a new age. The mechanistic understanding of change is sponsored by an agricultural and a military approach.

The *shoushi* chapter employs the seasonal agricultural metaphor of proper timing, revealing the less flexible, external, and formalistic understanding of time. The wording sounds like the *changgong* chapter.

> When the rivers and land are frozen solid, then Hou Ji would not sow. When Hou Ji sowed, he certainly waited for spring. Thus, if a person, although wise, does not happen on the right time, then he achieves nothing. When the leaves are abundant and beautiful, people don't know the end of it even after picking leaves all day long. When the autumn frost falls, all the forests will wither.[93] The ease or difficulty of an affair does not lie in its being important or trivial; rather, *the task of affairs lies in realizing the right time* (*zhishi*).[94] (emphasis added)

People cannot work well if they do not accord with the natural circumstances. From an agricultural perspective, it is always good to know one's limitations. This return to the agricultural model as the root metaphor of proper timing shows the *shoushi* chapter's concern for a practicable program, gaining success by articulating time.

The concern for precision in establishing policy and programs becomes comical in the following example, implying that wild animals avail themselves of proper timing and provide a context for social change.

> In the difficulties of Zi Yang of Zheng, a mad dog brought on the confusion. In the troubles of Gao and Guo of Qi, a stray ox caused the confusion.[95] The masses took advantage of these opportunities to execute Zi Yang, and Gao and Guo. If it coincides with the right time (*dang qi shi*), even a

> dog or an ox can take the lead on behalf of humans, how much better to have a human for a leader?[96]

Anyone can act in a timely fashion when it comes to attacking a despotic tyrant. The reader is challenged to *dangshi* (coincide with the right time) by leading the masses to attack a tyrant.

The *shoushi* chapter compares the people of a chaotic generation to starving horses or dogs who do not get excited until they see the hay or bones. "People of a chaotic generation are quiet because they have not seen a virtuous person. Once they see a virtuous person, their going to him cannot be stopped. That which goes to him is not their bodies, is it their hearts we refer to?!"[97] Although this may sound mechanistic, in that the people of a chaotic generation are driven like starved animals to accept a worthy ruler, we must be aware that this is an analogy concerning the people's social and spiritual desire to live in peace and safety. It is no overstatement to say that oppressed people flock to a worthy ruler and a well-ordered society.

The *shoushi* chapter discusses how the states Lu and Wei "met with the opportune time" and gained territory from larger states. "That in spite of the smallness of Lu and Wei, both got what they wanted from larger states is because they happened on their opportune times."[98] Here the text explicitly employs the expression "happened on their opportune times." This coincidence in meeting with the times displays the discipline of one's self-cultivation. To meet with the times then is in part something that happens to one, and yet one must be actively prepared and flexible enough to meet the challenges of the event—again, the waiting is a positive action that creates intrinsic timing. The chapter concludes with the watchword that in peaceful times one need not worry about rebellion, but affairs need to be conducted according to the times.

> Hence, the worthy ruler's and eminent knight's worrying about the common people coincides with a disorderly age. Heaven does not issue (the mandate) twice. The opportune time does not tarry long, and the capable do not perform two tasks simultaneously. Success in tasks coincides with the right time (*dangshi*).[99]

It is the sage ruler who can "match the times" (*dangshi*) and achieve success in the art of rulership. The *shoushi* chapter's presentation of *shi* as "proper timing" is complex enough in its own right. It has its own bias toward timing, and this bias is highlighted when compared to the highly creative art of contextualizing, *rujia*, paradigm of timing in personal conduct.

The concern for managing all affairs by creating timely action is very much in keeping with the use of proper timing in the *Zhongyong*.

> The authentic one is self actualizing, and the *dao* is one's self-realized *dao*. Being authentic is the beginning and end of affairs; without authenticity there is nothing. It is for this reason that the consummate person (*junzi*) venerates authenticity. Being authentic is not only one's own self-actualization, but it is also the means to actualize others. Self-actualization is accomplished through appropriate human relations, while actualizing others is completed through moral-wisdom. This is the virtuous-potency of human character and the way (*dao*) of uniting the inner and the outer. Therefore, proper timing is the fitting way to manage affairs.[100]

Self-actualization integrates others when consummate people create time in the management of state affairs. Although this is a representative passage of the *rujia* paradigm for articulating time, it is not a strong example, because part of the commentary tradition ignores the role of proper timing and interprets the character *shi* as an adverb. The *Yijing* and its commentarial tradition can be used to explicate the *rujia* paradigm of proper timing in self-cultivation.

The *Yijing*'s impact on pre-Qin thought is considerable, and its role in the content, especially the almanac-like structure of the LSCQ, requires elaboration. Timing is central in ancient or modern *Yijing* divination. From the earliest forms of oracle bone divination through the development of the yarrow stalk method and the writing of the *Yijing*, timing is of crucial importance. First there is the preparation time in which the diviner arranges the materials and oneself for the divination. The divination itself is a highly creative act of articulating time. Loaded with various time-related elements, the hexagram explains past and present events and predicts the future. Richard Wilhelm maintains that a whole hexagram constitutes a "time."[101] He describes four different notions of "time": Time as (1) movement—decrease or growth; (2) action or process; (3) law; and (4) symbolic situation. The person receiving the divination, usually a ruler in antiquity, will take what is learned from the divination and act accordingly, either advancing, altering, or ceasing the current project. One acts in such a way so as to articulate intrinsic time, influencing the world. At the same time, one performs an action in a timely fashion with extrinsic conditions. The composite makeup of the *Yijing* provides a model for interpreting the LSCQ.

The understanding of time in the *Yijing* represents a worldview of interdependent, multiple processes—particularly processes involving heaven, earth, and humanity. For example, hexagram eleven *tai* (Peace), which shows the trigram *kun* (The Receptive, female earth) above *qian* (The Creative, male heavens), represents the harmony of heaven and earth. It constitutes a "time" of peace and prosperity, both in nature and society. The *xiang* (image) reads:

> Heaven and earth unite: the image of peace. Thus the ruler divides and completes the course of heaven and earth. He furthers and regulates the gifts of heaven and earth. And so aids the people.

Wilhelm comments:

> Heaven and earth are in contact and combine their influence, producing a time of universal flowering and prosperity. This stream of energy must be regulated by the ruler of men. It is done by a process of division. Thus men divide the uniform flow of time into the seasons, according to the succession of natural phenomena, and mark off infinite space by the points of the compass. In this way nature, in its overwhelming profusion of phenomena, is bounded and controlled. On the other hand, nature must be furthered in her productiveness. This is done by adjusting the products to the right time and the right place, which increases the natural yield. This controlling and furthering activity of man in his relation to nature is the work on nature that rewards him.[102]

The *Yijing* advocates that there are interrelationships obtaining between human life and the environment. The *Yijing*'s perspective indicates that nature, especially heaven, sets the pace for earth and humans to follow. The commentaries align human activity with the natural, creative powers of *qian*. This is true even in the commentarial passages, which disclose the ability of the consummate person (*junzi*) to articulate creatively (*qian*) the accommodation of proper timing (*yinshi*). In the commentary to the third line of the *qian* hexagram, Kongzi is cited as saying that the consummate person "acts with care in actively and creatively accommodating proper timing."[103] The creative and active power of the consummate person is described in terms of the cosmic principle of *qian*. The *tuan* commentary to the fourth hexagram *meng* (Youthful Folly) explains the judgment's claim "folly has success" to mean that "one who succeeds hits upon the right timing (*shizhong*) for his undertaking."[104] The creative process of articulating time (*shizhong*) discloses a harmony between both an intrinsic and extrinsic manifestation of time. The *Yijing*'s position on proper timing is generally in agreement with the LSCQ's.

The practical application of proper timing is a predominant image in the LSCQ's social and political thought. Not only does the text provide a comprehensive discussion of timing, but the very structure of the LSCQ is arranged by the temporality of appropriating policy according to seasonal, historical, and personal timing. Proper timing grounds the program for social and political order in the LSCQ by successfully harmonizing various positions, such as the extrinsic "rule of law" paradigm and the intrinsic aesthetic paradigm.

The LSCQ was defined by its era, and it assisted in perpetuating that culture in a syncretic literary genre and consolidated philosophy, which we now think of as distinctly Han or Chinese. It sponsored the unification of prior philosophies and justified the reform of regulations and the transformation of dynasties while advocating the need for centralized government. The authors of the LSCQ accomplished all of this because of their ability to establish a paradigm of harmony under the guidance of proper timing. Certainly our world today is different. Or is it? Nations vie for power. Philosophers debate about the proper course to be followed or constructed. People speak of a unified world or a global government. Even though these are only superficial similarities, nevertheless, we may be able to learn something from the LSCQ. In the next chapter, I delineate some of the ways that the LSCQ's philosophy can be applied to contemporary issues.

Chapter 5

Applying Proper Timing to Contemporary Issues

In keeping with the temporal orientation of this book, rather than conclude, I want to begin a narrative in comparative philosophy. Thinking temporally affords contemporary philosophy an alternative approach for understanding the world and human life. The temporal approach contrasts sharply with theoretical analysis, integrating the differences among particulars in a changing world.

In practical ethics and political policy, "*when* to act" is of major importance. This question is rarely discussed in contemporary Western philosophy. "Cosmic harmony" is a major concern of most pre-Qin philosophy, and the LSCQ is one of China's earliest extant texts to develop a cosmology of social and political order derived from the ruler's personal application of timing. The philosophical perspective of "the right time" underlies and unifies the social, political, and ethical concerns of the LSCQ. The pre-Qin aesthetic order stands in opposition to most post-Kantian notions of ethical and political theory. The art of rulership that emerges from a study of the LSCQ presupposes a philosophy based on a programmatic understanding of the various contexts of human life. This is a radical alternative to "top down" political theory and constitutes a peculiar pre-Qin or "Chinese" style of organization.

Is Social and Political Philosophy Culture Bound?

There is a bias among certain thinkers, for example, Martin Heidegger and Kitar Nishida, who argue that philosophy is culture bound, and that the highest forms of philosophy are unique to their respective cultures. Others, such as

Kant, argue that reason is universal to all people regardless of cultural background, and so all people, at least potentially, participate in universal reason; but Kant's ethnocentrism did not allow him to extend that notion of universal reason very far from the Germanic people. Both positions are extremist and in need of modification.

To do comparative philosophy one must be self-conscious of personal and cultural biases. Being self-conscious of bias allows one to gain insight into other traditions, but this insight must be brought back home for the enrichment of one's own tradition. For Hans-Georg Gadamer, a hermeneutic study teaches us to guard against opinions leading to misunderstanding. He instructs us to reappraise the role of prejudice in understanding.[1] Gadamer opens a horizon for understanding past traditions. Prejudice expands our understanding of the temporal-historical nature of consciousness and the social-political orientation of the human life-world.

A hermeneutic study provides both avenues: historical criticism and human empathy. Giambattista Vico proposes that the imagination creates the possibility of empathizing with past cultures.[2] We can follow Vico's suggestion to enter ancient China. The historicity and temporality of consciousness offer an avenue to contemporize the past. We can gain access to different cultures by our political orientation and a "prejudice" to select the other.

Because philosophy and social-political theory are tied to historical context, they cannot properly be understood when separated from their cultural background and life-world. To the extent that a language frames philosophy, it is culturally relative. Language and philosophy can be transmitted from one culture to another. They are in part rational enterprises, and as such, they are the domains of rational creatures, regardless of culture. On the other hand, the translatability of languages and philosophies is not due to one's participation in universal reason but rather to one's creative ability to empathize with another—no matter how peculiar. The creative capacity of humans allows for the development and use of human language and philosophy. The creative use of our imaginations allows for translatability from one context to another. Creative beings can empathize with others, at least, through the power of imagination. Language, and thus philosophy, can be translated and transmitted from one culture to another.

Social and political philosophy are committed to relative cultural, historical, and economic parameters. One might be tempted to limit their scope of applicability to those relative contexts. This would place unnecessary limitations on our ability to discern and extract valuable ideas and meaningful content from another tradition that could possibly enrich our own. To fail to extract the ideas and insights of other traditions only limits our own creativity, our understanding of others, and, ultimately, ourselves. The sustained evolution of Western culture and philosophy from ancient Babylon to contemporary Euro-American thought is more myth than reality. What underlies this idea of sustained evolution is a complex exercise of creativity in appropriating and extracting the valuable and the meaningful across cultural, historical, and linguistic boundaries. The bias has been to limit the debts to those traditions that developed west of the Himalayas, but the time has arrived when we need to borrow and trade ideas and acknowledge past trading debts with those traditions east of the Himalayas. The purpose of this chapter is to extract an important concept of "proper timing" from pre-Qin philosophy that can enrich our own philosophy.

Contemporary Philosophy and the LSCQ

Contemporary theories of time are exclusive or one-sided in their approach: either they externalize time as a part of the world, or they internalize it as an aspect of consciousness. The LSCQ's unified, eclectic philosophy offers an alternative model. Theories that de-emphasize the dynamic achievement qualities of the social self can be enriched by adopting ideas from the LSCQ. Political theory, especially constitutional interpretation, and the LSCQ's blend of organic and instrumental approaches are used to develop an "organic contract" theory for the origin and justification of the state. In the realm of ethics, a social role ethic for citizens' obligations is established by blending Rawlsian and *rujia* approaches, which requires the articulation of timing in both personal and environmental relationships.

A Cross-cultural Narrative on Time

Some of the major theories concerning time are reviewed to generate a synthetic image of our role in articulating time. I want to continue Paul Ricoeur's study of time, but from the perspective of comparative philosophy.[3]

Theories of time in the West are generally classified into one of two camps: the phenomenological theory of time as an inner experience, and time as a category of nature, whether it is an objective, absolute time or a relative, context (velocity)-dependent phenomena.

Robert S. Brumbaugh notes that time was one of the major concerns of the twentieth century. He highlights the importance of time in the various sciences, literature, aesthetics, and philosophy.[4] Brumbaugh summarizes four general theories on time: (1) classical materialism; (2) the Aristotelian view of time; (3) the Platonic; and (4) the modern.[5] Despite the complexity and comprehensiveness of this classification, it clearly shows the bias mentioned above. Brumbaugh holds an objective position regarding time by ignoring the phenomenological approach. He discusses the psychological and aesthetic, and he demonstrates that psychology is an aspect of each theory. Phenomenology's nearest cousin, existentialism, is mentioned as an aspect of the modern understanding but not as a separate understanding of time. His analysis is biased by a preconceived notion of objective, external time.

The phenomenologists usually assume a bias going in the opposite direction. They place emphasis on the temporal nature of consciousness.[6] Aron Gurwitsch argues, "phenomenal temporality is a necessary condition of every act of consciousness and of whatever exists in and for consciousness . . ."[7] The phenomenologist pursues the temporal character of consciousness to its ultimate conclusions, namely, that objective time is an act of the unity of consciousness. Edmund Husserl argues this point,[8] and Gurwitsch describes it:

> *On the basis of the one, unique objective time*, in which the life-histories of all persons take place, *all the spatial surroundings of those life-histories are unified into one all-encompassing order of existence*, namely, *the one real, objective, spatio-temporal world*, the life-world of all human beings communicating with each other either directly or indirectly.[9]

The bias of the phenomenologist is that objective time is dependent on a unitary act of consciousness. Consciousness generates the structure of objective time. In Brumbaugh's four classical theories, objective time is the context of reality and the source of psychological experience. These examples of the realist and the phenomenologist perspectives represent the two mainstream interpretations of time. In light of the LSCQ's consolidated spirit, it is perplexing that the two positions are held in abeyance without recognizing some mutual dependence of the two different kinds of "times" discussed by these two perspectives.

Brumbaugh's four theories fail to acknowledge the religious perspective of time, especially timelessness, overlooking the anti-temporal and anti-historical movement of the twentieth century.[10] Douglas K. Wood argues that religious timelessness and the revolt against time are related.[11] Wood juxtaposes man's escape from time (the experience of eternal timelessness) with humans as prisoners of time, especially social-historical time. With Wood's analysis, time, both historical and natural, is something that humans must struggle against to prove themselves.

Brumbaugh's classification and Wood's analysis assume the independence of time-in-itself and the human experience of it. The dichotomy opens itself up to another possibility, that is, an alternative approach toward time that acknowledges the mutual determination between being-time, space-time, and action-time. The different theories of time can be unified. Beginning with the theory of relativity and its understanding of time as a contingency relative to a context, one can expand the model by drawing from Zen master Dōgen's notion of *uji* (the mutual dependence of having time, or having for the time being). Finally, one can blend in the LSCQ's insight that "time" is "articulated time," generated out of the interaction of particulars, especially human action.

With the theory of relativity, the modern conception of "space and time" is fundamentally reconstructed. Space and time are no longer understood in absolute terms but are relative to one's perspective, which is dependent on mass and velocity. Space and time become contingencies. However, the role of the human participant-observer in the construction of time has not been fully explored. Although Heisenberg's Uncertainty Principle notes the influence of the observer in measuring atomic particles, it is generally assumed that the relativity of space and time is due to objective (mass and velocity) conditions, or the phenomenologists might say intersubjective (phenomenological experiences, private and public) conditions. Modern physics is not willing to propose that space and time are or can be human creations. But it is close to drawing the conclusions of Zen master Dōgen that time and events are inseparable.

It is generally accepted in both the general and special theories of relativity that space-time is relative to and thus contingent upon mass and velocity. In quantum mechanics, Heisenberg's Uncertainty Principle (that the uncertainty in the measurement of the energy of a particle times the uncertainty in the time it exists can never be less than Planck's constant) establishes the relationship between energy and time.[12] General relativity proposes that clocks run slower near large masses or when subject to high accelerations.[13] The well-known thought experiment of the so-called twin paradox is often cited to express this dependence of time on velocity.[14] For example, if one twin takes a long, round-trip space journey traveling at high speeds, then upon her return she will discover that her sister is older because she was not subjected to the accelerations. This observation regarding the relationship between time and mass (or velocity) has led relativity theorists to propose that when the speed of light is approached, time reaches a stopping point, and mass becomes infinite.[15] Actually, mass and velocity are interchangeable, as in Einstein's famous formula, $E = mc^2$, mass (m) is equivalent to energy (E). Velocity is a form of energy set in motion (speed) toward some direction; velocity (V) is equal to distance (d—direction away from or toward) divided by time (t); $V = d/t$.[16] Time, or better yet space-time because mass always curves space, is dependent on mass that is equivalent to energy.

Time slows down as mass and velocity increase. Theoretically then, in physics, one can significantly alter or make "time" by adjusting mass or velocity.

Dōgen provides a historical and an intellectual bridge between antiquity and the present, although he does have a spiritual agenda. His conception of *uji* is grounded in both Buddhist and traditional Chinese thought, which accepts the pre-Qin and Han dynasty conviction that ritual action generates environmental and political conditions. Dōgen proposed that *u* (ch. *you*—"having," "the constancy of existence," often incorrectly translated as "being") is mutually determining with *ji* (ch. *shi*—"season," "time," or "timing"). For Dōgen, *uji* ("event time" or "having for the time being") is not the usual idea that events occur within time, but rather the time and the event, and the event and the time are not two separable processes within the flux of impermanence. Things do not change according to their season; rather, the season and process of transformation are co-arising.

> Passing seriatim are like spring, for instance, with all its many and varied signs. That is passing seriatim. You must learn in practice that passing takes place without anything extraneous. For example, springtime's passage invariably passes through spring. Passage is not spring, but since it is the springtime's passage, passing attains the Way now in the time of spring.[17]

The actions and their time of occurrence are not two separate measures; that is, the time of one's enlightenment is none other than the action of sitting meditation. As a Zen master, Dōgen's primary concern is enlightenment, which provides a key for unlocking his conception of *uji*. For Dōgen, practice and attainment are not different, and an event, especially oneself, and time are not different either.

> We set the self out in array and make that the whole world. You must see all the various things of the whole world as so many times. These things do not get in each other's way any more than various times get in the way of each other. Because of this there is an arising of mind at the same time, and it is the arising of time of the same mind. So it is with practice and attainment of the Way too. We set our self out in array and we see that. Such is the fundamental reason of the Way: that our self is time.[18]

Dōgen stresses how time is integral with the particular, especially the particular person, as a focus of consciousness. Things are time, and I am time. Time, from Dōgen's enlightenment experience, is not an independent container of things. Things and time are manifest together. "The *time* has to *be* in me. Inasmuch as

I am there, it cannot be that time passes away."[19] Time is dependent on active subjects. Dōgen's insight offers us a path to understanding an interactive articulation of time.

The pre-Qin concept of time, which is found in the LSCQ, accepts "time" as contingent. Time is dependent on both cosmic, especially environmental (*tian*), activity and human, especially the ruler's, ritual actions. These two forces, environmental and human, interact and mutually create each other. The mandate of heaven (*tianming*), the justification for political sovereignty, is verified by productive harvests and constructive competition among the masses. These can only be guaranteed by a ruler who controls his actions because of their impact on the environment and the livelihood of the people.

The LSCQ contains at least three different positions on "time." Some chapters have the extrinsic and mechanistic conception of time as a process of objective, natural events. The text contains a complex understanding that "time" entails nearly 2,000 years of cultural history, arguing for a theory of cultural and historical transformation. Finally, the LSCQ contains a unique perspective that "time" is something that humans, especially the ruler and ritual ministers, articulate through their performance of ritual action. The third perspective bears some similarities to the theory of relativity—both accept "time" as a contingency. Instead of mass and velocity, the third understanding of time from the LSCQ focuses on the social weight of the ruler's *position* and *performance* of ritual action. The term *position* is used to refer to the social significance, weight, or importance of a social role, office, or institution. The term *performance* means the appropriate enactment by an individual or a group of a ritual, policy, law, habit, or gesture. The relative dispositions and interactions among particular elements in harmony with each other articulate, create, and maintain time.

Humans constitute time through their *position* and *performance*. Human action is context dependent; it occurs within both environmental and social circumstances. These circumstances provide a ground or given in which actions take on significance and meaning. Ultimately, the function of the action is to bring the circumstances into harmony—a fruitful disposition. The actor and the conditions are mutually dependent and co-determining, so that human action generates the future continuity of both environmental and social circumstances. The ruler or state, which is sensitive to the transformations of history, can enact regulations and reform or abolish outdated statutes, and can be responsive to the role of human life adapting to the environment, performing actions that actually cultivate an environmental climate. The influence on seasonal factors and the ability to articulate time are proportionally correlative with the significance of the actor's position and the quality of one's performance. For many of the LSCQ's treatises, it is the ruler and the officials at court who hold the significant social and political positions and who have the ritual knowledge to properly enact the performance of ritual (legal, moral, or personal) actions that constitute both cosmic and social time.

If modern physics proposes that time is contingent upon mass and velocity, then using the LSCQ as a social and political critique, one could propose that the "truth" or "reality" of the physicists' proposal must depend on their position and performance. The "ritual" performance of experiment and statistical formula, that is, the "meaning" invested in it, and the socially significant position of the physicist constitute a critique of modern physics from a political perspective. Cosmologically speaking, the idea that time is an articulation of one's position and performance can be extended to signify that time is constituted by both the species and persons. Modern physics will not go as far as some treatises from the LSCQ are willing to go in attributing the generation of time to human activities, but as Lawrence W. Fagg points out, at least some physicists are willing to propose that, in an indirect sense, we are making time.[20] It is only in a very limited and specific sense that modern physics is willing to acknowledge our role in the creation and maintenance of articulating time. On the other hand, phenomenology does not fully acknowledge the role of the external environment. Dōgen's doctrine of "time" as "event-time" integrates both cosmic events and individual human events in the construction of "time," but he has a chiefly spiritual objective. The LSCQ goes beyond these approaches with a comprehensive understanding of the mutual interrelationship obtaining between humans, especially the ruler, and the environment in the articulation of time, joining the objective and subjective without the concern of Buddhist spirituality. Thus the LSCQ provides some distinctive insights concerning proper timing through which we can reconceive our philosophy of "time."

Reconceiving the Human Person

In our understanding of human development, time and proper timing play an important role. A temporal concept of human character underlies the LSCQ's political thought, especially where it describes people as social and political creatures pursuing both orchestration and attunement with cosmic and social forces. Collectivism emphasizes the priority of social realization over individual attainment, and individualism underscores individual realization as an end and social relations as a means to that end. What is peculiar about traditional pre-Qin philosophy, especially the *rujia* model, is that personal and political realization are seen as coextensive. One's attainment in self-cultivation sets the tone for the achievement of social harmony. For parts of the LSCQ, it is especially the ruler's self-cultivation that orchestrates social order, and the ruler's personal achievement in ritual action harmonizes the cosmos. The weight of the ruler's position is partly due to the fact that the ruler reflects and represents the concerns of the community.

An analogy is drawn in the *guisheng* chapter between cultivating one's character and the appropriate nature of the state, especially the fulfillment of life and political administration. For the LSCQ's hylozoistic philosophy, the means of promoting life permeates the world, and so personal attainment, especially the ruler's, must be assisted by social, in particular, political, institutions. The fulfillment of life occurs within the natural environment and simultaneously enhances those environs, promoting self-cultivation. The ruler as the consummate exemplar of humanity is the person who holds that pivotal position between the heavens above and the masses below. The ruler integrates with the environment and sets a model for the people to follow. The ruler must comply with the needs and feelings of the masses and create and maintain a social atmosphere of productive competition and an environmental climate conducive to agriculture. For the *rujia* constituents in the LSCQ, a person achieves personhood through the creative performance of ritual action, education, and other modes of self-cultivation. The ruler as a consummate model of humanity is not a given but an attainment, not an indivisible personal attainment but a creative act of integration that is conducive to the fulfillment of life in others.

Modern political theories hold an understanding of the person that is different from the pre-Qin. There is a strong tendency in contemporary political theory to emphasize individualism, freedom, equality, and independence. Because Immanuel Kant lays the groundwork for much of contemporary political theory, his thought is used as an example. Although Kant usually refers to rights as civil rights created under the social contract, he does allow for one innate right, namely, freedom, which is loaded with innate equality, and being irreproachable (*justi*) and being one's own master (*sui juris*), that is, independence.[21] Actually, the classic contractarians (Hooker, Hobbes, Locke, and Rousseau) give these three inalienable qualities of freedom, equality, and independence to precontractual individuals.

When Kant and others refer to an "individual," the reader reflects on such notions as rationality, autonomy, freedom, inscrutability, and so on. Borrowing from pre-Qin philosophy, when I employ the term *person*, the reader should consider such alternative images as parity, integration, human exemplar, and creative achievement by articulating proper timing.

Many conceptions of equality, especially mathematical equality, accept a static, nontemporal, and substantialistic approach. "Parity" is based on a dynamic understanding of an interactive articulation of time. For the sake of limiting the discussion, only three theories of "equality" will be interpreted. The three theories can be interrelated. In the spirit of the unifying approach of the LSCQ, an equal consideration of interests theory is reconstructed using the idea of parity.

The first theory of equality is the classic interpretation that declares equals as equal under a formal principle of identity. Those who hold this understanding usually cite Aristotle's *Nichomachean Ethics* (5.6) and *Politics* (1.2, 3.1) to establish a theory of justice requiring equal treatment of citizens under the law.[22] Even if one could establish a totally just constitution and law with a proper definition of "citizen," not excluding groups or individuals, nevertheless, the formal identity theory of equality runs the risk of not properly providing for the citizens in actual practice. Although it provides equal civil rights, it does not provide for a just distribution of other social goods. The formal identity theory of equality does not provide for, what John Rawls designates as the difference principle, the just distribution of goods. The identity theory of equality lacks a temporal understanding of human life by not accounting for change. So let us set it aside and turn to the next theory.

The "equal opportunity" theory of equality attempts to resolve the shortcomings in formal equality. Equal opportunity seeks to provide those social goods that are not properly distributed by ensuring that all groups, especially the poor, have the same opportunity to acquire social goods. Although the equal opportunity theorists recognize a basic difference between humans and attempt to provide a timely opportunity to ameliorate those differences, nevertheless, there is a serious flaw with this kind of thinking in that it subtly begs the question; it assumes that all people, including the impoverished, are equally prepared to take advantage of their "equal" opportunity. The theory of equal opportunity does not fully take into account the temporal character of humans—if given appropriate training in early childhood development, individuals might be in a better position to take advantage of and to create opportunities. But in fact everyone is not equally well-prepared to take advantage of an opportunity, so this theory too has its shortcomings.

The third, and perhaps the most defensible and morally and politically realistic theory of equality, "equal consideration of interests," acknowledges that people, having different interests, require different kinds of social goods to be treated, on balance, as legal and social equals, and to be properly prepared to take advantage of equal opportunities, again on balance. Equal consideration of interests has problems of its own. Conceptually, what counts as an "interest" is not always clear. Equally ambiguous is the means to be employed, and how much the state is supposed to cultivate and safeguard those interests. More importantly, the execution of the theory of equal consideration of interests may appear to run counter to self-interests, but this can be true only in immediate terms, because equal consideration of interests should in the long run, at least in theory, fulfill one's own self-interests. The equal consideration of interests theory then takes into account the long-term, temporal aspects of human life.

What seems to be needed is a worldview in which self-interest and other-interest are mutually determining and co-terminus. The pre-Qin organic, focus-field philosophies provide such a worldview, in which each particular exists in an existential parity with every other, and parity is a temporal concept. Particulars as different as they may be, because of their temporal interaction with each other, ameliorate and enhance those differences in a dynamic harmony. Parity is not identical sameness. It means that each particular contributes its uniqueness, but the particulars are not identical. Parity is not an equal opportunity, because some individuals will naturally take advantage of opportunities more skillfully than others, and they should be the leaders or rulers.

The concept of "parity" provides an existential perspective from which equal consideration of interests can be reconceived and defended. Existentially speaking, parity means that the importance of each unique, particular focus contributes to the field of interrelated processes in nature. The blade of grass and the mountain contribute to the environment, and the field of interrelationships changes with the alteration of either one, but their contribution is prioritized in that one will have a relatively smaller or greater effect from a certain perspective. Each contribution is significant, but each is different. Sociologically speaking, this conception of parity proposes that each citizen must be known to have equal significance and equal rights under the law. John C. H. Wu notes that there was a basic legal equality in practice under traditional Chinese law.[23] The truth here is limited to legal theory. A hierarchical social system, evidenced in traditional China, precludes legal equality. A social system based on parity recognizes that certain people, because of their social magnitude and position, require more social privileges and thereby have greater responsibility. For example, the officials of states require preferred access to the means of fulfilling life, because they presumably are in a position to deliver it to the masses who need it most.

This concept of existential parity develops a moral corollary—what I call the *existential commitment*. The "existential commitment" is a moral attitude of obligation to show concern and to provide care for the life project of others. The ontological and cosmological understanding of the interrelatedness of particulars leads one to acknowledge one's moral obligation to promote the interests of another. Within the perspective of existential parity, the value of others must be understood as having significance for oneself. This notion of existential commitment is similar to many traditional religio-philosophical positions that claim that people have a basic responsibility for others, for example, the "brother's keeper" idea. It is informed by the "respect for persons" notion developed from Kant through Ronald Dworkin in that one of our most basic forms of social responsibility is to respect others. The existential commitment is a stronger position because it is not merely a social convention, agreement, or theoretical starting point but rather a fundamental characteristic of existential parity—existing in a world of temporal interrelationships. Thus parity and an existential moral commitment provide a way for properly practicing equal consideration of interests, given the temporal character of human life. The abstract part/whole or individual/society relationship can be reconceived in terms of the mutually defining self-other or focus-field relationship.

Theoretically speaking, at least for some contemporary philosophers, logical positivists in particular, logic and its principles are supposed to be independent of ontological or existential significance. This point is clearly displayed in most Western social and political theory in sorting out the relationship between the individual and the whole of society. The one-many problem has been a distinctive feature of Western metaphysical theories, leading many philosophers to discuss the individual/society relationship in terms of the part/whole relationship: either they subsume the part under the whole (conservativism and collectivism), or others (usually liberals) violate the traditional part/whole relationship and are accused of committing the fallacy of composition—by proposing that what is good for the individual is good for society. Principles of logic bias our understanding of the individual/society relationship.

Traditional Western organic and holistic thinking led Aristotle to propose the holistic principle of a preference for the whole which is greater than the sum of its parts. Aristotle has a prejudice for self-sufficiency. He believes that such holistic, greater wholes are the self-sufficient. The idea of the greater whole means that the characteristics of the parts do not necessarily apply to the whole (guarding against the fallacy of composition), and attributes of the whole do not necessarily pertain to the parts (guarding against the fallacy of division). Aristotle said: "Further, the state is by nature prior to the family and the individual, since the whole is of necessity prior to the part."[24] Aristotle could be criticized for confusing logical priority with temporal priority. Because the whole as a logical concept must precede the part, he understands it to be a temporal order also. Thus he commits a category error of logical and existential priority (i.e., confusing logical necessity and temporal priority). Aristotle, like Plato, establishes the traditional Western organic position in which the individual is placed in service to the whole—slavery and other abuses are contained herein. Although Aristotle recognizes the need for the state to provide for the needs of the individual citizen, the priority of the whole still takes precedence. Since the whole is advanced by perfecting the quality of workmanship, he promotes perfectionism where society, for its own betterment, advances the development of superior personality types (*megalopsychia*). Aristotle may be guilty of a fallacy of division by imposing perfectionistic qualities of the whole onto the individual citizen. The fallacy of division clearly underlies the problem in Rousseau's "general will" theory, that is, when I discover that my vote dissented from that of the "general will," I realize that I did not even know my own opinion on the matter. Political liberals such as Jeremy Bentham and J. S. Mill can be criticized for committing a fallacy of composition when they claim that one's individual pleasure or good is that of the society's at large.[25] However, if we give the individual/society relationship serious reflection, the logical model of the priority of the whole does not ring true to human experience on the temporal and existential levels.

Insights from pre-Qin, especially *rujia*, social philosophy can assist in resolving these problems. From the focus-field perspective of *rujia* and *daojia* thought, the whole or field is not conceived of as prior to the part or focus; rather, the part/whole or focus-field relationship is one of integration, interdependency, interpenetration, and coextensiveness. David Hume also dabbled with these problems. For example, he cites the problem of identity over time with the example of a boat rebuilt at sea;[26] if we change every part of a boat during a long journey, in what sense is it still the same boat? For the pre-Qin organic perspective, especially Laozhuang thought, just by changing one part or focus, the whole field is changed. The concept of the "whole" is an abstraction. This is not to say that there is no "identity," but that it is defined in terms of continuity in relationships. For Laozhuang thought and the *Yijing* (*Book of Changes*), all things are interconnected to each and every other thing. The *Yijing* proposes: "All is one, and one is all."[27] For many of the pre-Qin thinkers, the "whole" would be considered an abstraction or a generalization about the overall interconnectedness and continuity of particulars. Their world is a plurality of coextensive, interrelated dependency of particular foci; it can best be described in terms of field and focus. The focus is any particular constituting the environment as field; the field is the dynamic processes of the interrelated foci.[28]

The focus-field worldview is ontologically homogenous; there is no imposed value structure in existence. This is not to say that there is no structure to existence, for there is a structure. There is a value-neutral hierarchical structure built into the world, in that the active (*yang*) principle moves first, and the passive (*yin*) responds—this hierarchical structure is especially true for Zuo Yan, the *rujia* philosophers such as Xunzi and the ritualists, and Huanglao, more so than Laozhuang, Daoists. The ontological priority of the *yang* principle positions heaven (*yang*) above earth (*yin*) and men (*yang*) above women and children (*yin*). I describe this as a value-neutral system, because it is not that things are "better" this way; for the focus-field philosophers, the existential priority of *yang* is *just* the way things are.

Society from the pre-Qin, especially the *rujia*, aesthetic perspective is a dynamic unity in the diversity of the various social roles in their harmonious interconnectedness—a dynamic union of diverse social unions. Kongzi was faced with the practical problem of adjusting social disorder that was starting to run rampant, so he was not overly concerned with abstract social theory; rather, he sought a person-to-person approach practiced and instituted through education. For *rujia* philosophers, society is defined in terms of the quality of the self-cultivated person's performance of social roles.

For example, the manner in which one behaves with one's neighbors defines the neighborhood one lives in. The criminal creates the criminal element in society: society, the interaction of roles, is criminal wherever the criminal preforms. However, this does not mean that the responsibility of the crime rests solely upon the criminal. Because roles are interdependent, other elements in society that allow for and maintain an unjust distribution of wealth are responsible for crime.

It will be difficult to accept this unique perspective of the foci-field relationship, because it is a deviant logic, but the ethnocentric presuppositions of (so-called nondeviant) logic cannot be overlooked. Here it is enough to grant that it might be possible to dissolve the traditional priority of the whole over the sum of the parts and to acknowledge from the perspective of existential parity that particular human existence precedes the species or society as a whole. If we adopt the perspective that the ancient pre-Qin *rujia* and *daojia* philosophers suggest and enhance it with a modernization of the classical *rujia* social role theory, developed below, we can unravel the Gordian knot of the individual/society problem and dissolve with it the problems of the priority of the whole and the fallacies of composition and division.

Once one accepts a worldview that does not assert the holistic priority of the whole over the sum of its parts, adopting a view of interrelated foci, that is, once one accepts an existential priority of the interdependent particular, one sidesteps the problem of perfectionism.[29] For example, the *rujia junzi* (consummate or authoritative person, often translated as "gentleman") is not a type of perfectionistic personality, because the *junzi* is in no sense a teleological product. The *junzi*, like any other social position or role, is defined in terms of her interrelationship with others; there is no pregiven model of the consummate person in *rujia* philosophy. The *rujia* consummate person is not the perfection of an ideal; rather, such a person is the completion or achievement of one's ability to create and maintain appropriate interpersonal relationships (*ren*) and appropriate behavior in undertaking affairs for the public good (*yi*). The *rujia* sage, like the *rujia dao*, way or tradition is not something fixed and preestablished; rather, it is negotiated, put into practice, and "traveled on" in one's particular interactions with others and events. These interactions never occur between bare entities of rights and liberties, or abstract individuals, but it is the interaction of persons, people fulfilling certain social and political roles, like family members, citizens, friends, and so on. These roles and interactions are always changing in a temporal context.

Generally, much of contemporary Western political theory begins with the assumption that the individual is discrete, atomic, and indivisible. The discrete individual is a rights' bearer. Such individuals are predisposed to be rational, self-interested agents endowed with freedom, equality, and independence to govern their own respective lives both personally, privately, and collectively in public as legislators. Henry Rosemont Jr. shows how the *rujia* perspective challenges the Western conception of an autonomous individuality.[30] Although most of the pre-Qin conceptions of the person are biased by a kind of feudal economy and social institutions that tend to devalue the individual's political position and civil rights, nevertheless, two points must be kept in mind: first, the notion of "parity" does not allow one to discredit the significance of the unique particular; second, many pre-Qin political thinkers are well aware that individuals *en masse* are the seat of political power. The LSCQ's *guigong* chapter is often noted for stating, "The empire is not one person's possession, but belongs to the people of the empire."[31] Thus the pre-Qin *rujia* and *daojia* perspectives need not necessarily conflict with the modern worldview.

One should try and take seriously, at least as a thought experiment, the notion that with democracy the individual becomes king. When one takes the position of the ruler, one acknowledges that self-cultivation makes significant contributions to the ambience and harmony of society. The achievement of citizenship assumes that the self-cultivating person attends to her or his existential commitment and behaves responsibly. There is always the threat that when people see themselves as discrete, equal, and independent actors that they will act solely out of self-interest in such a manner that they harm others or the environment, though without violating any legal code. In a society where people understand that one's actions as a person, enlightened or not, have sustained and broad impact, therein we might expect a wider moral base in society at large in which one could secure the integrity of the individual person within the political institutions. That is, where the majority of people are sensitive to the necessity of each particular contributing to social order, then the minority interests—even the individual person's interests—will be guarded. Fairness and due process would be bolstered in a society that orients its members toward the achievement of person making.

To the extent that contemporary political theory focuses on the "atomic individual" who is discrete, independent, and self-contained in reason and self-interests, such a conception stands in marked contrast to the pre-Qin *rujia* philosophy of the person as a social moral achievement, where "person" is defined in social and environmental terms. The general conception of the person in *rujia*, *Mojia*, and *daojia* thought is that one must practice different forms of self-cultivation to attain a degree of authoritativeness or genuineness. One's personhood is not a natural given. Rather, one must work at achieving and maintaining it through self-cultivation. This pre-Qin idea is not an "atomic individual" but one of achieving a level of person making in which the person is organically interrelated to all other particulars. To be engaged in the process of person making is to place oneself at the pivotal point of morality, both social and environmental.

The contrast is between the Western conception of the individual as "indivisible" opposed to the pre-Qin, especially the LSCQ's composite, understanding of the consummate model of person making as one who is an integrated, interconnected "administrator" of cosmic, historical, and social order. Achieved persons are in a sense extraordinary, not because they are self-contained and inscrutable, but because such people have opened up themselves to the social and environmental context in such a way that they are consciously and intentionally aware of their temporally interdependent and co-creative relationship with social and environmental conditions.

The rulers, or consummate models of person making, hold the highest and most powerful positions of authority and majesty in the state, and yet it must be clear that they do not rule by coercion alone or even in the main. Although they are persons of authority, they are not authoritarian. The rulers set the example of self-cultivation and person making, but they cannot dictate it; they are the authoritative "author" of both social and political order, but they are neither the strong arm nor the big man. The rulers provide for their people; they do not "possess" or "drive" them. It is through the ruler's achievement of self-cultivation that such a ruler is able to attract the knights of the way (*youdao zhi shi*) who will administer law and order for the people. The sage ruler is supposed to provide the authoritative model for the empire to emulate on the social level, and the ruler generates the social and physical atmosphere in such a manner that the masses may benefit from the bounty of the earth. David L. Hall and Roger T. Ames describe the "authority" of authoring oneself and correlatively one's context.[32]

Where the modern Western theories focus on the independent, inscrutable individual as rights bearer, the model extracted from the LSCQ focuses on developing an authoritative exemplar—a sage ruler. The sage rulers are able to maintain awareness of their pivotal position in co-creating self, others, and the world. Thus it is not a question of the ruler's inscrutability. In fact, the rulers are the most scrutable persons, because their actions have far-reaching, long-lasting social and cosmic effects. This type of sage ruler is not independent and inscrutable; he is totally interdependent and must be open to scrutinization and remonstrance from the ministers and masses. Because these rulers are the authors of social, legal, and political order and hold the crucial position of responsibility being open to scrutinization, they stand as an authoritative, historical-moral exemplar for the tradition. Because the rulers can be scrutinized, they leave their mark through historical transformations, either as a positive exemplar, a sage ruler, or as a negative one, a tyrant.

Again we need to contemporize the discussion by allowing that now every citizen holds a pivotal position that influences social, cultural, and environmental conditions. A person's political rights need to be safeguarded by such notions as independence and inscrutability, but on the social-moral level, the citizen as person must take responsibility for her or his own achievement of person making by maintaining awareness and the proper intentionality of both one's interdependency and one's responsibility for environmental, and especially social, conditions.

Western philosophers and theologians, generally speaking, have devoted much attention to the question of human freedom. Within the Judeo-Christian tradition, since Augustine at least, the concept of free will has played a central role. Many moral philosophers have assumed that people are predisposed to behave freely, at least when they act morally. Kant argues that freedom is our one and only given, innate right that grounds all moral and political actions.

It is significant that in the LSCQ the concept of "freedom" is not explicitly discussed. We can explicate the LSCQ's implicit position on freedom. For pre-Qin philosophy and the LSCQ, a person's "freedom" is directly correlated with one's ability to act spontaneously and creatively. One attains freedom *from* a naive, unreflective understanding of how one's social and environmental context conditions one's life *to* achieve a sustained awareness and an intentional understanding that one's context is just as dependent on one's own life as one is dependent on the environment. One achieves this freedom through the recognition that one's spontaneous and creative actions generate a moral atmosphere. The ruler, as one engaged in person making, achieves the deeper realization of freedom through a more highly developed expression of self-cultivation and refinement in ritual action. The free person is one who can cultivate the sense organs, biological drives, and desires to fulfill life in a spontaneous and creative fashion. Freedom is not an innate or a biological propensity; it is a human achievement that is gained through the quality of one's actions.

There has been a tendency in Western thought, following the notions of independence and individualism, to further assume that the core of human life is a simple, immortal soul, that the essence of human life is an unchanging spiritual substance that partakes of the eternal and the good or heaven. The pre-Qin *rujia* perspective is much more in keeping with contemporary social psychology, understanding the person not as a biological or an ontological given but as a social-cultural achievement. In this respect, the person, after death, does not live on in another world of unchanging forms or heavenly grace, but rather if we must speak of "living on after this life," then it is fulfilled indirectly through one's impact on the cultural tradition. The pre-Qin *rujia* and *daojia* conceptions of the person are not that of an ontological given. The person is seen as complex, constantly changing, and integrated with the social conditions so that he or she is mutually determining those conditions. As the *shiwei* (Appropriately Displaying Majesty) chapter proposes, the *shen* (spirit) who "survives" death is *not* an independent entity but is one's creative power to transform ancient ways and establish new social and cultural trends: "This is why the five emperors and the three kings were unopposed. They themselves had already died, but the later generations were transformed by them spiritually. This is because they carefully examined their people and the affairs of state."[33] One's "spirit" is not a disembodied substance but rather one's creative ability to transform human life by contributing to community and culture. Y. P. Mei notes that the pre-Qin concerns of immortality were not for personal but rather social immortality; he cites the *Zuozhuan* commentary, which relates that the meaning of "to suffer no decay" is to leave an example of virtue, service, and honesty for the future.[34] In this sense, the achievement of person making can extend beyond the grave, not as a transcendent soul but as an ongoing cultural process.

Pre-Qin philosophy offers a very different conception of what it means to be human. The dynamic flesh-and-blood perspective of pre-Qin philosophy contrasts markedly with the Western tradition of the abstract, autonomous individual. My intention is not merely to draw distinctions but to suggest a new understanding of what it means to be human. A newly conceived comprehension of human life is a prerequisite for reinterpreting the social and political order.

Constitutional Interpretation and Developing an Organic Contract Theory

Can the LSCQ's call for timely reform of regulations (*bianfa*) be applied in constitutional interpretation? Can we apply the LSCQ's amalgamated approach in blending the strong points of organic and instrumental political theories to be used to develop the theoretical construct of an "organic contract"? In both cases, the importance of time, especially cultural history, plays an important role. Constitutional interpretation and legal reform occur within the dynamics of history. Interpretation and reform constitute historical transformation. The "organic contract theory" is grounded in a historical understanding of culture, where human social life, though organic and natural, develops new contractual relationships to meet the needs of the ever-changing social and economic conditions.

The following oversimplification is commonly accepted, especially in the media, namely, that there are two major approaches to constitutional interpretation: the conservative approach, which attempts to interpret the constitution as it was intended by the original authors; and the liberal approach, which seeks to interpret the constitution to meet the needs of the present. The original authors did not believe that one eternally fixed document was the final solution in framing a new government. They allowed for the modification of the U.S. Constitution through the amendment process.

Since the crux of the issue is at rock bottom, whether or not the regulations and statutes of a state can be modified or transformed, it is clear that the constitutional tradition in America, embodied in both the original document and 200 years of practice, is in agreement with the LSCQ's commitment to reform regulations. The *chajin* chapter supports the open-ended modification of the statutes. Not only is our position and relationship with the environment ever changing, but those laws that govern political, social, and interpersonal relations must be flexible enough to meet the demands of the ongoing process of human interactions in cultural history. The crucial questions are: To what extent may one transform the regulations, statutes, or constitution? What standards are to be applied? Are we guaranteed achievement of our social ideals?

And most importantly, can we expect the basic principles of the constitution to work indefinitely, or will we have to prepare ourselves to reconstitute political order at regular intervals? Ronald Dworkin provides a contemporary and comprehensive perspective on this topic, so dialogue between the LSCQ and Dworkin seems appropriate.

In *Law's Empire*, Dworkin argues that the dominion of law is framed within the boundaries of an interpretative temporal and historical process. His analysis is not a thought experiment nor an imaginary empire; he "takes up the internal, participants' point of view . . . the judge's viewpoint . . ."[35] He seeks to ground his theory of law in the historical tradition of the U.S. Constitution. An important part of the dynamics of transformation and change over time is rooted in the process of interpretation. For Dworkin, the interpretative process is one that exercises what he calls "creative" or "constructive" interpretation.[36] Dworkin argues that the creative act of interpretation seeks to discover the "intention of the artist," but this intention is not some "conscious mental state" that caused the original work. The artist's intention is a complex matter of "purpose," and that "purpose" or "intent" can and will be transformed by further interpretation. Dworkin appeals to an example where a film critic has an imaginary discussion with Fellini about the similarity of a legend to one of his films; Fellini agrees that although he did not know about the legend, it does capture his intention, and "he *now* accepts it as part of the film he made."[37] Dworkin argues that constructive interpretation adds something that is only coincidentally new but in fact maintains the original intention.[38] Dworkin recognizes that history is the arbitrator of one's interpretation.[39] The power and beauty of Dworkin's theory is that it is a realistic one, seeking to explain the nature of ordinary, especially U.S. constitutional, politics. Thus for Dworkin, the object of political philosophy is not merely to describe an ideal, utopian social order, but rather it must, like the processes of politics, participate in historical interpretation and seek to provide the "best fit" in explaining and interpreting the tradition.[40] Dworkin advocates an evolutionary, almost a teleological, interpretation of political society. He argues that the principle of treating like cases alike does not meet the demands of political morality, and he argues for a "virtue of political integrity."[41] Integrity, for Dworkin, is a political ideal of operating with coherent principles of justice and fairness as they really are.[42] Because Dworkin is providing a rational justification for ordinary political processes, he is keen to acknowledge the historical evolutionary character of these processes. But he does not go far enough. He limits rational, principled behavior to maintaining the status quo of political order without the consideration that it might be overthrown or degenerate and need replacement. Dworkin assumes continued evolution without catastrophe, or at least a total alteration of the system, is beyond his project of explaining and justifying the interpretative process of law.

Integrity, for Dworkin, is a twofold principle, "a legislative principle, which asks lawmakers to try to make the total set of laws morally coherent, and an adjudicative principle, which instructs that the law be seen as coherent in that way, so far as possible."[43] Integrity must be seen as an independent ideal, because it will conflict with other ideals.[44] Dworkin attempts to ground our political and community obligations in commonly accepted moral obligations. His model community lives by principles; he needs the principles to set the model for the "best kind" of legislative and adjudicative legal system. Although Dworkin rejects the idealistic approach and seeks to work out the justification of ordinary politics, nevertheless, he is in keeping with mainstream Western political theory, which defends the independence of moral principles. Philip Soper points out an inconsistency in Dworkin's position; Dworkin asserts that there is no loss of coherence when we act on policy rather than principle, but then he claims that pragmatism must abandon the ideal of integrity.[45] The problem is that Dworkin emphasizes principle at the cost of policy, and this is the basic disagreement between Kantians and Utilitarians.

Dworkin's theory, then, begins to recede from explaining the interpretative process of ordinary politics in favor of establishing absolute principles, thus his position is an idealistic or utopian one of describing a perfect system rather than explaining the ordinary processes. A number of illuminating insights emerge from a comparison of Dworkin's position and the LSCQ's.

When Dworkin applies this interpretational theory of law to study the constitution, he points out that the traditional division of camps into liberal and conservative is both uninformative and incorrect. He sees the academic distinction between "interpretivist and noninterpretivist" camps as equally misguided, ignoring the fact that the law is an interpretative process.[46] Dworkin exercises his idea of law as interpretation to argue against historicist interpretivism and passivism, setting the stage for his Herculean judge.[47] He admires the U.S. Constitution as the most basic fundamental element of the legal system, and as such, it must be interpreted in a fundamental manner. But when Dworkin wants it to both "fit and justify the most basic arrangements of political power," he assumes that those arrangements of power could meet the conditions of justification. Although he is presenting a description of actual practice, nevertheless, he does not allow for the possibility of the U.S. Constitution itself needing reform or revision; Dworkin assumes that the revolutionary spirit exclusively underlies its formation. Once formed, it can only be interpreted in a historical evolutionary fashion, but never overthrown.

The LSCQ, in general, and the *chajin* chapter, in particular, differ from Dworkin in two fundamental ways. First, the LSCQ material is pro-policy, concerned with meeting functional needs. Second, the LSCQ's authors assume that at some point the political integrity will break down and have to be entirely reconstructed. In this regard, Dworkin is limited to the scope of his project, which is to show that the actual judicial system is one that seeks coherence and integrity in the law; he is not concerned with revolution and establishing a new social practice. Maybe Dworkin does not have to address the concern of revolution until the constitutional form of government is deemed unnecessary or detrimental to social integrity itself, but this is part of his problem, because he will inevitably side with principle rather than justice or policy and obstruct any revolution that overrides his idea of the virtue of integrity. Hercules will always defend those provisions in the constitution, which include the protection of democracy.[48]

One important lesson from Dworkin's position is that we must not only think of the citizen as king or legislator, but we should consider the legislative process as the main determinant in structuring social order over history. Dworkin's latent Kantian spirit leads him to make commitments to principles of equality and fairness which can be further strengthened by the *rujia* and *daojia* conceptions of parity. His notion of strengthening political obligations by relying on obligations toward others appears to anticipate an existential commitment.

Dworkin's constructivist approach to constitutional interpretations bears some resemblance to the constructivism in the modern Chinese constitutional tradition. The Chinese constitutions provide a more radical approach. In part this is due to the fact that since 1911, the Chinese have had eleven constitutions and constitutional drafts.[49] These provide an experiential base for their constructivist approach. Traditional cultural values have bolstered their constructivism. Throughout this book, we have seen the developmental achievement orientation in *rujia* and *daojia* social and political thought—individually and socially, one is what one makes of oneself. This kind of constructivist thinking emerges in the modern Chinese constitutions, most notably in regard to human rights. Andrew J. Nathan notes six points of commonality among these diverse constitutions: (1) rights are not derived from human dignity but political membership; (2) rights change over time; (3) rights are programmatic; (4) the government has the power to limit rights; (5) there is no check on the government's power; (6) the constitutions do not provide for an effective exercise of popular sovereignty.[50] In the Chinese constitutional tradition, rights themselves are constructed and constituted within the political context.

The Chinese and American traditions could learn from each other. Surely the Chinese constitution needs a system of checks and balances. The people require a means to exercise rights of popular sovereignty. The Chinese constitutional tradition in a sense inherited some of the more negative, exploitative, and tyrannical elements of the tradition. According to the LSCQ treatises, ideally the ruler reflects the needs of the masses, but in actual practice, the Chinese emperor or local branches of government acted upon narrow *fajia* principles of power tyranny. The American constitutional tradition could be enriched by acknowledging that at least some rights, especially welfare rights, change over time.

Traditionally, the organic and instrumentalist political theories have been seen as different in kind. The instrumentalist position does not accept that mankind is socially and politically oriented by nature, but rather it holds that civil society is formed under a social contract. Society and politics are seen as devices or instruments of a people. The organic and instrumentalist political theories can be synthesized. An "organic contract theory " explicates a social role ethic for citizens.

The problem is that for the past 400 years, most Western political theories have been based on a social contract theory that ignores the natural, organic basis of political society. This is a peculiar point in contract theory, because the contractarian is well aware that no actual society was ever solely formed by a contract. Even the most likely candidate, the United States, was not forged out of a precontractual state of nature or some version of a hypothetical, prehistoric or ahistoric "original" position. It too had its contingent cultural tradition, environmental factors, and predispositions conditioning its Constitution. There were the early colonial charters, establishing a tripartite division of powers. Although contemporary contractarians, like Rawls, have attempted to sidestep the "historical applicability" problem by positing a hypothetical "original position" prior to the contract, other problems concerning political obligation and morality arise because of the faulty starting point of the instrumentalists.[51] Usually a theory's hypothesis concerning the origin, in this case, political society, predisposes the theoretical limits on the character of that topic. That is, any theoretical stance, such as a divine creation, natural development, or social contract theories, concerning the origin of society places certain limitations on the character, nature, and justifications of political society and on political obligation and social ethics.

For example, for the divine creation position, because the physical world and society along with it are created by God, society should serve, worship, and obey the will of God. For the instrumental theory, since society is founded on the social contract, it should serve the needs of the contractors. For the traditional Western organic political theory, because individuals develop in society, they should serve the whole. Even if the implications concerning the hypothesis of the origin do not apply in other theoretical frameworks, it applies in social and political theory. The nature of society is predetermined to some extent by the theoretician's hypothesis on the origin of society.

An "organic contract theory" grounds social political theory in a comprehensive, social-scientific hypothesis, taking into account the historical and archaeological evidence that shows that our species and ancestors have been living in social groups for the past 6 million or more years. An "organic contract theory" takes into account the spectrum of archaeological, historical, and social science evidence concerning human life, especially our social-political arrangements. An "organic contract theory" is based on both the natural, organic origins of political society and the historical role that reason plays in creating and adjusting the constitutional apparatus of that society. These two points are united in acknowledging the organic, natural basis of reason in culture. The "organic contract theory" generates a social role theory for moral obligation, an ethic for citizens.

Traditionally, conservative Western organic theories, especially fascism, de-emphasize the role of reason in ordering society and overemphasize the value of society at the expense of the person, while social contract theories de-emphasize the role of culture and stress reason's role in constructing society. Generally speaking, classical conservativism and Western organic theories have the individual serve the good of the whole society or state. Classical liberals and instrumentalists have the whole society benefit the interests of the individual. An "organic contract" position recognizes strong and weak points on both sides, and it undertakes a synthesis by uniting the strong points and dissolving the weak ones.

An "organic contract theory" acknowledges the natural biological and environmental factors that make humans gregarious creatures. It holds that these biological and environmental factors, coupled with the gregarious nature of humans, lead to the *natural* development of culture, that is, the material and immaterial repository of understanding and relating to the world and others in a social and political manner, which is intimately part and parcel of language, both natural and artificial, and various combinations of culture and language generate art, religion, philosophy, and science.

Confining the discussion to the social-political dimensions, in the natural extended family loosely practicing exogamy, the small group or band becomes the first social and political arrangement, and in a sense the small group is always the fundamental arrangement in any society, regardless of its overall size—all large societies are composed of relatively smaller social units or groups. The extended family system or band creates and maintains the context into which the individual is raised. The individual redefines the group by participating in the social network. As the band grows in complexity and diversity through history, these participating persons find it necessary to think of themselves, their culture, and their world in new and different ways. It becomes necessary, because of chiefly environmental, economic, and social conditions, and the fact that social biology cannot be ruled out entirely, for people to restructure or create new social structures, arrangements, roles, institutions, and professions. For an "organic contract" position, social contracts are a natural development in restructuring or creating new forms of social interaction. The social contract grows organically as a natural human activity of reformulating and reinterpreting culture as a response to environmental, economic, social, and other factors.

For example, the development of social contract theory in the West can be seen as a reaction to social changes brought on by economic and scientific revolutions, and ideological and religious reformations, and in turn the contract position, as constitutionalism, creates the modern social order. Like Nietzsche, one could easily oversimplify the whole of contract theory as a political application of the merchant's business contracts, allowing for the trade boom of Renaissance Europe. At that time, there was a concern to eradicate deep-rooted religious or otherwise biased ideology from politics, especially state persecution of religion, and the contract theory guaranteed that.

An "organic contract theory" then overcomes the oversight of "reason" in many traditional Western organic theories, and it clarifies the ambiguous role of "nature and culture" in the contract theories. For the "organic contract theory," human life is basically natural, but mankind has a strong tendency to manipulate the natural environment and our own natural capacities through culture. In a sense, culture itself is the "organic contract," for to some extent culture is biologically and environmentally influenced, but to a large degree it is contrived by human activity and reasoning. Despite the growing body of evidence provided by the students of Jane Goodall, as far as we can tell, only humans have fully developed cultures, but human cultures are unique and various. One must be born human to fully participate in a culture, but simply being human does not guarantee one admittance to human culture and recognition as a person with civil rights.[52] One's role as a person is achieved through participating in culture, and yet culture is not fixed and unchanging—by participating in culture, one alters and changes it. The "organic contract theory" attempts to account for all of mankind's natural, cultural, and rational capacities that play a role in creating new social arrangements. For the "organic contract," humans qua humans have always lived in some social and political arrangement, and historically, those arrangements have been renegotiated in different organic and instrumentalist formats.

Given the basic shortcomings of traditional Western organic and social contract theory in accounting for the origin and nature of civil society, arguing for a synthesis of the two positions provides a comprehensive and precise hypothesis. An "organic contract theory" has advantages. It dispels some traditional problems, particularly the role of reason and culture, in social and political theory. The "organic contract theory" has ramifications for social role ethics. The "organic contract" grounds the moral responsibility of our roles in the necessary interdependency and interrelatedness of human life—our gregarious nature.

Ethics

The hylozoistic foci-field perspective of the pre-Qin *rujia* and *daojia* philosophies can inspire a reconceptualization of ethics. To the extent that humans "articulate time," they are responsible for the quality of that time and the other constitutive results of their action. Some LSCQ passages on timing describe the articulation of time that is generated out of one's social position and one's performance in action, usually highly significant social and political and ritual action. From the unified organic contract perspective, one can ground a theory of moral and political obligation in social roles.

The ethos or lifestyle characteristics of the citizen who is intentionally aware of the existential commitment, the political obligations grounded in the "organic contract," and who thus performs in social roles in such a way so as to enhance self-and-other-cultivation in a timely fashion, need elaboration. The "organic contract" perspective installs the role of citizen as our most basic social role. This confirms the need for a social role ethic for citizens. Our most basic natural and contractual role is that of group member. Speaking politically, that role is held by the citizen. As such, the quality of our performance in the role of citizen affects both the social articulation of time as cultural history, and will have, in fact, has had, environmental influences. The role of timing needs to be examined on both the personal and environmental levels.

A social role ethic for citizens can be developed by blending elements of pre-Qin and modern philosophy. For simplicity's sake, I focus on John Rawls and Kongzi. Following the unifying approach of the LSCQ, some of the best, but different, positions are united. A fuller elaboration of a social role theory should consider the contributions of symbolic interactionism, the school expanding G. H. Mead's social psychology, and emergent interactionism, the school expanding L. S. Vygotsky's social psychology.[53] In this regard, one might propose that a comparison between pre-Qin *rujia* thought and Alasdair MacIntyre may prove more fruitful, because they share a diachronic conception of virtue and social roles. However, MacIntyre will not suit my purposes, because he is in a sense too much an organic thinker, like Kongzi.[54] That is, I have chosen Rawls because he clearly holds a social contract position and a theoretical approach in contrast to the emergent foci-field order and aesthetic practical concerns of Kongzi. Their differences promise to make a engaging blend. Rawls has a developmental and diachronic understanding of the moral virtues of both the individual and society. It is this concern for proper timing that provides an important link between Rawls and Kongzi, opening the way for a social role ethic in harmony with an "organic contract."

Although Rawls is noted for his theoretical-atemporal approach, nevertheless, there is a practical side to his theory that draws one's attention to the significance of timing. On the practical side, the self-esteem one achieves by fulfilling one's temporal life plan is good, for Rawls, establishing one's sense of fairness and justice. Rawls does not fill in the details of such a life plan, but he does note the importance of fulfilling one's life plan in a timely fashion at the appropriate time.[55] Rawls acknowledges the historical and diachronic nature of social structures. He argues that humans can control the changes that social institutions undergo; at least to some extent one can shape one's social arrangements.[56] Rawls' theory has a practical element acknowledging the temporal and developmental context of human life.

The viewpoint of existential parity, the mutual interrelatedness and integrity of particulars, is grounded, for *rujia* thinkers, in the social institution of the family as the natural expression of human codependency. The natural basis of social roles is fundamental to both the "organic contract" and the moral justification of the existential commitment, the obligation to care for others. Rawls proposes a social contract theory, and in Kantian fashion, he is concerned to reconcile the *reasonableness* of free agents entering into the contract with the historicity of mankind. Kongzi, on the other hand, is not only a representative of a pre-Qin version of the organic foci-field theme, but he also develops the social role theme that the LSCQ borrows. The *rujia* and *daojia* organic approaches are not biased toward monotheistic or absolutistic tendencies. The foci-field relations can be employed in dissolving some fundamental problems in Western social theory. Kongzi's organic position indicates the need for a pluralistic society as a prerequisite for harmony (*he*). Furthermore, both Rawls and Kongzi hold a "social position" or social role theory to justify both moral and political obligations. Their respective understandings of the importance of social roles open the way for my social role ethic, harmonizing with the "organic contract theory."

Rawls' theory of social positions is implied in the original position where the rational agents are hypothetically ignorant of individual preferences, but they have some idea of the "relevant social positions" needed to build a just union of social unions—a well-ordered society. Though Rawls rarely uses the expression "social role," his expression "social position" is its equivalent.[57] Rawls implies that a social role theory is at work when he uses expressions such as the "relevant social positions" and working from the cases of "representative individuals or citizens." Basically his theory of justice secures individual liberties and attempts to ground the disparity of social positions in a just pluralistic union of social unions.

Because Rawls is approaching his theory of justice from a Kantian, contractual perspective, he naturally opposes the Utilitarian emphasis on personal individual preferences. He implies that a "person" is an individual in a social position. An "individual," following Bradley, is a bare abstraction.[58] For Rawls, we must work out the structure of just social institutions before determining a person's or a social position's obligations and duties. Rawls holds that this priority of institutions and positions before persons "shows the social nature of the virtue of justice..."[59] However, he has only gone part of the way toward the ultimate conclusion; his point exposes the social nature of human life defined in terms of the interaction of social positions. For Rawls, the living individual is a "person" holding a certain position in society, and the most general position is the representative citizen. Society is not a number of separate and distinct indivisible individuals; rather, a society is a union of social positions filled by persons or role players, individuals standing in relation to and with others. Operating under the veil of ignorance, Rawls narrows the moral agent down to a purely rational, nonemotional, self-disinterested judge. Even in the original position Rawls wants the disinterested parties to have long-term, multigeneration obligations. He describes them as "representatives or heads of families."[60] In the operating well-ordered society, the person is a performer in a certain position. As such, a person as a performer in a position is defined by the social context. The position of citizen is the most general role to be played, and it is defined in terms of other positions and institutions of the just society. Thus the role of the citizen provides the basis for establishing a social ethic for that position.

For Rawls, a social position is important, because it both simplifies the discussion and emphasizes the significance of the social and institutional nature of justice. It simplifies the discussion in that it only requires persuading one rational agent—hence, his book has the style of being written to one person—the reader is the rational agent. This is exactly the high level of abstraction that the social contractarians prefer to operate under, because at this level the moral judgment is stripped of personal biases and preferences. The agent is totally rational and morally self-disinterested. Since Rawls' project is to define a theory of justice, he focuses on an institution or a social position theory to establish a system, at least in theory, that will operate under the bare minimum of requirements. Certainly no special personality types will be required; Rawls argues against the "perfectionism" of traditional, conservative, Western organic theories.[61] The *rujia* and *daojia* concept of the mutually defining relationship obtaining between person and community, focus and field, precludes such perfectionism. The structure of society and the relevant social positions are, for Rawls, defined rather generally so that they will accommodate a wide variety of opinions and lifestyles. Rawls does not intend to limit the social positions to any particular form of life. The positions only have to meet the two principles of justice. He defines the positions as parts of the social institutions, and his definition of a social institution is general enough to subsume any traditional cultural practices, for instance, games, rituals, trials and parliaments, and economic systems and markets, as long as they are just.[62] By defining society as a union of social unions and by focusing on the general, relevant social positions and not on individual desires, Rawls emphasizes the contractarian advantages to a social position theory.

Rawls has not entirely overlooked the natural, organic basis of social roles. Although he focuses on the acquired positions, he acknowledges the importance of the naturally ascribed social roles. He delineates the diachronic process of moral learning to consist of two stages: first, the morality of authority, which is based on family ties; second, the morality of association, which is based on social relationships. Rawls accepts an ongoing developmental understanding. The family and social forms may not be the most preferable. They change over time. At one point Rawls even criticizes the family for allowing inequalities.[63] He describes a model of early childhood development and learning, grounding moral sensibility in the love and affection of family life.[64] At the second stage of moral education, the individual comes to regard the family as just one small association among other social and institutional forms of life.[65] He describes how the individual matures into an understanding of morality. The virtues of a good son or daughter develop into the virtues of a good student or classmate. "This type of moral view extends to the ideals adopted in later life, and so to one's various adult statuses and occupations, one's family position, and even to one's place as a member of society."[66] Rawls is well aware of the developmental nature of morality.[67] The sequence of positions, or stages of life, expands our historical horizons for acting morally toward others.

Being naturally predisposed to live and rear our children in groups, there are some social positions or roles that are not earned nor entered into contractually and rationally. Some roles are defined at birth, and some of these are ascribed birth-given roles; for instance, gender and family lineage, and other biological or environmental factors believed to be socially relevant, such as talents and capabilities, play an important part in one's future acquisition of roles. The organic perspective of the *rujia* philosophers cultivates a social and political theory in the parent/child relationship which, through a proper upbringing, develops the moral exemplar, authoritative person, leader, or ruler. Rawls notes the need for "moral exemplars."[68]

Kongzi's (551–479 B.C.E.) understanding of social roles was developed by Mengzi (371–289? B.C.E.) in the form of what is called the *wulun*, the five relationships. To make Kongzi meaningful to our present situation, the temporal nature of roles cannot be overlooked, and language needs to be contemporized, giving these pre-Qin thinkers some philosophical charity for not overcoming their own ethnocentrism and gender biases. For Kongzi and Mengzi, "culture" means the high composite culture of the Zhou dynasty. Tribal people may have "a way of life," but they did not have *wen* (the arts and letters of cultural refinement). They both assume that society can only take an exogamous patriarchal form. That is, writing in a chauvinistic language—written and read by men—Kongzi and Mengzi ground society in the *father/son* relationship. In fact, classical Chinese does not have generic terms such as "parent" and "child."[69] Kongzi and Mengzi may have focused on the father/son relationship because of ethnocentrism and because of the patriarchal practice of bequeathing inheritance to the eldest son. So the philosophers concentrated on the social-economic father/son relationship, rather than on the maternal. The popular tradition supplements this chauvinism with numerous stories, starting with the biography of Mengzi, in fact, concerning the importance of the mother/son relationship. The lack of information concerning Kongzi's mother, who apparently raised him for the most part, possibly as a widow, and Kongzi's own wife, should be taken as an indication of their appropriate position—they influenced their son or husband but did not make a *name* for themselves. To contemporize the *rujia* philosophy for modern discussion, the wording needs to be "desexized."

For example, where the *rujia* writers use the masculine gender, we can use a neutral expression. If their organic model holds, then this simple, charitable rephrasing should allow us to escape their ethnocentric, patriarchal system and generate a neutral position with application to patrilineal, matrilineal, and communal child/adult relationships. The social role must be left open for redefinition because of its temporal-contextual nature. Kongzi primarily discusses the father/son and ruler/minister, or more generally the ruler/subject, relationships. He mentions the elder-brother/younger-brother, and other rank-and-age relationships, like superior/inferior, teacher/disciple, and elder/younger in general. The text named after Mengzi depicts a systematic presentation of human relationships, or *renlun*. The *Mengzi* attributes the founding of the division of social relationships to the legendary minister of education, Xian, "who was to teach the people human relationships: loving respect between father and son; just appropriation between ruler and minister; the distinction between husband and wife; precedence of the old over the young; and credibility between friends."[70] We can contemporize the language by redefining the relationships as parent/child, spouses, siblings, and role model authority figures/uninitiated strangers and friends. In politics, the ruler/subject becomes legislator/citizen in a republic and citizen/citizen in a true democracy. The parent/child relationship is conducted around mutual, loving respect. The spouses seek open communication and consensus. Siblings should hold a concern for guiding each other, regardless of age. The role model authority figures set the example and educate the uninitiated again, based on ability and merit rather than age. Likewise, among friends and strangers, there would be a strong commitment to promote self-interest by promoting other interests. The lawmakers must have the interests of the citizens at heart.

The important thing for the *rujia* philosophers is that the state and its institutions are a natural extension of the family. L. Shih-lien Hsü and others point out that the *rujia* organic theory, concerning the state, views political obligation as a natural development and extension of the family.[71] The physical environment, the animal kingdom, and gender distinctions underlie the family as a social unit with defined roles; the family is the basis of human social and political life; the father/son relationship establishes both a chain of command and a patriarchal justification for inherited aristocracy and so grounds the traditional feudal political order. The natural social roles of the family operating with filial piety at home will produce the loyal, dedicated subject and minister. Acknowledging the temporal character of roles, we need to establish the biotic root of the state in the natural obligations of the child and young adult to their life providers, usually the "family," but it could be a "commune" or some other social organization, and because of the organic debt to life, that is, the existential commitment, human life must be revisioned in such a way so as to obligate one not simply to a patriarchal aristocracy but to any just social arrangement. In fact, Rawls recognizes the full effect that citizens have on each other in a well-ordered society, where they seek to benefit the interests of other individuals and the wider bonds of institutional forms.[72] The interrelatedness and ubiquitous impact of one's actions, which Rawls acknowledges, blends nicely with the notion of parity. The latter, more general, obligation cannot be established without introducing a contract theory into *rujia* philosophy, and this is where the "organic contract" supplements the traditional *rujia* social order. The *rujia* organic perspective directs our natural obligation to the social institution that provides life, that is, usually the family and, by extension, the state. This requires some immediate explication.

For the hylozoistic worldview of *rujia* philosophy, there is no clear distinction between organic and inorganic matter—this is a living world. The animated world is hierarchically ordered, but everything is interrelated and interconnected so that there are no independent, unrelated aspects in the world—every single thing or focus is defined in terms of every other thing. For *rujia* philosophers, the person and the community and the focus and field are correlative and complementary. The person and community are not, as Aristotle and almost every thinker who reads him holds, to be conceived of as cumulative. The whole is *not*, for the pre-Qin *rujia* and *daojia* philosophers, greater than the sum of its parts. Thus the hierarchical order of *rujia* philosophy does not imply a super-value or extra significance to the higher superiors or ruler in which the lower subjects do not share. Here it is important to note that the hierarchical cosmic structure develops a similarly structured family and public political order—male over female, husband/wife, ruler/subject. Moreover, the social and political order founded on the family is made up of social roles, that is, as we saw above, there is no independent abstraction of an individual, but there are actual persons performing roles.

Blending Rawls and Kongzi, then, one can define society as a union in diversity of pluralistic institutional positions and social roles temporally interdependent and correlative so that each is defined in terms of every other position or role. It is understood that some roles are given as a birthright. In a Rawlsian just society, birthrights entail the equal distribution of civil liberties governed by the first principle of justice. While other social roles are freely and contractually acquired, these fall under Rawls' difference principle, that is, the unequal distribution of social goods to the advantage of the least well off. By nature, people find themselves in temporal social and political relationships, and they creatively redefine those relationships both individually and collectively in a number of ways, the contract being one of the most just and historically effective, at least to date. The strength and beauty of an "organic contract theory" is that it grounds political obligation in our indivisible, gregarious nature, and it justifies a theory of citizenship obligations under the rubric of a social role ethic. The social position of citizen must be interpreted as a kind of political role which is at first ascribed to the infant as political family member and then grows with the individual through the articulation of time in the process of achieving personhood and acquiring roles of social responsibility. The position of citizen requires proper political training and preparation to both become aware of the significance of one's own person in the field network of social life and the environmental web of life at large. The training of the citizen awakens one's own personal integrity as a contributing and significant particular. When the citizen acknowledges his or her mutually defining relationship with others, the existential commitment, the moral obligation of concern and care for the integrity of others, provides an adequate ground for political and moral obligations.

For the "organic contract," one is obligated to the political arrangement one lives under, not because of coercion, choice, or religious or moral commitment but because ultimately that political arrangement is none other than one's own life. This is not to say that one must blindly accept the dictates of tyrants or dictators, nor that one cannot dissent from the majority or the authority. For simplicity's sake, let us assume that we are confining our discussion to people born into an ideal or at least (mostly) a just society. Under these conditions, the very natural obligations one owes to oneself—the fulfillment of basic needs and desires—one also owes to all other interdependent social roles. Because society is a unique network or field of interrelationships of each particular person's fulfillment of roles, one must regulate oneself to maintain social order.[73] In a disordered political community, this self-cultivation is even more important, for the cultivated person would be a rare exemplar of harmony. To defend oneself is to defend others, and vice versa; to feed others is to feed oneself, and vice versa. The hylozoistic focus-field basis borrowed from the *rujia* philosophers obligates citizens to assist in manifesting just social arrangements and positions that promote the continuation of socially healthy human life. Thus, any social system that does not advance the benefit of a complete range of diverse lifestyles, but clearly advocates promoting one position at an unjust disadvantage for another position would have to be rejected by the Rawlsian-*rujia* role player. Assuming that we are working within the framework of a just society, then, one's obligations are rooted in one's existential commitment to fulfill one's life plan in the full recognition that this cannot be accomplished without acknowledging and acting upon one's interdependency with other social role players. Since we are interpersonally defined, we are politically obligated to one another in the same way we are obligated to ourselves. At this level, "obligation" may not be a strong enough term to capture the depth of commitment one owes others for one's life and existence. A shortcoming here is that everyone will not intuitively experience this interdependency and act accordingly, and so education plays an important part in maintaining an "organic contract."

Being existentially committed to our social roles as our self-concept and our self-understanding and being obligated by our interdependency with others to strive for the most just institutions achievable in order to promote the fulfillment of the widest range of lifestyles, herein lies the foundation for a citizen ethic based on social roles. In other words, if one can accept that society is formed by the interaction of obligated social roles, then a system of a role ethic organizes the moral interaction between role players.

Furthermore, even if we suspend judgment, for the time being, on the exact origin of society and the existential commitment, and if we just accept the minimal position here, namely, that at least humans are defined in terms of their interaction with others because a developing person needs significant others to identify with, a person could not achieve roles of greater social responsibility, thus one could argue that as role players we are obligated to act appropriately according to our given and acquired roles. In other words, when one is acting within the capacity of a social or political role, one is obligated to behave appropriately, that is, to abide by a citizen ethos, and at least to fulfill the minimum requirements of one's position.

For example, in the parent/child relationship, the parent has a duty to provide for and appropriately raise the child, and the child has a right to such provisions. It should be understood that the child's life is extending the parent's life, the society, and the species at large. In turn, the child is conditioned not only by significant others but also environmentally and socially. The existential commitment works both ways: the parent is defined by the child, and the child is defined by the parent, hence both are obligated to each other. To the extent that the state is an extended family system, this two-way obligation applies between the person and the state. The degree of commitment depends on the size of the social organization and the particular role one holds. For example, in a relatively small social group under unjust military attack, every able body should be obligated to defend the group, because the destruction of the social organization would entail one's own termination, either one's death or the end of one's social self, one's self-concept and understanding, especially where the war captives are put into slavery or prison. However, in a larger social organization with a standing defense system, it should not be the obligation of every able-bodied person to defend the state, because the defense institution could be designed to handle such attacks without calling out the entire civilian population, but this does not rule out the possibility of certain large-scale national emergencies where the entire population may be required to assist.

The individual is not obligated to obey unjust parents or an unjust state, because in being unjust they have violated the existential commitment—they are not fulfilling their duty to raise a person or to maintain a community, but rather they are abusing liberties with the unjust *use* of other people. On the other hand, if the individual violates the existential commitment, then the state has the duty to punish, but care must be taken to reform any unjust institutions, or to punish and reform significant others who influence the criminal, because the principle of interrelatedness acknowledges that people do not act in a vacuum, but that other people, and social institutions in general, influence them.

Turning to acquired social roles, like one's profession, one is obligated to perform appropriately because of the existential commitment and because of the necessary interrelatedness and co-conditioning of social roles. Whether one freely chooses one's acquired roles or not, but especially where one has voluntarily selected the position, one is obligated to act appropriately. If one does not appropriately abide by the accepted forms of behavior, then one is apparently either attempting to redefine the social structure or subvert it. If good reasons can be given for the subversive actions and the need for change, then the unjust conditions that gave rise to their breach of the existential commitment must be corrected, and those who initiated the reform should not be punished. If no good reason can be given for restructuring society, that is, if the reorganization will not make the society more just, then that so-called reformer and the significant others who influenced the rebel must be subverting the social harmony, and they have a right to be punished.

This social role ethic is based on the recognition that the harmony of society is maintained by each role player, not the bare abstract individual, effectively contributing to the well-ordered society by fulfilling the duties of his or her respective positions. There will be no absolute moral laws or formalism applicable to all roles for all time, nor can one simply rely on social or cultural relativism or situational ethics. It should be clear that ethical absolutism is too general a theory to meet the needs of unique roles; for example, the captured soldier may be obligated to lie to the enemy. Ethical relativism is too general, and the society at large is not skilled enough to determine the special moral principles applicable to each role. For example, though a whole society may condone lying, it would not be advantageous for those in the role of messengers to practice it when delivering a message. Situational ethics cannot be applicable, because it is not one's own personal decisions that matter but one's role decisions; it is not a personal matter of doing one's best but a social matter of fulfilling one's role to the best of one's ability.

In another sense, however, all three ethical positions are applicable to a limited degree. Some moral principles will be absolutely applicable to every member of a social position or role under any conditions; for example, a health care provider should never take advantage of a patient. Any social role ethic will, in a limited sense, take the form of a "role" relativism, in that the codes are only applicable to that social position or role; for example, the parent is responsible for providing for the child's physical, emotional, and intellectual needs; while the educator must be sensitive to the latter two, she need not provide for the physical needs of food and shelter, although the department of education may have to fulfill that need. Finally, a social role ethic is similar to situational ethics, in that the citizen or role player must be sensitive to unique conditions, and a citizen ethic will always be confined to certain roles or social positions under certain unique conditions.

A social role ethic is based on the acknowledged importance that society is a diverse union of various social unions, roles, and social positions that change over time. Since people rarely, if ever, interact as bare individual to individual, a social role ethic assumes the need for moral guidelines to direct the interaction of roles. For social role ethics, the moral question is not what should I do to be moral? Rather, the question is what is required of my role? or, what is required of me to be a good citizen?

The role of timing in personal behavior and social roles has not been fully acknowledged in the philosophical journals. Timing is usually recognized as an aspect in business, especially in market investment. Timing in government policy must be recognized as a moral responsibility—if certain government actions are not made in a timely fashion, the common weal will not be served. Social role ethics should consider a general code of behavior that requires citizens, and special social positions, professionally trained or not, such as doctors, lawyers, investors, politicians, and so on, to behave with moral responsibility and proper timing. In fact, every social position has its deadlines that are met or not, due to one's job performance. If we cannot accept the actuality of time as an achievement, as something that is made by one's performance, then one might still be open to acknowledging that one should consider acting "as if" one's behavior had ubiquitous influence and a moral responsibility accompanying such influence. We must be conscious of not only choosing the right time but *making* the right time for moral action.

Doing the right thing at the wrong time or without having constituted the right time would be an evil from the perspective of moral proper timing. Proper timing in moral theory opens up a new vantage point and an alternative to relativism and contextualism, and it could help resolve the problem of conflict of principles in absolutism. That is, if one takes timing as the primary director in moral action, then principles could be prioritized according to the proper time. The check against blind cultural relativism and lack of direction for doing one's best as a contextualist could look to proper timing as a guideline. Proper timing supported by the idea of parity in the existential commitment allows one to become aware that enhancing the interests of others is correlative to one's own self-interest.

If the pre-Qin perspective, which was extracted from the LSCQ, on the human's role in articulating time is taken as an "as if" hypothesis for moral insight, then one would have to seriously entertain the idea that one's personal articulation of time contributes to the social-historical conditions. The significance of one's social position as citizen, and the quality of one's performance in that role, articulates a certain "time"—not only as a social context but also as a historical event. The "kind of time" one articulates in one's personal life contributes to the social milieu one lives in. To the extent that we interpret history on the basis of creative accomplishments and deeds, the impressions one leaves behind fashion the basis for historical interpretation. In describing his understanding of existential subjectivism as a kind of intersubjectivity, Jean-Paul Sartre states that in choosing for oneself, one chooses for all people.[74] For Sartre, a person creates oneself and creates all of mankind. One's actions, choices, and lifestyle make the individual person, and it involves all of humanity. In a similar manner, our personal manifestation of timing involves all of humanity and the environment at large. One's personal articulation of time contributes to both the present social context, and it generates historical patterns of interpretation for the future. One's timely and untimely actions affect the quality of the environment.[75]

Many authors in environmental ethics argue for the *rights* of animals, the environment, and the rights of future generations.[76] The attempts are not well grounded. Traditionally, to be a rights bearer one either had to be a "legal person" or be able to "claim" one's rights, and it is difficult to see how non-human animals, trees and mountains, and the unborn can make a claim or be classified as persons. However, not to be able to defend and protect animals and the environment seems incorrect. The unified eclectic and organic positions found in the LSCQ provide alternative perspectives that could be incorporated into contemporary issues in environmental ethics. The organic, dynamic, focus-field philosophy of the LSCQ assumes that humans and their environment are interdependent and mutually related, thus environmental issues must be seen as integral to one's own existence.

It is difficult to accept Eugene C. Hargrove's claim that "the fact that human actions could damage the environment on a large scale went unrecognized in the West until George Perkins Marsh pointed it out scarcely a century ago. . . ."[77] When the Romans salted the earth at Carthage, they were well aware of what they were doing. Even in places where deforestation took generations, cultural memory in the form of legends and literature records the existence of ancient forests. If what Hargrove says is true, then it is only true of his conception of the West, or "large scale" denotes the globe. Hindu legend notes the destruction of the land by destroyer goddesses who are interpreted to be the power of ethnic groups. Certainly the Great Wall, the ancient irrigation system in western China, and the ancient canal system in eastern China are evidence that they were aware that humans can alter the environment on a large scale, and they can benefit from the results of the successful manipulation of nature. The importance of the leading chapters of the *shierji*, the *Liji*'s *yueling*, and the LSCQ itself is that they present an understanding of the world in which the natural environment and human life are intimately related and mutually determining, that is, a worldview in which human actions do in fact influence the environment on a large scale. The LSCQ's consolidated approach contains some of the earliest extant cosmological and environmental material from the pre-Qin period.

Roger T. Ames argues for interpreting "*de* as the integrity and integration of particular foci."[78] Arguing that the pre-Qin philosophers provide an alternative philosophy based on an aesthetic paradigm, he draws an analogy to the culinary arts and cites the LSCQ's *benwei* chapter as an example of the significance of the particular in forming an aesthetic composition.[79] What needs to be explicated is the notion of "proper timing" contained in the phrase "there must be an order in the mixing." The notion of "an order in the mixing," literally "a first and an after" shows that, for the LSCQ, the cook or social orchestrator must articulate timing in the temporal priority chosen in integrating the particulars. Each particular ingredient or focus must be integrated in a timely fashion to fully enhance its contribution to the social and environmental field. One should be sensitive to temporal priority in environmental issues.

From the perspective of existential parity, one involved in self-cultivation acknowledges the importance of environmental factors, both influenced by oneself and also influencing one's development. Awareness of parity predisposes one to be sensitive to environmental issues. The self-cultivating person becomes aware of the expanding contexts in which his or her actions have influence; one's existential commitment to family, relatives, neighbors, society at large, and humanity in general grows with the achievement of creative living. This program of self-cultivation expands through social integration into an environmental, cosmic integration, where one's commitment extends to the natural environment. In this sense, one develops an obligation to protect the interests of other creatures and to protect the environment within which and upon which they and oneself live.

These are arguments for an existential and ontological basis for our moral obligation to protect and preserve a natural balance. These arguments respond to Richard T. DeGeorge's attempt to argue for individual and collective obligations toward the environment and to clarify that the basis of both individual and collective obligations is developed in the existential commitment on the most basic, existential level of parity of particulars and equal consideration of interests.[80] Likewise, J. Baird Callicott and Roger T. Ames argue that it is necessary "to construct or adopt a *different worldview and a different set of values and duties*" to successfully deal with environmental issues.[81] The dynamic field-focus perspective of the pre-Qin period, especially as it is embodied in the composite content of the LSCQ, provides an appropriate cosmology from which the defenders of environmental ethics can construct a new *ethos* or lifestyle. Whether or not our "prejudices" will invite this strange guest to stay with us remains to be seen.

An even stronger case can be made for establishing our environmental obligations both individually and collectively by rooting them in political obligations. Although moral obligations usually provide a more rational justification and universal appeal, nevertheless, they notoriously avoid the practical issue of instituting policy. The "organic contract" and social role ethic acknowledge the significance of establishing legal obligations and a code for social roles, particularly a code for the citizen. This entails the protection and appropriate modification of the environment. The political obligations of the state and the collective mass of society should establish laws grounded in the "organic contract" to protect the dynamic web of life—social as well as biological. The social role ethic of the citizen establishes both a ritual code and a moral code of conduct in regard to the environment and its creatures to guide the citizen, especially as hunter, camper, and exploiter of nature, in appropriating and integrating with the environment in a mutually enhancing manner. The citizen, as a contributing particular, and the legal attitude of the society at large should be committed to the protection and enrichment of the environment, especially when the fulfillment of self-interest can be enhanced in the process. The existential commitment and social concerns for the environment naturally entail a need for proper timing on various fronts. There would be a concern, as there is now, for the seasonal migration and breeding patterns of various species, and there would be a greater concern for our own influence on climatic and seasonal conditions.

Despite shortcomings, these arguments have implications regarding theories of time, social political order, and our own self-understanding, in that they attempt to reclaim our identity as both interrelated aspects of nature, and especially as temporally interrelated social creatures. The pre-Qin philosophy contained in the LSCQ can expand our horizons, opening up new ways of thinking about and dealing with contemporary problems.

Appendix I

Phenomenological and Etymological Conceptions of Timing (*Shi*)

One can reconstruct a conception of an archaic experience of "time" through archaeology. A philological and semantic analysis of archaic Chinese characters or words provides a means for gaining insight into an ancient concept. Friedrich W. Nietzsche, Martin Heidegger, and John L. Austin, among others, have proposed that contemporary words still bear their ancient, etymological meanings, and that a study of a term's etymology reveals something of the "old idea."[1] If this is true of Indo-European languages, it becomes more significant and more complex in the Chinese language, which is structured in organically related clusters of cognate terms. It is more complex in the Chinese case because the "old idea" is a core in a cluster of terms rather than a single term. It is more significant in that it enables a term to be defined genetically and morphologically. This kind of etymological analysis is only suggestive and heuristic. The ultimate argument must rely upon philosophical coherence that can only be sought in a specific text, framed within a larger cultural context.

Time—as the duration of natural phenomena—constitutes one of the most primordial experiences of the animal kingdom. The duration of the moon's orbit about the earth, and the earth's wobbling, elliptical spin around the sun, comprises the passage of light and dark, high and low tides, fluctuations in temperature, and the seasons. Life as we know it on our planet has developed in response to the cycles of day and night, tide, and season. From the daily life activity (feeding, mating, and sleeping) to reproductive patterns and the overall life cycle, a creature's existence is maintained in and through its response to time—the duration and motion of natural phenomena—light, tide, temperature, season, and so on. The human organism, like any other creature, must appropriate the duration of light, tide, and season. This type of phenomenological conception of time as an organism's "creative response" to the earth's changing environment underlies the pre-Qin conception of time.

A phenomenological experience of time grounds the archaic use of the word time as the quality of an organism's response to its environment, that is, time as the appropriate action for a situation. According to the *Oxford English Dictionary*, the Old English *tíma* (and the Old Nordic *tími*) and its contemporary derivative "time" not only denote the measurement of duration but the "fitting or proper time" and "good time." Of course, "time" is a word rich in connotation and varied usage, but its root *tí*, which means "to extend," "to stretch," underlies both the quantitative measurement of an extent of time and the qualitative experience of constructing or making time, that is, extending time through one's activity. It is interesting to note that *tí* is the root for the word "tide," which reveals a strong link between the concept of the "extent" of the natural phenomena of the ocean tide and "time" in Old English. In its contemporary usage, "time" usually connotes quantity, especially in science, and less so the quality of "proper time."

It is characteristic of the classical Greek philosophical vocabulary that the logical aspect of the "old idea" was developed, while the more aesthetic and rhetorical denotations were undervalued. For example, now it is popular to think of *cosmos* primarily as "order," but it did mean "elegance," and *logos* not only meant *ratio* but also *oratio*. This is true of "time." The ancient Greeks had a separate vocabulary for the expression of "proper or critical time" (*kairos*) as opposed to the more familiar "duration of events" (*chronos*). In its general usage, *kairos* means "proportion," "fitness," or "due measure," and when used in reference to a place, it denotes the "right place," especially vital parts of the body, or wounds. In reference to time, *kairos* denotes the "proper time or season for action." It is the "exact or critical time," "the right point of time" to take action. The Latins used the expression *opportunitas* to express *kairos*. Its most positive expression is still preserved in Pindar's proverbial: "Time and tide wait for no man."

The Sophists primarily used *kairos* as a rhetorical concept. Gorgias in particular "made *kairos* the cornerstone of his entire epistemology, ethics, aesthetics, and rhetoric."[2] The Pythagoreans, Plato, and later Cicero used the concept *kairos*. James L. Kinneavy argues that the term fell out of use because of the impact of Aristotle's concern for the "art of rhetoric" instead of the "act of rhetoric," which calls for *kairos*.[3] I propose that Aristotle and his interpreters were influential in directing attention toward *chronos* as the measurement of duration, thereby undervaluing the qualitative aspects of time and timing.

The character *shi* 時, like the Old English *tíma*, denotes both the *quantity* of duration and the *quality* of the "proper time" in taking action. In its broadest meaning, the English term *time*, carries both the abstract, quantitative, and engaged quality connotations of *shi*. Too often, however, we are prone to dichotomize. John Smith points out that a neat division between *chronos* (quantity time) and *kairos* (quality time) "will not do; both aspects of time are ingredients in the nature of things and both have a practical import."[4] Smith's analysis apprehends the pre-Qin impression of "time." When "time" is used as a translation of *shi*, a conception of the correlativity of the quantity and the quality of "time" must be maintained and kept in mind.

The Chinese language is notoriously dynamic, focusing on processes of change as opposed to the more static conceptions of causal states or phases, and Chinese characters often denote a complex web of bipolar activity.[5] "Time/*shi*," in the pre-Qin period, expresses the dynamic process of the active subject engaged in and with the world. This dynamic conception of time as the "proper season-time" is conceivably rooted in the agricultural culture of ancient China. China is often noted as a long-standing agrarian civilization. The Longshan stone age pottery culture and the archaic Shang bronze culture were based on a flourishing agricultural, socioeconomic structure. This deeply rooted agricultural nucleus of the Shang and later the Zhou peoples influenced their religious, philosophical and political worldviews.

From the agricultural perspective, the character *shi* 實 means "fruition"—the achievement of a bountiful harvest. It is often translated as "reality." The harvest *is* reality which was surely part of the archaic Shang and Zhou worldview in that such ancient characters as *shi* 實 and *guo* 果 refer to "fruit," and they also mean the "real," or "really" and "truly." For pre-Qin people, "reality" is not a given. What is "real" is the process of maturation and efficacy. The pre-Qin organic, agricultural culture yields a dynamic field ontology. It is a radical process of the beginningless and endless unfolding of the interrelationship of heaven, earth, and man.

The *Book of Changes* (*Yijing*), the core of which is thought to date from the early Zhou, is a fair representative of this process (*yi* 易) worldview. It is not enough to simply say that "things change." The quantitative measurement of duration or change is made in order to gain insight into the appropriate qualitative moment to take action. The "way things are" is the way they have been "made" through successful or unsuccessful participation in the natural processes. With such an achievement-in-process worldview, "time" is not fully distinguishable from spatial circumstances. The world is a spatiotemporal matrix of interrelated changing particulars. In this tradition, chronological time is always fused with "kairological" time, that is, the appropriation of "critical timing" or "seasonableness" in initiating, maintaining, and completing an activity with efficacy.

The character *shi* (時) is a "combined meaning" (*huiyi* 會意) character, which means that each component of the character carries semantic force. It was originally written as *shi* 旹, which shows *ri* 日, the sun, under *zhi* 㞢 or 止, a "foot" or the idea of "to abide for a while," "to stagger," "to rest," or "to remain." *Zhi* (foot) is also written as *zhi* 之, "to go to."[6] *Zhi* (止) can mean "to stop an action," and it carries the connotation of *perpon* (propriety or fitness) when it is used to mean "proper deportment" or "courteous." As is the case with characters that have multiple meanings, one must strive to arrive at an understanding of the central idea that conjoins them. Rather than exclusive disjunctions, each reading must be qualified by the other connotations. In this case, "to stop," "to abide," "to settle," and "proper deportment" collaborate to suggest "abiding in a position negotiated to achieve greatest efficacy."

In summary, the archaic etymological image that emerges from the pictograph *shi* 時 is that season or time is the "proper phases" (*zhi* 㞢) of the sun (*ri* 日)—equinox and solstice—the quantitative duration coupled with a perspectival appropriation. There are other bone graph depictions of *shi*, namely 㫑 or 㫑, which are predecessors of the modern graph. The character on the right (寺) is chiefly phonetic, but note that it retains the *zhi* 止, which is above *cun* 寸, "a thumb," or "to measure, as an inch." The phonetic *si* (寺) presents the image of "measuring" (*cun* 寸) "according to the proper phases in an activity" (*zhi* 止), that is, "waiting for motion-activity," or "appropriating the measurement of duration." Claude Larre, following the *Shuowenjiezi*, associates *zhi* 止 with sprouting vegetation.[7] This links *shi*, the pre-Qin conception of time, to an agricultural root of appropriating season time.

To appreciate the connotations of *shi* (時), we should examine its cognates and other terms that have semantic similarities. Many of the cognates of *shi* are composed of the phonetic *si* (寺), and they direct our attention toward the mutual interrelatedness of subject and event, actor and action. *Shi* (侍), as "waiting" or "appropriating duration," entails a mutual codependency of the waiting subject properly seizing a changing state of affairs. The character *shi* 侍 means "to wait upon," "to accompany." It is closely related to *dai* 待, "to wait, await," or "to treat," "to behave." The binomial *dai shi* (待侍), "to await the right opportunity," is an ancient compound, and it plays a major role in the program of appropriating critical timing in social and political action, especially in the LSCQ's *shoushi* chapter.

These terms are related to *zhi* 徛, "to provide," "to prepare," where "waiting" is making "preparations." Hence the "waiting" is not entirely passive but entails a contributory element on the part of the person waiting, which influences the "rightness" of the time. Time, generally speaking for the pre-Qin world, is basically waiting for the opportune moment to take action. So temporal concepts are often related to "waiting," like *hou* 候 (to wait), which forms the modern binome *shi hou* 時候 (time). In addition to this seminal notion of "waiting upon," which is passive, is the more active connotation of "grasping" and "interdependency."

Season or time (*shi*) lies at the heart of the constellation of concepts relating to interdependency. The character *shi* 恃, "to depend on" or "rely on," is a cognate. The notion of interdependency is reinforced by another constellation of characters—though not cognates, they bear semantic similarities—that frequently appear with *shi* 時 or are associated with "timely efficacy" in a more general sense. *Yin* 因, "to rely upon" or "to make the best of," fits in this constellation, and as such, it must be read as a spatiotemporal, co-creative, and integrative activity of availing oneself of "conditions." *Shi* 勢, "purchase," "leverage," or "the force of circumstances," holds a pivotal place in this concept cluster of interdependency and spatiotemporal conditions. *Shi* 勢 is etymologically an agricultural concept denoting the force or leverage one gains in "grasping and planting." This discloses the interrelatedness of the active subject "making" one's world by properly allocating and taking advantage of spatiotemporal conditions. *He* 和, "to harmonize," "to attune," "to make the correct proportions, or proper blend" holds a place in this cluster of concepts, displaying a process of interrelated co-creative responses or proper allotment of a particular within a spatiotemporal context of focus and field. *Zheng* 正, "attunement, to straighten out," relates to this cluster not only as a harmony concept, but also because it is constructed out of *zhi* 止, "abiding and proper." Where harmony is "putting things in order," then *deng* 等, "to classify," "to rank," or "to wait," joins this constellation.

Although many of the cognates of *shi* (時) give the impression that one simply awaits (*dai* 待) the conditions, nevertheless, the reciprocity and mutual interrelatedness of the interactions of particulars and the determinative influence of their participating in the process of change must not be undervalued. That is, the ontological status of any "thing" is always negotiated and is not fixed or pregiven. The phonetic *si* 寺 fashions other cognates of *shi* (時), enhancing the idea of mutuality and the controlling, directive elements implicit in the phonetic *si* and the concept "time" itself. For example, *te* 特, in addition to various other meanings, denotes "a mate," that is, "one of two" or "a match for." And this brings *yu* 遇, "to meet with," and *dang* 當, "to match," into the "season/time" concept cluster, and the binome *yu he* 遇合 is the title of a chapter in the LSCQ that considers the significance of timely encounters between ruler and minister as affecting social and political order, and the binome *dang shi* 當時 "matching or meeting the proper time" plays a significant role in the LSCQ. The character *chi* 持, "to hold" or "to grasp," introduces the "grasping" connotations of *si* (寺). The "subject" or particular focus, which must be thought of as a complex organization of other particulars, is not merely propelled nor environmentally determined, but it also has conditioning efficacy on its environs.

Within the constellation of *shi*, there is a cluster of concepts that relates "time" to discourse. When spoken words (*yan* 言) come together with a harmonious rhythm/rhyme (*si* 寺), they constitute poetry (*shi* 詩). The discourse of poetry is a season-evoking experience. A large part of the early classical corpus is associated with seasonal matters: planting, harvesting, festivals, and so on. Of course, historical record is another expression of time as discourse. The cognate character *zhi* 誌, composed of "words" (*yan* 言) of "purpose" (*zhi* 志), denotes the "records." The characters *zhi* 誌 ("record") and *zhi* 志 ("purpose," "aim," "spirit," or "mind," which is used for "record") are related to *shi* through the meaning-invested phonetic *zhi* 止 or *zhi* 之.[8] These characters instruct our attention to examine the active participation and mutuality of the human subject in the record of history and poetry directed at the active expression of "an existential purpose in the achievement of goals" (*zhi* 志). In Chinese historiographies, there is a relationship between narrative and perspective, which tends to make history didactic.

Shi, season or time, the patterns of sun and moon, three moons for each season, does not reference an objective natural event as opposed to some human subjective impression, but rather "*shi*" is manifested seasonability in the human activity of appropriating a natural phenomenon. A season is not an empty Newtonian dimension in which events arise; rather, the occurrences of events are the manifestation of time. This interdependency of time and activity is a basic presupposition of Chinese and Japanese thought. The LSCQ displays this interdependency of time and activity in the *mengchunji* (Record of Early Spring) chapter when it says: "If the summer ordinances are carried out in the early spring, then the winds and rains will not be timely. The plants will wither early, and then there will be apprehensiveness in the capital."[9]

The *Liezi* and the *benwei* chapter of the LSCQ relate a story of a music master who alters the weather conditions by playing certain melodies.[10] This story metaphorizes the idea that human actions can influence the seasons, just as the seasons influence humans. Activity and time are mutually dependent.

Time (*shi*) is rightly "season" or "time," which is both a cosmic and a social event. The cosmic event is the duration of the phases of the sun and moon; the social event is the human's appropriation of the "seasonability" of a project, especially in agriculture, warfare, and ritual sacrifice. Season or time is appropriated time, that is, time in which one avails oneself of the natural events just as much as one contributes to the creation and sustenance of those events. "Waiting for the right time" (*dai shi*), waiting for the proper moment to act, is a form of articulating time itself—in making preparations (*zhi* 偫), one is waiting (*shi* 侍). The critical season or time cannot exist in its fullest qualitative significance, if a person, but especially the ruler as the people's model, is not prepared to undertake an activity or a project. In undertaking one's project, such as a ritual or planting, one modifies the meaning and value of the specific season and history in general. Human activities contribute to and creatively cooperate with the season. The LSCQ implies this in its pattern of spring planting, summer weeding, autumn harvesting, and winter storage.

The archaic Shang and Zhou concept *shi* (time) is not dependent on a posited, cosmogonic origin or a mythico-ritual attempt to reenact those cosmic origins. As one might expect, the absence of cosmogony suggests a noncyclic, nonlinear conception of time. The radical field cosmology, representative of many of the pre-Qin teachings, coupled with a chiefly agrarian and ancestor cult concerns, yields a conception of time that is profoundly organic, programmatic or goal oriented. Lacking cosmogonic roots, the conception of *shi* is dynamic and organic, and it promotes an emergent, creatively negotiated, spatiotemporal cosmology that is aesthetically arranged through an emergent order of spontaneous harmony. Such a cosmetic cosmology, or *ars contextualis* ("the art of context"), does not underplay the significance of time. Time is a composite of interdependent and mutually determining factors. The degree of success is a function of the quality of one's personal integration, harmonization, and co-creation of those factors.

As a heuristic model, the classical pre-Qin conception of time can be thought of or modeled as a spiral. The spiral should be seen as a beginningless double helix of interacting bipolar forces (*yinyang*) culminating in the present, which unfolds into an endless future of changing possibilities. Each loop in the spiral can be read as the yearly cycle of the four seasons. However, the yearly cycle of the seasons is never an exact repetition. Lawrence W. Fagg, in the *Two Faces of Time*, comes close to this spiral model when he proposes that "Chinese time has both linear and cyclic aspects."[11] The cycle of the seasons has been misconstrued, leading some to elide the "Chinese" understanding of time with other conceptions that focus on returning to the *in illo tempore* in a grand cycle.

For the dynamic, organic modes of pre-Qin philosophy, "origins" are rooted in the unfolding of the present. The "origins" are not temporally nor ontologically prior. Chaos and order are always intimately interlinked in the tension of bipolar forces. Though the present is a culmination of the past, it is not deterministically realized; rather, the present and the unfolding future are again creatively negotiated. The efficacy of one's integration with the emergent spatiotemporal arrangement and duration of events makes one a participant in an open-ended process of *creatio ab initio*. The creative appropriation of proper timing is explicated in the discussions concerning human character and society in Chapters 2 and 3.

Appendix II

A Study of *Xingming zhi Qing* in the LSCQ: The Achievement of One's Character (*Xing*) in One's Natural Relations (*Ming*)

In addition to *xing*, the concept *ming* is most important in understanding the LSCQ's worldview, especially its conception of how human life interacts with cosmic and political forces. *Ming*, one's natural relations (usually translated as "fate" or "mandate"), is closely related to the concept *xing*. This relationship is expressed in the phrase *xingming zhi qing*, that is, "the reality, or contextual conditions (*qing*) of life (*xingming*)—one's achieved character (*xing*), in the context of one's natural relations (*ming*)."

The term *ming* literally means "to mandate, or command"; it is also used as a nominal, meaning "a decree, a command," or "a government notification." Moreover, it has the meanings of "life," and it was associated with the mandates of the Son of Heaven, or nature itself as the throne of the deceased emperors—the emperor or nature mandate life and death. *Tianming* (the mandate of heaven) dispenses the decreed relationships of nature, which establish and maintain a ruler's reign.

Recall from Chapter 2, Tang Junyi's interpretation of *ming* as the interrelated and co-dependent *relationships* obtaining between *tian* (nature) and *ren* (humans), so that *ming* takes on dynamic contextual significance.[1] Socially and politically speaking, *ming*, then, means the relationships of conducting one's personal behavior or the state's administration to bring about certain results. When *ming* is abstracted from the political arena, it carries with it the connotation of a "commanding relationship" toward some end. It should be noted that in the pre-Qin context, the "end" or "result" is not something absolute, permanent, and perfect; it is not a *telos*. The end in view here is establishing a dynasty—a few generations of proper rulership; it is always understood that the ideal cannot be maintained for long, even though the traditional wish was that it would last 10,000 years. The art of rulership proposed by those passages in the LSCQ that sponsor unification of the empire is concerned with developing techniques that will promote the establishment of an imperial command over the central plains of China.

The social and political significance of *ming* is not limited to the efficacious self-cultivation of the ruler alone. Some of the LSCQ's passages take the opportunity to point out the benefits of self-cultivation among the scholar-knights (*shi*), especially the *youdao zhi shi* (the scholar-knights who possess or comply with the Way). The *guanshi* (Reflecting on the Age) chapter gives a detailed example of Master Liezi as a self-actualizing knight of the Way. The story depicts Liezi and his family living in near starvation, and yet Liezi is unwilling to receive gifts from the corrupt ruler of Zheng. Though his wife could not understand Liezi's actions at first, he proves to be a master of timeliness and foresight. This story occurs in the *Zhuangzi*, the *Xinxu*, and the *Liezi*. After the LSCQ's version, the following comment is appended, emphasizing that penetrating (*da*) into the reality of one's character and the correlative natural relations (*da xingming zhi qing*) plays an important role in Liezi's ability to appropriate circumstances.

> Was not Master Liezi's rejection of what is not right and his avoidance of noncompliance penetrating?[2] Moreover, when one is suffering the calamities of cold and starvation, and yet one does not take things improperly, this is to foresee transformation. To take action already foreseeing the transformation coming is to be fully penetrative with the reality of one's character and natural relations (*xingming zhi qing*).[3]

The *zhongji* chapter emphasizes the need for one's self-cultivation practices to lead one to penetrate (*da*) into a thorough understanding of the actual conditions of one's achievement of character and the natural relations of one's life. After a careful discussion of three important considerations, namely (1) wealth and poverty, (2) distinguishing between the significant and insignificant, and (3) safety and danger, the text relates the following comments.

> The above three cases are what those who possess the Way consider seriously. There are those who consider it carefully, but on the contrary they harm it (life). This is because they did not penetrate into the depths of the reality of their character and natural relations (*ta xingming zhi qing*).

> Not penetrating into the depths of the reality of your character and natural relations, no matter how seriously you consider it, what is the advantage?![4]

In the Daoist context, careful consideration is not as good as the existential integration and practice of self-cultivation. Bare theoretical consideration without praxis will put one in jeopardy in the political arena.

Cosmically speaking, *ming* denotes interdependent-cause, which is not the one-for-one correspondence of classical causation, nor a statistical probability, as in modern causal theory; rather it is somewhat similar to the Buddhist *pratitya-samutpada* (codependent arising).[5] *Ming*, which I have been translating as "natural relations," is the outcome of "events" both psychological and natural. The natural relationships that constitute *ming* are not "innate" or "fated," but rather they are creative possibilities that the enlightened ruler or scholar-knight of the Way must enhance. The psychological aspect is captured in *ming*'s relationship with *xing*, character, of both the Emperor issuing mandates and the masses revolting as in Mengzi's conception of *tianming* as the people's will. The degree to which one successfully practices self-cultivation and develops and refines the natural tendencies without excess influences the net result of one's life. One's interrelatedness to the environment and one's success at ruling are also a direct outcome of self-cultivation. For those classical pre-Qin philosophers who share an organic interpretation of the hylozoistic world, interrelatedness to the environment is a reciprocal relationship so that one not only influences the physical environment, for instance, opening new canals, roads, fields, and so on, but also in a reciprocal relationship the natural environment plays a role in shaping one's own developing life.

The *zhifen* (Knowing Distinctions) chapter employs an interesting piece of lore about Yu the Great, which makes this point concerning the interrelatedness of achieving one's character (*xing*) within the context of one's natural relationships, especially in the case of the emperor. Yu is noted for draining the floods of antiquity by altering the terrain. He is thus an exemplar ruler, that is, one who establishes and maintains his rulership by harmonizing the natural environment through his own self-cultivation. In the *zhifen* chapter's story, Yu is fording a river in a boat full of people when a yellow dragon emerges from the river, lifting the boat on its back. The people are frightened out of their wits.

> Looking upward to the firmament (*tian*), King Yu sighed, "Since I have received the mandate (*ming*, the scope of his natural relationships) from nature (*tian*, heaven), I should exhaust my energy to nourish the people.

> My life depends on character (*xing*); my death depends on the mandate (*ming*). Why should I worry about this dragon?" Lowering its ears and drooping its tail, the dragon left.[6]

Here we see that King Yu's self-cultivation has a direct bearing on his understanding of the course of his life and death and his ability to command the environment due to heaven's mandate that he rule. The chapter continues with the following comments:

> In this sense King Yu really understood the distinctions between life and death, and the guideline of benefit and harm.
>
> All people and things are the transformations of yin and yang. The interaction of yin and yang is what nature gets going and completes.[7] Nature inherently has its aspects of declining, deficiency, abolishing, and collapsing, but it also has the aspects of flourishing, fullness, arising, and growing.
>
> Humans have the aspects of failure, distress, exhaustion, and deficient, but they also have the aspects of being filled, solid, communicative, and successful. These are all patterns of things (*wu li*) allowed by nature (*tian*), and natural phases (*shu*) which cannot be other than they are. The ancient sages would not allow the motives of personal desire to harm the spirit. They waited in tranquility.[8]

This correlative unity is especially true in the case of the Son of Heaven and the *tianming* theory, where the Mandate of Heaven is displayed in the natural environment with "timely rains" and good harvests or untimely frost and poor harvests. If the emperor is not practicing self-cultivation, then bad weather and popular rebellions will bring on the downfall of the imperial house.

The ruler is in a unique position to co-creatively engage *ming*. The *junshou* (On What the Ruler Should Protect) chapter explicitly states that it is the Way (*dao*) of the ruler to obtain or integrate (*de*) with the environmental relations (*ming*).

> Hence, there is the old saying: "The one who creates suffers the worry; the one who acts accordingly enjoys peace." Only the Way of the ruler obtains the reality of the natural relations (*weibi jundao de ming zhi qing*—the essentials of the mandate). Hence, he will be responsible for the empire without any compelling. It is this that is called an intact person (*quanren*).[9]

The person who integrates with *ming* can rule the state without coercion, and this is the embodiment of a consummate ruler.

With the appropriate self-cultivation, moreover, the emperor could affect not only good weather and resulting good harvests but also draw in proper officials for the governing of bureaucratic affairs. This point is made in the *zhidu* (Knowing the Proper Standards) chapter:

> When a ruler submits to the reality of his character and its natural relations (*fu xingming zhi qing*), gets rid of his personal likes and dislikes, and employs being vacuous and acts with non-purposeful-action (*wuwei*) as the roots to receiving useful advice, this is called the proper functioning court (*zhao*). Whenever there is a proper functioning court (the ruler and officials) mutually promote pattern and rightness (*liyi*), and they mutually establish standards and statutes (*faze*).
>
> If the ruler submits to the reality of his character and its natural relations (*fu xingming zhi qing*), then the knights (*shi*) of pattern and rightness will flock, and the application of proper standards and statutes will be established. The crooked and depraved will withdraw, and the avaricious and deceitful gangs will be kept at a distance.
>
> Hence, the crux of ruling the empire properly lies in rooting out depravity. The crux of rooting out depravity lies in ordering the offices properly. The crux of ordering the offices properly lies in the Way of achieving political order (*zhidao*).[10] The crux of the Way of achieving political order lies in being aware of the character and its natural relations (*zhixingming*).
>
> Hence, our Master Huazi said, "Being generous but not over doing it, one should sincerely preserve the One (fundamental) affair (i.e., the Way).[11] His correct character (*zhengxing*), this he delights in. Since the masses never display their abilities universally, they must be accomplished in a specific ability. After accomplishing things by thoroughly exhausting their abilities, then the four tribes will be pacified. Only the Heavenly Tally (*tianfu*, an auspicious event) is universal by not being universal. This is what Shennong used to be the leader, and what Emperors Yao and Shun used to be outstanding."[12]

The ruler's self-cultivation is a natural determinant in structuring a well-ordered society and an effective administration. The ruler's self-cultivation, particularly controlling "the reality of his character and natural relations," will attract officials who practice appropriateness and rationality. The basic conditions for ruling the empire are obtained in the ruler's self-cultivation of *xingming zhi qing*. When the ruler is fully communicative with the actuality of his character and the natural correlative relations, then the proper fulfillment of desire can follow.

The benefit of the ruler's self-cultivation is not limited to himself, but rather when the ruler cultivates his own *xing*, he is interconnected to the myriad things. This point is made in the *youdu* (On Possessing Proper Standards) chapter.

> Jizi said, "All of those who were able to properly govern the empire were certainly well versed (*tong*) with the reality of their character and its natural relations; they were certainly without any partiality." . . . The disciples of Kongzi and Mozi filled the empire. They all instructed the empire in the methods of human kindness and rightness (*renyi zhi shu*). If you had no where to practice the teachings, then you still cannot practice the method—so how much less can those whom you taught! Why is this? It is because the methods of human kindness and rightness are external. Using the external to conquer the internal, even a commoner cannot practice it, how much less can a ruler? If one is well versed in the reality of one's character and natural relations, then the methods of human kindness and rightness will be practiced of themselves.
>
> The former kings were not able to know all. By grasping the One, the myriad things were in order. That which causes people to be unable to hold fast to the One is due to their being stimulated by things.[13]

This passage is highly eclectic. The chapter presents a modified *fajia* approach, revealing such sympathies in criticizing the way of the early sage kings and the methods of appropriate human relationships and rightness (*renyi*), but it acknowledges the appropriateness of those virtues, provided the ruler has cultivated *xingming zhi qing*.

The *wugong* (On Not Getting Personally Involved) chapter makes the point that effective administration is the result of the ruler harmonizing with *xingming zhi qing*.

> Now when facing south, the various depravities would be self-corrected, and all in the empire would return to their essentials (*qing*). The dark haired masses to the last one enjoy their aspirations and securely cultivate their characters (*xing*); none among them were not completed (*cheng*). Hence, if the one who is adept at serving as a ruler respects and submits to the essentials (*qing*) of his character and his natural relations, then the various officials are already well-governed; the dark haired masses are already close; and names and titles are already manifested.[14]

The ruler's cultivation not only sets the exemplary model for the empire to follow, but it also has a transformative influence on both the people and the natural environment. If the ruler is appropriately responding to his own natural desires and the people's desires, then he can set the world in harmony. The ruler's position provides the pivot on which the harmonization of the masses and nature concurs, and of course the ruler's ability to properly manage affairs of state by appointing the proper personnel holds an important position in the LSCQ's political thought.

The *jinting* (Listening with Care) chapter contains the final passage we shall examine on the ruler's use of *xingming zhi qing* as a guideline for proper administration. The *jinting* chapter focuses on the ruler making proper use of counsel, especially in taking proper advice on appointing worthy ones. It has been noted that the ruler must be able to accept remonstrance to rule appropriately.[15] The chapter goes so far as to propose that the cultivated ruler can arrive at the reality of one's character and natural relationships by listening carefully.

> How could Emperor Yao casually appoint Shun in obtaining a worthy one for the empire; how could Shun casually appoint Yu in obtaining a worthy one for the empire? They judged them merely by hearing about them. Hearing about someone can be used to make a judgment; it is a return[16] to the reality of one's character and natural relations. Now, first, a confused one does not know to return to the reality of his character and natural relations, and second he does not know to examine the means by which the Five Emperors and Three Kings consummated their reigns.[17]

The enlightened ruler is aware of the need to have appropriate officials administer the state, and the ruler should also be aware that a worthy one's reputation precedes him. The attentive ruler will recognize the presence of a worthy one by hearing about his reputation first, appointing him accordingly, and maintaining harmonious order in the state.

These passages supplement our understanding of human character (*xing*) as an achievement concept. They also connect the achievement of one's character to the limits of one's correlative relationship to one's natural course (*ming*). The expression *xingming zhi qing* is clearly an important concept in LSCQ political philosophy.

Notes

Chapter 1

1. When I mention a "philosophical consolidation" or a "unified eclectic philosophy," the reader should *not* have the impression that discrete "schools" existed. The different philosophers or masters (*zi* or *tzu*) disputed about the Way (*dao* or *tao*), and Mengzi (Mencius) differentiated his alignment with Kongzi (Confucius) verses Mozi (Mo Tzu), Yang Zhu (Yang Chu), and others. The notion of discreet "schools" was developed by later interpreters, such as the author of chapter 32 of the *Zhuangzi*, and Sima Tan and Sima Qian, the principal authors of the *Shiji*. Certainly the "disputers of the *dao*" had their differences (A. C. Graham, *Disputers of the Tao* (La Salle, Ill.: Open Court Press, 1989). They were not at "war" with each other, as later interpreters have proposed. In the arts of rulership and statesmanship, it is pragmatic to amalgamate various diverse positions. The historians and bibliographers developed the label *jia* (school) to classify the various books. During the Han dynasty, when imperial policy was configured by conflicting philosophical schools, now referred to as the Modernists and the Reformists, there was an anachronistic tendency to read this kind of contention back into ancient history. During the pre-Qin period, either rulers did not take the philosophers seriously (Kongzi is the classic example) or when they did pay attention to academics, they supported a broad spectrum of them, which is seen in the Jixia academy's compilation of the *Guanzi* and Lü Buwei's *Lüshi chunqiu* (LSCQ). Therefore, when expressions such as *daojia*, *fajia*, or Daoism are used, I do not contend, nor should the reader imply, that there was an organized school or systematic philosophy of "Daoism," or so-called "Legalism." Those expressions are convenient labels. "Huanglao" is a handy tag for comparatively similar political teachings of the so-called Yellow Emperor texts, the *Huangdi sijing* and the *Laozi*. The term *Laozhuang* is a convenient designation for the comparatively similar teachings on self-cultivation from Laozi and Zhuangzi. These were not systematic "schools." That notion developed later. For the debate between the Modernists and Reformists during the Han dynasty, see Denis Twitchett and Michael Loewe, eds., *The Cambridge History of China*, vol. 1, *The Ch'in and Han Empires*. (Cambridge: Cambridge University Press, 1986) 104–06, 128, 144, 488–89, concerning the misleading bibliographical classification systems, see 651–52.

2. Qin shihuangdi adopted the symbol of water to show that he had extinguished the Zhou symbol of fire. Derk Bodde discusses this and refutes criticisms against the claim that Qin did not adopt the symbol of water in Twitchett's and Loewe's *The Cambridge History of China*, 77, 96–97. For the significance of this symbol in the Han dynasty, see 119, 208, 729–30, 737. However, as far as I can tell, no one else has drawn

the connection between this passage in the LSCQ and the First Emperor's claim to legitimacy. See the passage to Chapter 3, Note 92, below. Michael Loewe cites evidence that passages from the LSCQ describe a symbol that would enable the possessor to control the empire, but he does not give details. See *Ways to Paradise: The Chinese Quest for Immortality* (Taibei: SMC Publishing, 1994), 74.

3. The *Guanzi* and its composite nature are well known, though the text was usually classified under *fajia*. See the *Guanzi* in the *Sibu beiyao* (Taibei: Chung Hwa Book Co., 1982), and W. Allyn Rickett, *Guan tzu: Political, Economic and Philosophical Essays from Early China: A Study and Translation* (Princeton, N.J.: Princeton University Press, 1985). Scholars may balk at the reference to the *Shizi*. However, we do know from the biographies of Mengzi and Xunzi in the *Shiji* that Shi Jiao's work was well known at that time. Shi Jiao was chief advisor to Shang Yang, but the *Shizi* is not a *fajia* text. The dynastic histories from the *Hanshu* to the *Songshu* list the *Shizi* under the *zajia* (unified eclectic or syncretic) heading, containing twenty volumes (*juan*). Although the *Shizi* was lost by the Southern Song, its fragments were collected and about 10 to 20 percent of the original text was reconstructed in the Qing dynasty by Sun Xingyan and his friends, including Zhang Zongyuan. Wang Jipei edited Sun's edition and wrote a commentary for it. See Shi, Jiao, *Shizi* in *Baibu congshu jicheng*, vol. 7, ed. Yan Yiping, (Taibei: Taiwan Yinshuguan, n.d.). Shui Weisong produced a modern Chinese translation using both Sun's and Wang's editions. See Shi, Jiao, *Xinyi Shizi duben*, Shui Weisong and Chen Manming, eds. (Taibei: Sanmin, 1997). Kung-chuan Hsiao briefiy discusses Shi Jiao, in *A History of Chinese Political Thought*, trans. F. Mote (Princeton, N.J.: Princeton University Press, 1979) 369, 371 and 551.

4. Michael Loewe discusses the preoccupation of time and timing in Han divination and its use for choosing the proper time to undertake activities. See *The Cambridge History of China*, 674, 677, 677, n. 68. *Lüshi chunqiu*'s concern for proper timing was defined by the spirit of the times and in turn provided textual support to maintain that spirit.

5. The terms *Confucian* or *Confucianism*, created by Europeans, have no equivalent expression in Chinese. *Ru* (scholars or Literati, followers of Kongzi) comes close, but that term is usually not used to refer to the so-called "Confucians" of the Song, Ming, and Qing dynasties. For a compelling analysis of the fabrication of "Confucianism," see Lionel M. Jensen, *Manufacturing Confucianism: Chinese Traditions and Universal Civilization* (Durham, N.C., and London: Duke University Press, 1997).

6. The postscript, or *xuyi* chapter, states that the work was completed "in the eighth year of Qin . . ." What year "the eighth year" refers to is still debated. Hu Shi (Hu Shih) and others use King Zheng's enthronement in 246 B.C.E. to propose that "the eighth year" refers to 238 B.C.E. Qian Mu's argument is more convincing. He begins the calculation at 249, the year of Lü Buwei's appointment, thus I follow his date of 241. See Qian Mu, "Lü Buwei zhushukao," appended to the editor's preface to *Lüshi chunqiu jishi deng wushu*, Yang Jialo, ed., (Taibei: Ding Wen Publishing, 1997) no page numbers—hereafter, this text is cited as LSCQ in the notes. Qian Mu's study is discussed by Hsiao, *A History of Chinese Political Thought*, 557, n. 19. Also see Michael Carson and Michael Loewe, "*Lü shih ch'un ch'iu*," in *Early Chinese Texts: A Bibliographical*

Guide, Michael Loewe, ed. (Berkeley: The Society for the Study of Early China, and the Institute of East Asian Studies, 1993).

7. Fung Yu-lan uses the LSCQ to reconstruct the philosophy of Yang Zhu (Yang Chu) and Zuo Yan (Tso Yen) in *A History of Chinese Philosophy*, vol. 1, Derk Bodde, trans. (Princeton, N.J.: Princeton University Press, 1952), 133ff. Kung-chuan Hsiao uses it to explicate Huang-Lao philosophy. See *A History of Chinese Political Thought*, 552ff. Joseph Needham is impressed with the LSCQ's scientific information. See *Science and Civilisation in China*, vol. 2 (Cambridge: Cambridge University Press, 1956), 36, 56. G. E. R. Lloyd is fascinated with its argumentation in *Adversaries and Authorities* (Cambridge: Cambridge University Press, 1996), 191. Michael Loewe cites it for early literary references concerning immortality and divination in *Ways to Paradise: The Chinese Quest for Immortality*, 143, n. 173, and 146, n. 61.

8. In particular, other texts should be analyzed as composite, being composed of many teachings, following A. C. Graham's study of the *Zhuangzi*, for example. I recommend an examination of the role of "proper timing" in other pre-Qin texts.

9. The binome *zhixing* (knowing and acting) appears in the *Zhongyong* and the *Xunzi*. The reciprocal interdependence of knowing and acting appears in the *Zhuangzi*, especially the opening of ch. 6. David L. Hall and Roger T. Ames argue that a reciprocal interdependency of theory and praxis is assumed in the *Analects*. See *Thinking through Confucius* (Albany: State University of New York Press, 1987), 47–55.

10. For compelling discussions of "time" and the "intrinsic quality of time," see John E. Smith, "Time and Qualitative Time," *Review of Metaphysics*, 40 (September, 1986); "Time, Times, and the 'Right Time:' *Chronos* and *Kairos*," *The Monist* 53:1. See also Eliot Deutsch, *Creative Being: The Crafting of Person and World* (Honolulu: University of Hawaii Press, 1992), or *Personhood, Creativity, and Freedom* (Honolulu: University of Hawaii Press, 1982).

11. David L. Hall and Roger T. Ames discuss these problems and offer innovative solutions. See *Anticipating China: Thinking through the Narratives of Chinese and Western Culture* (Albany: State University of New York Press, 1995), and *Thinking from the Han: Self-Truth and Transcendence in Chinese and Western Culture* (Albany: State University of New York Press, 1998).

12. "For the Chinese the real world was dynamic and ultimate, an organism made of an infinity of organisms, a rhythm harmonizing an infinity of lesser rhythms." See Needham, *Science and Civilisation in China*, vol. 2, 292, note d. Needham reserves the idea of an organic worldview for Song neo-Confucianism (see pp. 2, 27); he discusses *Xunzi*, *Zhuangzi*, and *Yijing* as forms of organic philosophy (see pp. 27–28, 51–54, and 291ff).

13. A. C. Graham, "The Background of the Mencian Theory of Human Nature," in *Studies in Chinese Philosophy and Philosophical Literature* (Singapore: Institute of East Asian Philosophies, 1986), 8. Sarah Allan explicates the dynamic root metaphors of Chinese philosophy in *The Way of Water and Sprouts of Virtue* (Albany: State University of New York Press, 1997), 17.

14. The field-focus image from "particle physics" and "field physics" inspired my

original conception of the foci-field model. See my "Three Models of Self-Integration (*tzu te*) in Early China," *Philosophy East and West* 37:4. Hall and Ames challenge Needham's terms *organismic* or *organicism*, proposing a model for a focus-field self. See *Thinking from the Han . . .* (Albany: State University of New York Press, 1998), 35–37, and 39–77. They did not challenge Needham's explication of organic philosophy in the *Zhuangzi* (see Needham, *Science and Civilisation in China*, 51–56. Needham supports the denial of teleology, 55). He rightly shifts the metaphor from a living organism (291–92) to a bureaucratic organism (337–38) to explain the *Yijing* and the development of Song dynasty philosophy. He misses the analogy of organ and office (*guan*) in the LSCQ. Because of the analogy developed in the LSCQ (discussed in Chapter 2) between the organs (*guan*) of the body and the offices (*guan*) of state, and the pre-Qin perspective of the firmament (*tian*) and the earth (*di*) as living creatures, I retain the term *organic* as an abbreviation for the foci-field image of the living world to frame the pre-Qin world picture.

15. See my articles "*Lüshi chunqiu*," in *Routledge Encyclopedia of Philosophy*, E. Craig, ed. (London and New York: Routledge, 1998) and "Lü Buwei," in *Great Thinkers of the Eastern World*, Ian McGreal, ed. (New York: HarperCollins, 1995). See Michael F. Carson's "Introduction" in *A Concordance to Lü-shih ch'un-ch'iu* (Taibei: Chinese Materials Center, 1985), and Michael Carson, and Michael Loewe, "*Lü shih ch'un ch'iu*," in *Early Chinese Texts: A Bibliographical Guide*, Michael Loewe, ed. (Berkeley: The Society for the Study of Early China, and the Institute of East Asian Studies, 1993).

16. Qian Mu, *Xian Qin zhuzi xinian* (Hong Kong: Hong Kong University Press, 1956), 485–89. Guo Moruo, *Shi pipanshu* (Peking: Kexue chubanshe, 1962), 387–460. See also Derk Bodde, *China's First Unifier: A Study in the Ch'in Dynasty As Seen in the Life of Li Ssu* (Hong Kong: Hong Kong University Press, 1967), 1–22. These are discussed at length by John Louton, *The Lü-shi chun-qiu: An Ancient Chinese Political Cosmology* (University of Washington, unpublished diss.), 22ff. See Twitchett and Loewe, eds, *The Cambridge History of China*, vol. 1, 40–43, 95.

17. For a critical appraisal of the traditional claim that the scholars were "buried alive," see Twitchett and Loewe, *The Cambridge History of China*, vol. 1, 95–96.

18. It is interesting to point out that although Lü Buwei (d. 235) was dead long before the unification, he did have some indirect effect on King Zheng's reign, in that he most likely used the LSCQ to educate the young king. Hu Shi proposes that Lü Buwei supported Li Si in his early days in Qin and helped Li Si attain infiuence at the Qin court. See "Du *Lüshi chunqiu*" in *Hu Shi wencun*, vol. 3 (Taibei: Far Eastern Book Co., 1961), 227ff.

19. Hsiao, *A History of Chinese Political Thought*, 558ff.

20. Hu, "Du *Lüshi chunqiu*" in *Hu Shi wencun*, 227ff.

21. Sima Qian, *Shiji xuan*, "Lü Buwei *liezhuan*" (Taibei: Wenyi Publishing Co., 1975). The same translation and classical Chinese text are found in *Selections from the Records of the Historian*, Yang Xianyi, and Gladys Yang, trans. (Peking Foreign Language Press, 1979).

22. *Zhanguoce*, *Qince* 5, 61.

23.The *Shiji* declares that Lü Buwei persuaded Lady Huayang's elder sister, but the *Zhanguoce* states it was her younger brother.

24. Louton discusses Qian Mu's and Guo Moruo's arguments for rejecting the *Shiji* passage, which incriminates Lü as the father of Zheng, the First Emperor to be. See, *The Lü-shi chun-qiu: An Ancient Chinese Political Cosmology*, 22, 33–34, 40 ff. Derk Bodde concurs in *The Cambridge History of China*, vol. 1, 95.

25. In fact, scholars have speculated that Lü may have been responsible for the death of at least the last two Qin kings; Friedrich Hirth cites Hu Anguo's accusation; see his *The Ancient History of China* (New York: Columbia University Press, 1908), 328.

26. See Sima Qian, *Shiji xuan*, "Lü Buwei *liezhuan*," 309, 310.

27. See Sima Qian, *Shiji xuan*, "Lü Buwei *liezhuan*," 309, 310. The reference to the "two-hundred thousand character" length of the LSCQ led to speculation concerning a longer version of the text, but this seems unlikely. The present text has over 100,000 characters, which may have led the historian to exaggerate (many numbers in the *Shiji* are exaggerated), or it is a copier error, mistakenly writing "one" as "two." For incorrect numbers in the *Shiji*, see Bodde's discussion in *The Cambridge History of China*, vol. 1, 98–102.

28. A. Wylie, *Notes on Chinese Literature* (Taibei: Bookcase Shop, 1970, reprint), 157–158. Burton Watson believes the form of the LSCQ conveys a message on the unity of heaven, earth, and man, but the content has ". . . little or no relation to the elaborate formal structure." See Watson, *Early Chinese Literature* (New York: Columbia University Press, 1962), 186–189. H. A. Giles is silent on the LSCQ, *A History of Chinese Literature* (New York: Grove Press, 1928).

29. Derk Bodde rendered *zajia* as "the Miscellaneous School" in translating Fung Yu-lan's *A History of Chinese Philosophy*.

30. Kung-chuan Hsiao attempts to clarify the meaning of *zajia* along similar lines in *A History of Chinese Political Thought*, 551. Part of the problem in attempting to grasp an adequate understanding of the term *zajia* is that three of the books, namely the LSCQ, the *Shizi*, and the *Huainanzi*, listed under that label are philosophical texts representing a unified, eclectic philosophy, while the rest of the texts under the *zajia* label do not contain a unified, eclectic approach, nor are they philosophical texts.

31. John Louton mounts a case against a "simple eclectic" reading, arguing that the LSCQ is eclectic, syncretic and synthetic. See *The Lü-shi chun-qiu: An Ancient Chinese Political Cosmology*, 5, n. 4. I agree that a "simple eclectic" reading does not do justice to the LSCQ. The unified eclectic approach entails the "syncretic and synthetic." Although I apply those terms, I am not partial toward them as descriptors of the LSCQ. "Syncretic" carries the connotation of the unity of the Cretans, who were in confiict but proved to be a united force when under attack. "Synthetic" implies an artificial, chemically produced product. "Synthesis" caries Hegelian and Marxian baggage. Hence I opt for "unified eclectic" or "consolidated and amalgamated philosophy."

32. Yang Jialuo discusses Liu Xiang's description of *zajia* and the LSCQ's incorporation of the other teachings in his preface to Lü Buwei, *Lüshi chunqiu jishi deng wushu* (Taibei: Ding Wen Publishing Co., 1977), the first unnumbered page of text.

33. I gained this insight from a discussion with D. C. Lau in Honolulu in 1982.

34. The LSCQ chapters that constitute the *Liji*'s *yueling* chapter are also found in the *Huainanzi*'s *shize* chapter. Although there are important differences, this material bears some resemblance to the calendar system in the *guanyou* chapter of the *Guanzi*, but the details are different. The *hongfan* chapter of the *Shujing* bears certain similarities in structure and correspondence, but the content is very different from the LSCQ, *Liji*, and *Huainanzi* chapters.

35. With the then-recent death of three Qin kings, it is not too surprising to find material supporting the Mohist idea of frugal funerals in the LSCQ. See the second and third chapters of the Early Winter section "Discipline in Mourning" (*jiesang*) and "Safety in Death" (*ansi*), LSCQ, 386, 394. Jeffrey Riegel analyzes these chapters in his "Do Not Serve the Dead as You Serve the Living: The *Lüshi chunqiu* Treatises on Moderation in Burial," *Early China*, 20: 301–30. Lucky for archaeologists, the First Emperor did not heed these concerns in preparing his own tomb.

36. I noted above that Burton Watson thinks the text lacks structural coherence, and A. Wylie argues that it is contradictory. For the claim that the LSCQ is an encyclopedia, see Wolfgang Bauer's introduction to the reprint of Richard Wilhelm's translation of *Frühling und Herbst des Lü Bu We* (Düsseldorf: Eugen Diederichs Verlag, 1979), and Paul Pelliot's "Review of Richard Wilhelm's *Frühling und Herbst des Lü Bu We*," *T'oung Pao* 27: 68–91 (1930). The LSCQ is an anthology rather than an encyclopedia. See Louton, *The Lü-shi chun-qiu: An Ancient Chinese Political Cosmology*, 5, n. 4.

37. LSCQ, 251–53. In Chapter 2, this passage is discussed at length.

38. The *youshilan* has only seven chapters. Apparently the last chapter of that *lan* is missing, and I believe some of the material from that missing chapter has been appended to the *xuyi* (postscript) at the end of the *shierji*. Bi Yuan notes that an old edition entitles the postscript as *lianxiao* (Incorruptible and Filial); see LSCQ, 478. The postscript abruptly concludes with a story of Zhao Xiangzi (see p. 477). Although some commentators believe that that passage belongs to the previous chapter, it could just as well be a fragment from the missing eighth chapter of the first *lan*, which could have been entitled *lianxiao*.

39. Yin Zhongrong opens his edition of Lü Buwei, *Lüshi chunqiu jiaoshi* (Taibei: Guoli bianyi, 1979), with the *balan*, placing the *shierji* last, after the *lulun*.

40. Watson, *Early Chinese Literature*, 186–89.

41. Wilhelm, trans., *Frühling und Herbst des Lü Bu We*, xviii. See also Eugen Feifel, "Review of *Frühling und Herbst des Lü Bu We*," *Philosophy East and West* 25:1:112–15, and Watson, *Early Chinese Literature*, 186–87. Pre-Qin society was very much concerned with fixing the proper time to engage in activities. Actual pre-Qin almanacs or tables were discovered in the Shuihudi excavation; see Twitchett and Loewe, eds., *The Cambridge History of China*, 677.

42. Xu Fuguan, *Lianghan sixiangshi*, vol. 3 (Taibei: Student Bookstore, 1982), 54ff, 63ff.

43. See my article, "The 'Cosmic Talisman' of Liturgical Taoism: An Analysis of the Structure and Content of the *Ling-pao chen-wen*," *Chinese Culture* 24:3:57–69. Isabelle Robinet notes the "cosmological and calendrical theories derived from Han thought that run throughout Taoism." See her *Taoism: Growth of a Religion*, Phyllis Brooks, trans. (Stanford, Calif: Stanford University Press, 1997), 167. She misses the fact that those theories originally were derived from the LSCQ.

44. For a fuller analysis, see my "On the Myth of Cosmogony in Ancient China," in *Analecta Husserliana* (Boston, Mass.: Kluwer Academic Press, 1995).

45. For instance, Henri Maspero, Wolfram Eberhard, Derk Bodde, and Charles Le Blanc, but this is especially true of Mircea Eliade's student, N. J. Girardot's work, *Myth and Meaning in Early Taoism: The Theme of Chaos (hun-tun)* (Berkeley: University of California Press, 1983). The cosmogonic approach is used in many of the anthologies on ancient mythology. This may have infiuenced Bodde and Maspero to apply this approach in their interpretations of China. In spite of his careful and critical analysis, Loewe is also partly drawn in by Bodde's approach. See Twitchett and Loewe, *The Cambridge History of China*, vol. 1, 657ff. David L. Hall gives an insightful critique of this paradigm in "Logos, Mythos, Chaos: Metaphysics as the Quest for Diversity," in *New Essays in Metaphysics*, Robert Neville, ed. (Albany: State University of New York Press, 1986). David L. Hall and Roger T. Ames have expanded that critique in great detail in *Anticipating China: Thinking Through the Narratives of Chinese and Western Culture*. In chapter 1, they mention the possibility of criticizing Eliade's interpretation of mythology. I offer my appraisal of Eliade below.

46. Frederick W. Mote argues that China is unique in "having no creation myth"; see "The Cosmological Gulf between China and the West," in *Transition and Permanence: Chinese History and Culture*, David C. Buxbaum and F.W. Mote, eds. (Hong Kong: Cathay Press, 1972), 7.

47. Giambattista Vico, *The New Science*, Thomas Goddard Bergin, trans. (Ithaca, N.Y.: Cornell University Press, 1948).

48. Clifford Geertz, "The Uses of Diversity," in *The Tanner Lectures on Human Values*, vol. 7, Sterling M. McMurrin, ed. (Salt Lake City: University of Utah Press, 1986), 253–75.

49. John S. Mbiti, *African Religions and Philosophy* (New York: Anchor Books, 1970), 10.

50. Mote, "The Cosmological Gulf between China and the West," 7.

51. See, for example, Charles Le Blanc, "A Re-examination of the Myth of Huang Ti," *Journal of Chinese Religion* 13–14 (1985–1986): 58–59.

52. Derk Bodde, "Myths of Ancient China," in *Mythologies of the Ancient World*, S.N. Kramer, ed. (New York: Anchor Books, 1961), 369–70.

53. Ibid., 372.

54. Henri Maspero, "Légendes mythologiques dans le *Chou king*," *Journal Asiatique* CCIV:1–100 (1924) cited in Derk Bodde, "Myths of Ancient China," 372–74.

55. For descriptions of Shang culture and divination, see Kwang-chih Chang, *Shang Civilization* (New Haven: Yale University Press, 1980), and *Art, Myth, and Ritual: The Path to Political Authority in Ancient China* (Cambridge, Mass.: Harvard University Press, 1983). Also see Te-k'un Cheng, *New Light on Pre-historic China* (Cambridge: Cambridge University Press, 1966), and *Archaeology in China*, vols. 1–3 (Cambridge: Cambridge University Press, 1959, 1960, 1966); Li, Liu, "Mortuary Ritual and Social Hierarchy in Longshan Culture," *Early China* 21:1–46 (1996); David S. Nivison, *The Ways of Confucianism: Investigations in Chinese Philosophy* (Chicago and La Salle: Open Court Press, 1996), chapter 1.

56. Sarah Allan, "Shang Foundations of Modern Chinese Folk Religion," in *Legend, Lore, and Religion in China*, Sarah Allan and Alvin P. Cohen, eds. (San Francisco: Chinese Materials Center), 3. See also Emily Ahern, *Chinese Ritual and Politics* (Cambridge: Cambridge University Press, 1981), 1.

57. Bernhard Karlgren, "Legends and Cults in Ancient China," *Bulletin of the Museum of Far Eastern Antiquities* 18: 199–365 (1946).

58. Mircea Eliade, *The Myth of the Eternal Return, or Cosmos and History*, Willard Trask, trans. (Princeton, N.J.: Princeton University Press, 1874), 39.

59. Douglas K. Wood, *Men Against Time* (Lawrence: University of Kansas Press, 1982), 50, citing Nikolai Berdyaev, *The Meaning of History* (Cleveland: Living Age Books, 1962), 31.

Chapter 2

1. Parts of this chapter were previously published as "Seasonality in the Achievement of *Hsing* in the *Lü-shih ch'un-ch'iu*," reprinted with permission of the editor of *Asian Culture Quarterly*.

2. "Hence, in commanding the masses in a disordered state, one won't discuss the people's character (*xing*); one won't restore the natural conditions of their lives (*qing*)" (quoted in LSCQ, 899).

3. Tang Junyi, *Zhongguo zhexue yuanlun: Yuanxingpian* (Hong Kong: New Asia Press, 1968), 6; cited in Roger T. Ames, "The Mencian Conception of *Ren Xing*: Does It Mean 'Human Nature'?" in *Chinese Texts and Philosophical Contexts*, H. Rosemont, ed. (La Salle, Ill.: Open Court Press), 152.

4. Ames, "The Mencian Conception of *Ren Xing*," 152.

5. Tang Junyi, "The *T'ien Ming* (Heavenly Ordinance) in Pre-Ch'in China," *Philosophy East and West* 11:4:195.

6. Ibid.

7. Pre-Qin philosophers discuss the correlative relationship between human life,

xing, and nature, *tian*. Mengzi (Mencius) contends that by "understanding character, one knows nature/heaven." See, *Mengzi yinde*, in *Shisanjing yinde* (Taibei: San Min Publishing Co., 1941), 7/A/1.

Although Xunzi draws a sharp distinction between humans and nature, he acknowledges their interrelatedness. In the *tianlun* (Discourse on Nature) chapter, it is the human ability to work with nature that allows people to form a "triad with sky and earth (*tiandi*)." People form a union with nature by employing the natural conditions. Xunzi's practical approach calls on the ruler to employ what is natural to fulfill the human (*Xunzi duben* (Taibei: San Min Publishing Co., 1981), 257, 260.

For the Laozhuang Daoists, nature is amoral and, accordingly, humans are too. Moral codes are thus unnatural and disruptive. Where people become a "companion with *tian*," they are one with the myriad things, co-creating the environment (Zhuangzi, *A Concordance to Chuang Tzu* (Cambridge, Mass.: Harvard Unversity Press, 1956), 16/6/20, and 18/6/74. Roger T. Ames takes a different tact but comes to a similar conclusion "The Relationship between 'Heaven' and 'Humanity'," in Lau and Ames *Yuan Dao: Tracing Dao to Its Source* (New York: Ballantine Books, 1998), 29–36.

8. Ames has a different interpretation. See "The Mencian Conception of *Ren Xing*," 154–55. A. C. Graham, "Reflections and Replies" in *Chinese Texts and Philosophical Contexts*, H. Rosemont, ed. (La Salle, Ill.: Open Court Press), 288.

9. LSCQ, 182.

10. Ibid., 57.

11. A. C. Graham addresses the dynamic connotations of Chinese concepts. See "The Background of the Mencian Theory of Human Nature," 7, 45.

12. Gaozi is noted for defining *xing* in terms of *sheng*. As a naturalist, Gaozi's equation of *xing* and *sheng* removes the normative import of *xing*. *Sheng* has been misunderstood to mean "inborn." *Xing* refers to the natural "developmental process of life" (Graham, Ibid.).

13. D.C. Lau, "Theories of Human Nature in Mencius and Shyuntzy [Xunzi]," *Bulletin of the School of Oriental and African Studies* 15:3 (1953): 541–42.

14. Fu Sinian, *Xingming guxun bianzheng*, in *Fu Sinian quanji*, vol. 2, Kong Decheng, ed. (Taibei: Lianjing Publishing, 1980).

15. Xu Fuguan, *Zhongguo renxinglunshi* (Taizhong: Donghai University Press, 1963). Zhang Dainian *Zhongguo zhexue dagang* (Peking: Chinese Academy of Social Sciences Press, 1982); Donald J. Munro, *Concept of Man in Contemporary China* (Ann Arbor: University of Michigan Press, 1979) and *Images of Human Nature—A Sung Portrait* (Princeton, N.J.: Princeton University Press, 1988).

16. Discussed below, these expressions are found in the *bensheng*, *dangbing*, and *chenglian* chapters, to name a few.

17. This expression is found in the *dangbing*, *chenglian*, and *guidang* chapters.

18. As was mentioned in Chapter 1, note 1, when I use the expressions *daojia*, Huanglao, and Laozhuang, I am not contending that there was an organized school or systematic philosophy of "Daoism." I merely use the expression as a convenient label.

Huanglao is only employed as a label for the comparatively similar political teachings of the so-called Yellow Emperor texts and Laozi, and Laozhuang for the comparatively similar teachings on self-cultivation from Laozi and Zhuangzi. For a study and translation of the Yellow Emperor texts see, Edmund Ryden, *The Yellow Emperor's Four Canons* (Taibei: Guangji Press, 1997), and Leo S. Chang, and Yu Feng, *The Four Political Treatises of the Yellow Emperor* (Honolulu: University of Hawaii Press, 1998).

19. Although the monthly ordinance chapters for the spring address agricultural practices and rituals, nevertheless, the subsequent chapters do not deal with agriculture specifically. They are, however, concerned with the "cultivation" of the ruler. The last four chapters of the *lulun* volume deal extensively with agricultural techniques.

20. Hu Shi, "Du *Lüshi chunqiu*," 234.

21. The *lisilan* (Distinguishing Customs) chapter provides the expression *ai li* (love and benefit), which Hu Shi uses to typify the LSCQ's brand of utilitarianism. The key passages are discussed in Chapter 3. See Hu Shi, "Du *Lüshi chunqiu*," 235, 237, 238, and LSCQ, 868, 889, 902.

22. LSCQ, 67–68.

23. Ibid., 475–76.

24. Zhuangzi, *A Concordance to Chaung Tzu*, 9/4/18; Burton Watson, trans., *The Complete Works of Chuang Tzu* (New York: Columbia University Press, 1962), 56. I modify Watson's translation. *Tian*, in the *Zhuangzi*, means "nature," "the heavens," or "sky." It does not mean "Heaven" in the Literati sense of a moral world. *Tianzi* is the "Son of Heaven" or "emperor."

25. Roger T. Ames, "Is Political Taoism Anarchism?" *Journal of Chinese Philosophy* 10:1 (1983): 27–48.

26. This story also appears in *Zhuangzi*, chapter 28.

27. LSCQ, 97. *Zhuangzi*, 76/28/3, and compare *Laozi*, 13.

28. Ibid., 96. Fung Yu-lan, *A History of Chinese Philosophy*, vol. 1, cites the first part of this passage, p. 138, and Kung-chuan Hsiao, *A History of Chinese Political Thought*, cites the opening sentence, p. 561.

29. Gao You suggests reading *tian* as *xing*, that is, "he endeavors to keep intact human character," LSCQ, 57.

30. Gao You states that the character for "life," *sheng*, should be read as *xing*. This was a common practice in the Han. Following his interpretation, the phrase means "offices were established to keep human character intact." Ibid., 58.

31. Ibid., 57–61.

32. Ibid., 74.

33. See A. C. Graham, "The Background of the Mencian Theory of Human Nature," 59–65, and R.T. Ames, "The Mencian Conception of *Ren Xing*," n. 49. Although I agree with Ames concerning the morphological import of *qing*, I believe that Graham

was heading in that direction, because he opposed the notion of "essences" in pre-Qin philosophy. When I translate *qing* as "the essentials," I mean that something "genuine" is given its interdependent relations, not its underlying, genetic essence. For example, when one says "the essentials of cooking are heat, utensils, and food," one does not describe the genetic or underlying essence. The "essentials" of developing one's character are controlling one's desires and senses.

34. Or the predicate could be rendered as "desire them the same," LSCQ, 104.

35. Ibid., 103–04.

36. Ibid., 216–17.

37. Ibid., 96.

38. Laozi, *Konkordanz zum Lao tzu* (München: E. Schmitt, 1968), 9/16/5, 27/42/2, 38/62/3.

39. "If one is impartial, the common people will be pleased." *Lunyu yinde*, 41/20/1.

40. For the *Shizi*'s discussion of *gongxin*, see the *guang* (Vastness) chapter, and for *wusi*, see the *zhitianxia* (Managing the Empire) chapter in Shi Jiao, *Shizi* in *Baibu congshu jicheng*, vol. 7, or Shi Jiao, *Xinyi Shizi duben*.

41. For the *jingfa* text in the Yellow Emperor documents, see Ryden, *The Yellow Emperor's Four Canons* and Chang and Feng, *The Four Political Treatises of the Yellow Emperor*. Robin D. S. Yates argues that the silk manuscripts are yin-yang texts, not Huanglao. See *Five Lost Classics* (New York: Ballantine Books, 1997).

42. LSCQ, 539, 540.

43. Ibid., 74.

44. Ibid., 143–45, 149. For further discussion of self-integration, see my "Three Models of Self-Integration (*tzu te*) in Early China," 372–90.

45. Tao Hongqing suggests reading *li* (pattern) as *shu* (technique).

46. LSCQ, 476–77.

47. Ibid., 75.

48. Ibid., 76.

49. Ibid., 77. See the Zhuangzi, *A Concordance to Chuang Tzu*, 19/7/2–4; Watson, *The Complete Works of Chuang Tzu*, 92 note 1.

50. See Laozi, *Konkordanz zum Lao tzu*, 34.

51. Ibid., 2/2/4–5, 6/10/6, 31/51/5, 20/34/2.

52. Ibid., 39/59/3.

53. Gao You's commentary recapitulates the above text to explain that the early emperors modeled the greatness of heaven and earth and benefitted the people. He concludes by comparing the meaning of this passage to "the sage is not kind (*ren*), he treats the people like straw dogs." See, *Laozi*, 3/5/2.

54. The story also occurs in the *Zhuangzi* 67/24/51–57; Watson, *The Complete Works of Chuang Tzu*, 269–70. Liezi, *Liezi duben* (Taibei: San Min Publishing Co., 1981), 198. Graham, *The Book of Lieh-tzu*, 126–27, *Guanzi*, chapter 26, *jie*, 5a.

55. See *Laozi*, 74.

56. See Ibid., 68. Here the idea is similar to the *Laozi* concept of *wuwei*. See *Laozi*, 27.

57. LSCQ, 80–81.

58. This phrase could also be interpreted to mean "try to be well dressed."

59. LSCQ, 81.

60. Ibid., 82.

61. The character *sheng* literally means "sound." I render it as "music." It can mean "to be heard of" or "to be famous," so the statement could be translated, "In matters of fame prohibit excess."

62. LSCQ, 82.

63. Ibid., 86–87.

64. Ibid., 607–08.

65. Yao sat in the subservient position; usually the emperor faces South.

66. LSCQ, 631–632.

67. Hsu Wen-ying, *The Ku-ch'in* (Taibei: Central Book Co., 1979), 18.

68. A third-generation Confucian, Shi Shi is supposed to have held that some people are born good, and others are born bad. The early Han saw a rekindling of interest in the debate on *xing* with Dong Zhongshu holding, according to Wang Chong, that people have the beginnings of goodness, and that their *xing* is good, but their feelings are bad. Liu Xiang held that human character was bad, but the feelings were good. Yang Xiong believed that human character is a mixture of good and bad. See Wing-tsit Chan, *A Source Book in Chinese Philosophy* (Princeton: Princeton University Press, 1963), 293–96. I avoid using the term *evil* because of its obvious theological connotations, which are not relevant in Chinese philosophy.

69. This phenomenon is similar to what Wolfred Seller called the "myth of the given." See Munro, *Images of Human Nature—A Sung Portrait*, 9, 151–52.

70. Jacques Gernet, *China and the Christian Impact*, Janet Lloyd, trans. (Cambridge: Cambridge University Press, 1985), 147.

71. K. E. Brashier, "Han Thanatology and the Division of "Souls" *Early China* 21: 125:58.

72. Roger T. Ames develops a similar understanding with regard to the achievement of divinity in pre-Qin religion. See "Religiousness in Classical Confucianism: A Comparative Analysis," *Asian Culture Quarterly* 12:2:7–23. See also David L. Hall and R. T. Ames, *Thinking through Confucius*, 260–61.

73. LSCQ, 896.

74. See my "Three Models of Self-Integration (*tzu te*) in Early China"; Roger T. Ames, "The Common Ground of Self-Cultivation in Classical Taoism and Confucianism," *Tsinghua Journal* (December): 65–97; Allan, *The Way of Water and Sprouts of Virtue*, chs. 1, 3, 5; Hall and Ames, *Thinking from the Han*, 171 ff.

75. Allan, *The Way of Water and Sprouts of Virtue*, 5.

76. LSCQ, 104.

77. Ibid., 904. Gao You's commentary suggests reading *tian* (nature, heaven) as *shen* (behavior or person).

78. Gao You suggests reading "character" (*xing*) as "body" (*ti*).

79. LSCQ, 1079.

80. Ibid., 923–24.

81. Ibid., 104.

82. Ibid., 561.

83. Ibid., 174.

84. Ibid., 529. See my "The *Lü-shih ch'un-ch'iu*'s Proposal of Governing by Filial Piety," *Asian Culture Quarterly* 13:1:43–61. For an analysis of filial piety in pre-Qin *rujia* thought, see Keith N. Knapp, "The *Ru* Reinterpretation of *Xiao*," *Earl China* 20:195–222.

85. Hu Shi, "Du *Lüshi chunqiu*," 233–34; LSCQ, 532.

86. In the context of discussing the meaning of an obscure character in the text, Xu Weiyu mentions his teacher, Mr. Liu's, comment that "among the compilers of LSCQ there were many disciples of Xunzi, and so the two books share similar expressions" (LSCQ, 175).

87. Gao You's note suggests that *zhi* be read as *chi* "to order," or "instruct."

88. The text reads *shi* (affairs), but Zhen Changqi's note suggests following the same passage in the *Huainanzi*, which has *ren* (people) instead of *shi*.

89. LSCQ, 1114.

90. This line is very similar to two other passages that discuss *xing* as "that which is received from nature." See the *chenglian* (On Sincerity and Discipline) chapter: "Being hard and being red are had as their character (*xing*). Character is what is received from nature (*tian*); it is not that one is doing something after making a choice" (LSCQ, 464, and see note 127 below). Also see the *dangbing* (On Mobilizing the Military) chapter: "That there is awesomeness and strength in the people (*min*) is from their character (*xing*). Character is what is received from nature (*tian*). It is not something humans themselves can construct. One who is martial (*wu zhe*) cannot alter it, and a capable artisan cannot change it" (LSCQ, 282–83, and see note 112 below).

91. LSCQ, 209–10.

92. Hu Shi, "Du *Lüshi chunqiu*," 238–39.

93. However, the *Shizi* may have been the original source of this kind of eclecticism. I say "may have been" because the extant text is composed of reconstructed fragments that are believed to be from the fourth to third centuries before the common era. Those fragments clearly advocate an eclectic blend of *mingjia*, *fajia*, *Mojia* and *rujia* philosophy. See especially Shizi's *fen* (On the Allotment of Duties) chapter, Shui Weisong, ed., *Xinyi Shizi duben*, 47 ff, or Wang Jipei's edition of the *Shizi* in *Baibu congshu jicheng*, vol. 7, 10b ff.

94. LSCQ, 889.

95. Ibid., 903–04.

96. Ibid., 168.

97. Ibid., 251–53.

98. This passage could be read as "*yue bu yue*" (music was not music), as Gao You suggests, or it could be read as "*yue bu le*" (the music was not enjoyable). I have incorporated both readings with "enjoyable music."

99. Liu Shifu's note suggests reading *sheng* (life) as *zhu* (ruler). The two characters are similar in form.

100. Bi Yuan's note says that an old edition has *wang* (king) instead of *sheng* (life). Because those two characters are somewhat similar in shape, it could be a copier's error.

101. Though there is no commentarial note here, the text has "life" (*sheng*), but "ruler" (*wang* or *zhu*) makes more sense in this context than it does in the context to the above two notes. So I read *sheng* (life) as "ruler" here.

102. Both Chen Changqi's and Tao Hongqing's notes want to read *xing* as *sheng*.

103. LSCQ, 214–15.

104. Ibid., 182.

105. Gao You's note says that "root," *ben*, should be read as "original nature" *benxing*.

106. LSCQ, 184.

107. Ibid., 278. *The Li Ki*, James Legge trans., 283–84.

108. Ibid., 279–80.

109. See my "On Mobilizing the Military: Arguments for a Just War Theory from the *Lü-shih ch'un-ch'iu*," *Asian Culture Quarterly* 11:4:26–43.

110. LSCQ, 282.

111. Ibid., 282–83.

112. Ibid., 1004. "Human life has come down from long ago; to treat it lightly and lose it, is it not a pity?!"

113. Ibid., 532.

114. The five criteria are: first, be fully authorized by the ruler's court and be victorious in battle; second, apply consistent standards in rewarding and punishing soldiers to promote morale; third, timing is very important, especially not hesitating; fourth, concentrate fully on what to do in battle; and fifth, plan well and know the enemy's weak points. The *Sun Bin bingfa* also counsels going ". . . to war only at the appropriate time." D. C. Lau and R. T. Ames, trans., *Sun Pin The Art of Warfare* (New York: Ballantine Books, 1996), 153.

115. LSCQ, 322–23.

116. For a detailed study of these chapters see Riegel, "Do Not Serve the Dead As You Serve the Living," 301–30.

117. LSCQ, 386–87.

118. Ibid., 411.

119. From this day, *yang* begins to revive and all life with it.

120. LSCQ, 421–22.

121. It appears as though the parallel structure has been broken. Tao Hongqing proposes that based on the subsequent passage (namely, "Hence if you thoroughly know the present, it is possible to know antiquity. If one knows antiquity, it is possible to know the future"), the last phrase here should read: "Likewise the future is to the present just as the present is to antiquity" (LSCQ, 442). Chen Qiyou offers a different interpretation, proposing that it should read: "Likewise the present is to the future just as antiquity is to the present." Lü Buwei, *LSCQ jiaoshi*, Chen Qiyou, ed., (Shanghai: Xuelin Pub. Co. 1984), 606. Because the text does make sense as it stands, I have translated it without incorporating Tao's or Chen's notes.

122. "Backward" and "forward" are literally "up" and "down" (LSCQ, 442–43).

123. The scholar-knights (*shi*) were the leaders of the commoners. The character *shi* looks like the character for "ten" above the character for "one." Thus the interpretation is that a *shi*, scholar-knight, is "the best"; that is a "ten" or the "first" among people. The *shi* held such positions as knight, scholar, foreman, butler, and so on; the *shi* were at the bottom of the feudal administration. The Son of Heaven (*tianzi*) was assisted by the feudal lords (*zhuhou*), who in turn were ministered to by the officials (*daifu*). The *shi* were the outstanding commoners who served the officials. When the feudal system began to break down during the Warring States period (403–221 B.C.E.), the *shi* were able to gain social mobility through loyal service by displaying military prowess or intellectual ability. By the time the LSCQ was written, it was not unheard of for a commoner, for instance Lü Buwei, to become a prime minister.

124. It must be possible for a ruler or an emperor to employ these able knights sometimes. Gao You's commentary to this line interprets it to mean that in some instances rulers (e.g., Yao, Zhou, and Han Gao Zi) cannot obtain the worthy officials they need.

125. LSCQ, 455–56.

126. Ibid., 464.

127. LSCQ's version of the story is paraphrased in the following:

> Bo Yi and Shu Qi left Guchu to serve King Wen, but they arrived after his death. So they observed King Wu's behavior. After observing him swear two blood oath contracts which helped strengthen the tyrant's position, they related the following before going off to starve at the foot of Mt. Shou Yang: "Ah! How strange it is! This is not what we call the Way. In the past when Shennongshi possessed the empire, he performed timely prayers with the utmost reverence, but he did not pray for good fortune. In his relations with others he demanded dedication and trustworthiness in fulfilling proper governing, but he did not seek more from them." (LSCQ, 464–66)

128. LSCQ, 467.

129. I follow Wang Niansun's reading of this passage; he supports this interpretation by citing similar passages in the *xiaxian*, *zhidu*, and *youdu* chapters of the LSCQ, and passages in the *Yanzi chunqiu* and the *Hanfeizi*'s *gufen* chapter.

130. LSCQ, 468–69.

Chapter 3

1. Gao You suggests reading *tian* as *xing*.

2. Gao You states that the character *sheng* (life) should be read as *xing* (character). This was a common Han practice.

3. LSCQ, 57–58, cited in Chapter 2.

4. Ibid., 96; cited above in Chapter 2.

5. Ibid., 162–63.

6. Derk Bodde and Clarence Morris present their hypothesis in the first chapter of *Law in Imperial China* (Philadelphia: University of Pennsylvania Press, 1967).

7. Fung Yu-lan took this approach, and others still interpret "the emperor on high" (*shangdi*) as "God." See his *History of Chinese Philosophy*, vol. 1, and see Wing-tsit Chan, *A Source Book in Chinese Philosophy*, chapter 1. For counter-arguments, see Sarah Allan, "Shang Foundations of Modern Chinese Folk Religion" and *The Way of Water and Sprouts of Virtue*; also see Hall and Ames, *Anticipating China*.

8. For a discussion of the theory of spontaneous order in Hume, see Ronald Hamowy, *The Scottish Enlightenment and the Theory of Spontaneous Order* (Carbondale: Southern Illinois University Press, 1987), 10–13. Hamowy does mention briefly the similarity to some pre-Qin philosophies, especially Zhuangzi.

9. Neither Hooker, Hobbes, Locke, or Rousseau argue for the historical event of the social contract. Commenting on Hooker, Michael Curtis states that the contract was not historical. See *The Great Political Theories*, vol. 1 (New York: Avon Books,1961),

324. Toward the end of chapter 13, Part I of the *Leviathan*, Hobbes asserts that the state of nature was not a historical fact. John Locke basically agrees in *The Second Treatise of Government*, (Indianapolis: Bobbs-Merrill Co., 1952), chapter 2, section 14. Rousseau notes that the social compact may "never (have) been formally set forth," *The Social Contract, and Discourse on the Origin of Inequality* (New York: Pocket Books, 1967), book 1, chapter 6.

10. Rawls blends Kantian contract theory with Utilitarian organic theory. Kant himself blends contract theory with his naturalistic and organic ontology. Following Hooker and Hobbes, Locke's contractarianism blends with natural rights and natural law. Rousseau's compact resides amid Romantic naturalism and natural rights.

11. *Analects*, 1/2, 2/21. See my article "The *Lu-shih ch'un-ch'iu*'s Proposal of Governing by Filial Piety," 43–62.

12. Leonard Shih-lien Hsü, *The Political Philosophy of Confucianism* (New York: E. P. Dutton & Co., 1932), 30.

13. Roger T. Ames, *The Art of Rulership* (Honolulu: University of Hawaii Press, 1983), 6. Kang Youwei advocated that Confucius was a progressive thinker.

14. Hsü, *The Political Philosophy of Confucianism*, 30. See Richard Wilhelm and Cary F. Baynes, trans., *The I ching* (Princeton, N.J.: Princeton University Press), 328. Wilhelm blurs the organic model by quoting a passage from the *Bohutong*, which is instrumentalist, 329.

15. *Zhouyi benyi*, "*xizizhuan*," section 3, p. 19b; see Wilhelm and Baynes, *The I ching*, 334–35.

16. Allan, *The Way of Water and Sprouts of Virtue*, chapter 1; Sellmann, "Three Models of Self-Integration (*tzu te*) in Early China," 372–75; Ames, "The Common Ground of Self-Cultivation," 65–97, and Hall and Ames, *Thinking from the Han* (Albany: State University of New York Press, 1987), 171 ff.

17. Hu Shi, "Du *Lüshi chunqiu*," 228–29. He briefly sketches this idea. I propose that as the legend of the primordial man came into the central plains of China either from South China, or possibly from India, then the myth of Ban Gu, the cosmic man, developed. Ban Gu is currently worshiped at popular Daoist-type temples.

18. A. C. Graham argues that chapter 80 is not Daoist but Agriculturalist; see "The *Nung-Chia* 'School of the Tillers' and the Origin of Peasant Utopianism in China," *Bulletin of the School of Oriental and African Studies*, 42:1:66–100. I propose a different approach below.

19. Ames, "Is Political Taoism Anarchism?," 37, and *The Art of Rulership*, 7.

20. See Watson, *The Complete Works of Chuang Tzu*. A world government is implied at the origins, p. 172, and a sage ruler is implied, 106–12. The text paraphrases instrumentalist material, p. 327, and even anarchy, p. 117. These passages occur beyond the inner chapters ascribed to Zhuangzi.

21. Hall and Ames criticize Rubin in "The Common Ground of Self-Cultivation in Classical Taoism and Confucianism," 93–94, and in *Thinking from the Han*, 174.

22. Ames concludes a discussion of the Laozhuang conception of history with this proposal. "Although this discussion has been based on the antique utopia depicted in the *Lao Tzu* 80, the notion of historical decline is one of the most popular and consistent themes in this kind of early Taoist literature" (*The Art of Rulership*, 9).

23. Jan Yün-hua, "Tao, Principle, and Law: The Three Key Concepts in the Yellow Emperor Taoism," (*Journal of Chinese Philosophy* 7:3:215. See also Ryden, *The Yellow Emperor's Four Canons*, chapter 9; Chang and Feng, *The Four Political Treatises of the Yellow Emperor*, 100.

24. Jan Yün-hua, "Tao, Principle, and Law,", 215.

25. Ibid., 218–19.

26. Hou Ji is mentioned five times in the LSCQ; see pp. 557 (2); 752, 1162, 1167.

27. LSCQ, 1160, 1162. This position contrasts with the *xiaoxinglan* proposal that filial piety is the root of instruction. See my "The *Lü-shih ch'un-ch'iu*'s Proposal of Governing by Filial Piety," 44, note 5.

28. J. J. L. Duyvendak, trans., *The Book of Lord Shang* (Chicago: University of Chicago Press, 1963), 57.

29. Scholars disagree on the significance of iron in Zhou culture. See Twitchett and Loewe, eds., *Cambridge History of China*, vol. 1. Derk Bodde denies its impact on weaponry (p. 47); while Nishijima Sado stresses its innovation in agriculture (p. 546).

30. Hsiao, *A History of Chinese Political Thought*, 235.

31. The subject is missing in chapters 1 and 2. In a parallel passage in chapter 3, *tian* is the subject. Y. P. Mei argues for inserting "heaven," noting that some argue for a democratic origin. See *The Works of Motze*, 112.

32. Y. P. Mei, trans., *The Works of Motze* (Taibei: Confucius Publishing Co., 1980), 110–14, and 118–22, and 142–44. This book also contains the Chinese text. F. Mote apparently follows Y. P. Mei's translation in Hsiao, *A History of Chinese Political Thought*, 235–36. I modify both translations, explicating the meaning of *yi* as "standards of rightness."

33. Hsiao, *A History of Chinese Political Thought*, 237. There is a textual problem with this view, because the *Mozi* does not say "to issue laws," but rather it says "to issue *zhengli* (the political leader of a village). Either Hsiao misquoted the text, or F. Mote overtranslated it.

34. Mei, *The Works of Motze*, 112, 116.

35. LSCQ, 162, 211, 308, 606, 664, and 787.

36. Even Han Fei acknowledges that the early kings established laws, and in some contexts, he praises this. See Burton Watson, trans., *The Basic Writings of Mo Tzu, Hsün Tzu, and Han Fei Tzu* (New York: Columbia University Press, 1967), 26.

37. "Hsün Tzu [Xunzi] believed that the state existed because man was a social animal who could not survive without societal institutions." See Henry Rosemont, Jr.,

ed., "State and Society in the *Hsün Tzu*: A Philosophical Commentary," *Monumenta Serica* 29:44.

38. *Xunzi duben*, 159. See a similar passage in the *wangzhi* chapter, p. 141; see also Watson, *The Basic Writings* . . . , 46.

39. Xunzi, *Xunzi duben*, 144; Watson, *The Basic Writings* . . . , 44.

40. Xunzi, *Xunzi duben*, 143; Watson, *The Basic Writings* . . . , 42–43.

41. Xunzi, *Xunzi duben*, 291; Watson, *The Basic Writings* . . . , 106.

42. Xunzi, *Xunzi duben*, 293; Watson, *The Basic Writings* . . . , 110.

43. *Zhanguoce*, chapter 3, p. 18. See also James I. Crump, (trans), *Chan kuo ts'e* (London: Oxford University Press), 56. Sun Bin, *Sun Bin bingfa jiaoli*, Zhong Zhenze, ed., (Peking: Zhonghua, 1984) chapter 2; the names differ there. Lau and Ames render the *Sun Bin* passage differently. See *Sun Pin, The Art of Warfare*, 128, 130.

44. LSCQ, 282–83. See also my article "On Mobilizing the Military," 28–30, 41.

45. LSCQ, 283–84. Actually, according to the legends, Chi You is supposed to have invented cast molding; in that sense, he was the first to make metal weapons.

46. Ibid., 284.

47. *Guanzi*, *Sibu beiyao*, section 11, chapter 31, p. 1a–1b. See also Rickett, *Guan tzu: Political, Economic and Philosophical Essays from Early China*, 412–13. This passage is cited by Hsiao, *A History of Chinese Political Thought*, 335–36.

48. Citing the *Guanzi*, Hsiao, Ibid., 336–37.

49. Hsiao, Ibid., 37.

50. Duyvendak, *The Book of Lord Shang*, 235–37. Hsiao, Ibid., 391–92.

51. Ames proposes that the Legalist idea of history is not evolutionary because it has no sense of progress. See his *The Art of Rulership*, 13.

52. *Hanfeizi*, Shi Zhao, ed., Burton Watson, trans., (Taibei: Confucius Publishing Co., 1979), 126, 127, contains the Chinese and English. See also Watson, *The Basic Writings*, 97; Hsiao, Ibid., 390.

53. *Hanfeizi*, 124, 125; B. Watson, *The Basic Writings of Han Fei Tzu*, 98.

54. *Hanfeizi*, 132, 133.

55. Ibid., 130, 131.

56. Ames, *The Art of Rulership*, 214–15, n. 35.

57. LSCQ, 923–24; partly cited above in Chapter 2.

58. Ibid., 925.

59. Bodde and Morris, *Law in Imperial China*, chapter 1.

60. LSCQ, 474. "LSCQ's Philosophy of History" and "A Justification of the Origin

and Function of the State" are reprinted from my article "The Origin and Role of the State According to the *Lüshi chunqiu*," *Journal of Asian Philosophy*, 9:3:193–218, with the permission of the publisher.

61. LSCQ, 474–75.

62. Ibid., 476.

63. Ibid., 511, and the first phrase is repeated in the LSCQ, 680.

64. Ibid., 617. The passage literally says "they all perished." In fact Qi, and Chu, called Jing, still existed, while Wu and Yue had perished.

65. Hsiao, *A History of Chinese Political Thought*, 568.

66. LSCQ, 808.

67. Ibid., 888.

68. Ibid., 782.

69. Ibid., 283.

70. Ibid., 179.

71. Ibid., 576, 931, 963, 1042.

72. Ibid., 576, 931.

73. Ibid., 352–53, 556, 568, 576, 607, 865, 1095, 1146.

74. Ibid., 556, 568, 1136.

75. Ibid., 568, 593–94. Michael F. Carson, *A Concordance to Lü-shih ch'un-ch'iu*, 603 ff.

76. Ibid., 677.

77. Ibid., 911.

78. Ibid., 971.

79. Ibid., 679.

80. Ibid., 924.

81. Ibid., 196–97.

82. Hsiao, *A History of Chinese Political Thought*, 568–69.

83. Modifying F. Mote's translation in Hsiao, Ibid., 568–69, LSCQ, 568–69. Concerning the interpretation of the title, *changgong*, I follow Chen Qiyou, who interprets the character *gong* (attack) as *zhi* (to order). He rejects Sun Qiangming's and Xu Weiyu's interpretation of *gong* (attack) as *gong* (achievement). See Chen Qiyou, ed., Lü Buwei, *LSCQ jiaoshi*, 793.

84. Hsiao, Ibid., 569.

85. Correlated with almost everything in the universe, the five phases, sometimes called the five elements or five agents, are: wood, fire, metal, water, and earth.

86. A. C. Graham proposes that the LSCQ is basically a *yinyangwuxing* text. I gleaned this insight from a personal discussion with him in Honolulu in 1989.

87. The *yingtong* chapter is considered by some to be the second chapter of the LSCQ. Because the *Shiji* lists the *balan* first and the *shierji* last in describing the LSCQ, Yin Zhongrong, ed., *LSCQ jiaoshi*, opens his edition of the LSCQ with the *youshilan*.

88. A. C. Graham, *Yin-Yang and the Nature of Correlative Thinking*, (Singapore: Institute of East Asian Philosophies, 1986), 80–81. Graham apparently follows Wilhelm, ending the quote after the first statement "The energy of the earth is dominant."

89. The commentary by Yu Yue proposes that these phrases are a later interpolation.

90. The commentaries propose that this line may be an interpolation.

91. Following Xu Weiyu's suggestion to read *gu* (solid) as *tong* (same).

92. LSCQ, 491–93.

93. Ibid., 496–97.

94. Kung-chuan Hsiao, *A History of Chinese Political Thought*, 568.

95. Hu Shi, "Du *Lüshi chunqiu*," 234.

96. Gao You interprets this line to mean that winter is cold and short (of daylight); summer is hot and long (of daylight); spring is mild (lit. soft); autumn is severe (lit. hard).

97. Graham cites most of this passage as an early example of yin-yang evolution. See *Yin-Yang and the Nature of Correlative Thinking*, 67.

98. I follow Xu Weiyu, reading *shang* (above) as *zheng* (attunement).

99. The original contains a rhyme, so I indent that part (LSCQ, 206–08).

100. This line is similar to two other passages; see LSCQ, 464, 282–83 discussed above in Chapter 2.

101. LSCQ, 209–10, cited above in Chapter 2.

102. Hu Shi, "Du *Lüshi chunqiu*," 238–39; cited above in Chapter 2.

103. Hsiao, *A History of Chinese Political Thought*, 231–32.

104. Ames, *The Art of Rulership*, 155.

105. *Laozi*, 10/19/1.

106. LSCQ, 186. The *Shizi* claims that rightness necessarily entails benefit. See Shi Jiao, *Xinyi Shizi duben*, (Taibei: Sanmin, 1997), fragment 87, p. 240.

107. LSCQ, 1007. I follow Gao You's note reading *bian* (convenient) as *li* (benefit) and *xing* (operate, practice) as *wei* (do, done).

108. Ibid.

109. Ibid., 1008. I follow Gao You's note interpolating *li* (benefit).

110. Ibid., 1008.

111. Ibid., 1009.

112. Ibid., 1011.

113. Ibid., 1013.

114. Ibid., 868, cited above Chapter 2.

115. Ibid., 896.

116. Ibid., 372–73.

117. Following Xu Weiyu's commentary, literally the text reads "rooted in rightness (*yi*), not in (selfish) love (*ben yu yi, bu yu ai*)." Based on the following line, and passages in the *lisi*, p. 686, *yongmin*, p. 893, and the *shiwei*, p. 896, chapters that discuss the importance of *aili*, Xu Weiyu suggests reading this line as *ben yu li, ben yu ai*.

118. LSCQ, 504–05.

119. Ibid., 646.

120. Ibid., 893.

121. I translate these lines in reverse order. A literal translation would be: "If he (the ruler) complies with *yi* but is insufficient to (have others) die (for him), or uses reward and punishment but is inadequate to (determine whether the people will) leave or stay, then as for a case such as this, one who is able to employ the masses, in the past and the present, never has there been one."

122. LSCQ, 887.

123. Ibid., 888.

124. The passage is obscure. Apparently it means that when the king is trustworthy, then those who make insincere promises will end up keeping them and being rewarded—the ruler's honesty will become contagious. Chen Qiyou proposes that "to reward" (*shang*) should be read as its cognate and synonym, "to indemnify, to fulfill a promise" (*chang*). He takes the line to mean: "If honesty is setup, then insincere words can be fulfilled or compensated for" (*LSCQ jiaoshi*, p. 1304, note 4). Chang Shuangdi et al. propose reading "reward" (*shang*) as "to distinguish, to judge" (*jianbie*)—"If honesty is setup, then insincere words can be distinguished"—(*LSCQ shizhu*, p. 691, note 4, p. 693). These seem highly speculative.

125. LSCQ, 908.

126. Ibid., 889.

127. Ibid., 891. I follow Bi Yuan's suggestion and interpolate an additional *bu*, making a double negative. As it stands the text reads "cannot examine this root."

128. The title *yongzhong* (Employing the Multitude) is given in one edition as *shanxue* (adept at study), which are the first two characters of the chapter.

129. LSCQ, 195.

130. Ibid., 196–97; cited above.

131. Ibid., 197–198.

132. Ibid., 888.

133. Ibid., 888.

134. Ibid., 888–89.

135. Ibid., 889; cited in Chapter 2.

136. Ibid., 894.

137. Ibid., 894.

138. Tao Hongqing argues that this line was miscopied even before Gao You's note; Tao reads it as a paraphrase of a *Zhoushu* passage: "If it is not like this, then he cannot possess them."

139. LSCQ, 894–95. Literally, the statement says, "from this (they) were produced," but I follow Gao You's note, which interpolates "enemies."

140. Ibid., 897.

141. Ibid., 503.

142 LSCQ, 902.

143. Ibid., 906.

144. Ibid., 903–04; cited in Chapter 2.

145. Ibid., 677.

146. Ibid., 1133.

147. Ibid., 1133–34.

148. Ibid., 1134.

149. Ibid., 1134–35.

150. Ibid., 1085–86.

151. In another sense, the LSCQ is somewhat like the composite character of the *Book of Genesis* in the *Old Testament* in its ability to create a new orthodoxy out of a diversity of older ideas.

Chapter 4

1. LSCQ, 56.

2. Loewe, *Ways to Paradise*, 1–2. See also Twitchett and Loewe (ed.s), *The Cambridge History of China*, vol. 1, 683ff.

3. LSCQ, 1188–89.

4. Hsiao, *A History of Chinese Political Thought*, 568–69.

5. LSCQ, 569.

6. John S. Major argues that in some cosmological contexts *xing* (conventionally rendered as "punishments") must be interpreted as "recision," and *de* (conventionally "rewards") should be "accretion." See, "The Meaning of *Hsing-te*," in *Chinese Ideas about Nature and Society: Studies in Honour of Derk Bodde*, (Hong Kong: Hong Kong University Press, 1987), 286.

7. LSCQ, 908–09.

8. Ibid., 1172, 1173–74.

9. This passage is a paraphrase of the *Laozi*, chapters 1, 25.

10. Gao You suggests reading *tian* as *shen* (body, himself), that is, "he will fulfill himself."

11. LSCQ, 210–11.

12. Ibid., 560–61. A. C. Graham commented on this passage, pointing out that the expression "something caused then" (*hou shi*) also occurs in the *Zhuangzi* and the *Guanzi*'s *baixin* chapter.

13. LSCQ, 151.

14. Ibid., 744.

15. Ibid., 367.

16. *Zhuangzi*, 15/6/12. Watson, *The Complete Works of Chuang Tzu*, translates this passage as "he who looks for the right time is not a worthy man," 78.

17. *Laozi*, 4/8/2–3.

18. LSCQ, 77.

19. Ibid., 119.

20. Ibid., 791.

21. Ibid., 816.

22. Ibid., 503.

23. According to Xu Weiyu's note, one edition titles this chapter *benzhi* (Wisdom As Basic) and another renders it as *buyu* (Not Meeting).

24. This story also appears at the opening of the *shanmu* (Mountain Tree) chapter of the *Zhuangzi*, 51/20/1–9.

25. Following the *Zhuangzi* version, I have taken the expression *zhigong* ("the duke of" or "the gentleman of") to mean "the host."

26. Again, I follow the *Zhuangzi* passage.

27. LSCQ, 594–96.

28. This is the conclusion given in the *Zhuangzi*; the LSCQ passage ends abruptly.

29. LSCQ, 502. This passage is the conclusion to a discussion between Yan Hui and Kongzi found in *Zhuangzi* 49/19/26, and in the *Liezi duben*, 85.

30. LSCQ, 792.

31. Ibid., 683–85. See *Zhuangzi*, 78/28/31–35; A. C. Graham, *The Book of Lieh Tzu* (London: John Murray, 1960), 162, and Liu Xiang, *Xinxu jinzhu jinyi*, Lu Yuanjun, ed. (Taibei: Taiwan Commercial Press), 238–39. The *Xinxu* version varies the most, interpolating part of the LSCQ's comment into Liezi's closing words.

32. LSCQ, 685–686.

33. Gao You suggests reading "superior and inferior" (*shangxia*) as "ruler and minister."

34. The "vital essence and life force (*jing qi*)" might be interpreted as one concept, e.g. "the quintessential energy." A. C. Graham suggested translating this line as "The quintessential energy once rises and once falls, going round and round, without halting or pausing anywhere."

35. The line of thought here appears to be that one's *fen* (lot in life, or one's externally given and internally acquired designation) gives one *zhi* (duties or dispositions) that limit one's realm of action. The *fen* chapter in the *Shizi* also links *fen* and *zhi*. See Shi, *Xinyi Shizi duben*, 48.

36. This line is obscure; literally, it says "not able to mutually make" (*bu neng xiang wei*). Gao You's note reads it as *bu neng xiang jian*, "not able to mutually unite." A. C. Graham translates it as: "they are not able to do each other's job."

37. LSCQ, 158–59.

38. Gao You interprets *jing* to mean "the light of the sun and moon." Both Sun Qiangming and Yang Shuda cite the *Shuowen* to argue that *jing* means *xing*, "stars," or "star light." A. C. Graham translated it as "The quintessence proceeding through the four seasons."

39. I am tempted to interpret *xing* (operate) as *qi*, given the above *jing qi* usage, and the following passage', "one up, one down," implies that the operations of both *jing* and *qi* are being discussed, not just the operation of *jing*.

40. "Stored" (*cang*) is interpreted by Gao You as *jian*, "retire, lay in hiding, store." The idea is that the seed and root are stored in the earth or granary, awaiting their return to the soil.

41. LSCQ, 159–60.

42. Ibid., 540. See the discussion in Chapter 2.

43. Ames, *The Art of Rulership*, 56–57, 59, 142, 146–48, 151, 176, 181, 188–89, 235 note 9.

44. LSCQ, 1086.

45. Ibid., 651.

46. Chan, *A Source Book in Chinese Philosophy*, 254. Note "the Yaos" refers to the sage rulers.

47. LSCQ, 330.

48. *Lunyu yinde* (3/2/14). Roger T. Ames and Henry Rosemont Jr. render this passage: "Reviewing the old as a means of realizing the new—such a person can be considered a teacher." See *The Analects of Confucius: A Philosophical Translation* (New York: Ballantine Books, 1998), 78.

49. René Dubos, *The Torch of Life* (New York: Pocket Books, 1998), 50.

50. Hu Shi, "Du *Lüshi chunqiu*," 251–52.

51. Ibid., 253, 254.

52. Duyvendak, *The Book of Lord Shang*, 170, 173, 274, respectively.

53. H. G. Creel notes that this passage is more like *The Book of Lord Shang*, and it is found in the *zhiguo* chapter of the *Guanzi*. He points out that its style and content are unlike Shen Buhai's other fragments. See *Shen Pu-Hai* (Chicago: University of Chicago Press, 1974), fragment 12, pp. 361–62, notes 1–3.

54. Ibid., 361–62.

55. Ames, *The Art of Rulership*, 13.

56. The phrase "cannot follow the standards of the early kings" is a distinctly *fajia* motto.

57. LSCQ, 664.

58. Ibid., 665–66.

59. Ibid., 667–68.

60. Ibid., 670.

61. Ibid., 665.

62. Ibid., 668.

63. The concept *yin* ("according with the circumstances or requirements of a situation") was a major contribution of Shen Dao. See P. M. Thompson, *The Shen Tao Fragments* (Oxford: Oxford University Press, 1979). This concept is used extensively in other chapters of the LSCQ. For example, the *guiyin* (Venerating Being in Accord with Situational Factors) chapter makes extensive use of the concept *yin*.

64. The expression "worthy ruler" might seem out of context in a *fajia* document, but here "worthy" should not be understood in the Confucian or Mohist sense as a "virtuous person" but rather as a "versatile person."

65. The commentary says that the number should be seventy-two sage rulers; also see the *Hanfeizi*.

66. LSCQ, 669. The emphasis on proper timing (*shi*) and situational factors (*shi*) is a basic concern of both the *fajia* and *bingjia* writers. These were especially put into practice by Li Si in abolishing feudalism and burning the books. Hu Shi notes that the last line here is paraphrased in Li's memorial on burning the books. See Hu, "Du *Lüshi chunqiu*," 254.

67. LSCQ, 586. A shorter draft of "timely encounters" and "priority on timing" is reprinted from my article "The *Lüshi chunqiu* on the Ruler's Use of Proper Timing," *Asian Culture Quarterly*, 27:1:59–71, with permission of the editor.

68. I follow Tao Hongqing, who argues against omitting the character *shi*, "time," as Bi Yuan and Chen Changqi suggest. If one prefers to omit *shi*, then the timely element in a proper encounter is still present in the character *dai* (to wait).

69. LSCQ, 584.

70. Following Wang Niansun's commentary, I place the consequent clause after the conjunctive "or" clause. In the text it comes before the "or" clause.

71. LSCQ, 592–93.

72. Ibid., 593.

73. Ibid., 585–86.

74. Ibid., 586.

75. Ibid., 588.

76. Ibid., 588–90.

77. Ibid., 591.

78.Gao You's commentary suggests reading *zhi* (intention) as *de* (virtue).

79. LSCQ, 593.

80. The commentary cites an old edition that titles this chapter *xushi* "Depending on Timeliness," which sounds like a more appropriate title given the many phrases that convey that idea.

81. LSCQ, 552.

82. Ibid., 552.

83. Ibid., 553.

84. Ibid., 553–56.

85. Ibid., 556.

86. Chung-ying Cheng, "On Timeliness (*shih-chung*) in the Analects and the *I ching* . . ." (unpublished manuscript, August 1980).

87. The sage always takes action at the right time. Compare the story of the fool who dies trying to escape his shadow and foot prints in the *Zhuangzi*, chapter 31.

88. LSCQ, 556–57. This passage resounds the *changgong* chapter's wording.

89. Fung, *A History of Chinese Philosophy*, vol. 1, 371, 372, 391.

90. D.C. Lau, *Mencius* (Middlesex, England: Penguin Books, 1970), 79.

91. Zhuangzi, *A Concordance to Chuang Tzu*; 80/28/84. Watson, *The Complete Works of Chuang Tzu*, 322.

92. *Lunyu yinde*, 8/13, modifying the translation in both D. C. Lau, trans., *The Analects (Lun Yü)* (Middlesex, England: Penguin Books, 1979), 94, and Ames and Rosemont, *The Analects of Confucius*, 123.

93. The idea here is that seasonality or time cannot be controlled by humans, but people can avail themselves of it.

94. LSCQ, 557–58.

95. The stories behind these lines tell us that the oppressed people under these tyrants employed the confusion of a mob trying to round up a mad dog and a stray ox to overthrow their rulers.

96. LSCQ, 558–59.

97. Ibid., 559.

98. Ibid., 559.

99. Ibid., 559–60. I follow Wang Niansun's commentary, which proposes that the final character *zhi* ("this") is a mistake and should be *shi* (time). Otherwise, the sentence would read: "Completing affairs lies in according with this." The cognate relation between *shi* and *zhi* is well known.

100. *Zhongyong*, in *Sishu guangjie*, Chen Jizheng, ed. (Tainan: Zonghe publishers, 1981), 46. Most translations render *shi* as an adverbial, temporal particle "whenever" or "often," so that the last sentence reads "Whenever he employs them, actions will be right."

101. Wilhelm and Baynes, *The I ching*, 359.

102. "The situation represented by the hexagram as a whole is called the time. This term comprises several entirely different meanings, according to the character of the various hexagrams." Wilhelm/Baynes, *The I ching*, 49.

103. *Zhouyi yinde*. in *Shisanjing yinde*, Nie Chongqi, ed. (Taibei: Sanmin Publishing Co., 1941), *Yijing*, 2/1/*yan*, and 3/1/*yan*; Wilhelm and Baynes, *The I ching*, 381.

104. *Zhouyi yinde*. 5 and 4 and *tuan*; Wilhelm and Baynes, *The I ching*, 406.

Chapter 5

1. Hans-Georg Gadamer, *Philosophical Hermeneutics*, David E. Linge, trans. and ed. (Berkeley: University of California Press, 1977), 9.

2. See, Giambattista Vico, *The New Science*.

3. Paul Ricoeur, *Time and Narrative*. 3 vols. (Chicago: University of Chicago Press, 1984). Helga Nowotny explicates the significance of "proper time" (Eigenzeit) in European philosophy. See *Time: The Modern and Post-modern Experience*, Neville Place, trans. (Cambridge, U.K.: Polity Press, 1984).

4. Robert S. Brumbaugh, *Unreality and Time* (Albany: State University of New York Press, 1984), 9.

5. Ibid., 11–13.

6. Aron Gurwitsch, *The Field of Consciousness* (Pittsburgh: Duquesne University Press, 1964), 3 and 6.

7. Ibid., 347.

8. Charles M. Sherover, *The Human Experience of Time* . . . (New York: New York Press, 1975), 501–02.

9. Gurwitsch, *The Field of Consciousness*, 387, citing Edmund Husserl's *Erfahrung und Urteil*, 191.

10. For a discussion of timelessness, see Lawrence W. Fagg, *Two Faces of Time* (Wheaton, Ill.: Theosophical Publishing House, 1985), 144 ff.

11. Wood, *Men against Time*, 20. Wood cites Hayden White, "The Burden of History," in *Tropics of Discourse* (Baltimore: Johns Hopkins University Press, 1978), 27–50.

12. Fagg, *Two Faces of Time*, 31.

13. Ibid., 21.

14. W. H. Newton-Smith argues convincingly through mathematical formula that this is not a paradox, *The Structure of Time* (London: Routledge & Kegan Paul, 1978), 187–195.

15. Fagg, *Two Faces of Time*, 21.

16. L.R.B. Elton and H. Messel, *Time and Man* (Oxford: Pergamon Press, 1978), 68.

17. Dōgen, "*Shōbōgenzō Uji* (Being Time)," N. A. Waddell, trans., *Eastern Buddhist* 12:124 (May).

18. Ibid., 117–18.

19. Ibid., 119.

20. L.W. Fagg, *Two Faces of Time*, 37.

21. Immanuel Kant, *The Metaphysics of Morals*, John Ladd, trans. (Indianapolis: Bobbs-Merrill Educational Publishing, 1965), 43–44.

22. See S.I. Benn and R.S. Peters, "Justice and Equality," in *The Concept of Equality*, W. T. Blackstone, ed. (Minneapolis: Burgess Publishing, 1969), 54–81, for a detailed analysis of this notion of equality.

23. "From the Hans to the Manchus, there were some mediocre and weak monarchs, but there have been no despots and tyrants who placed themselves above the law. In this it can be truthfully asserted, that under the old system all persons were equal before the law." John C.H. Wu, "The Status of the Individual in the Political and Legal Traditions of Old and New China," in *The Status of the Individual in East and West*, C. A. Moore, ed. (Honolulu: University of Hawaii Press), 396.

24. Aristotle, *The Basic Works of Aristotle*, Richard McKeon, ed. (New York: Random House, 1941), 1129.

25. John Stuart Mill, *Utilitarianism* (Indianapolis: Hackett Publishing Co., 1979), 34.

26. David Hume, *A Treatise of Human Nature*, L.A. Selby-Bigge, ed. (Oxford: Oxford University Press, 1980), 257.

27. *Zhouyi benyi*, 1. A similar idea occurs in Buddhist causality. Especially in Chinese Chan (Zen) and Huayan Buddhism, Fa Zang proposes that removing one brick from a house changes the whole house. See F. H. Cook, *Hua-yen Buddhism: The Jewel Net of Indra* (University Park: Pennsylvania Sate University Press, 1977), 75 ff.

28. I was first inspired by particle physics for this focus-field image before I read *The Tao of Physics*.

29. Although I agree that perfectionism is distasteful and to be argued against in a just society, nevertheless I disagree with Rawls' reading of F. W. Nietzsche, discrediting him as a perfectionist. See *A Theory of Justice* (Cambridge, Mass.: Belknap Press of Harvard University, 1971), 25, 325. I agree that Aristotle and others hold a doctrine of perfectionism. However, if it is true that Nietzsche's point of view is basically "existential"—particular truths precede universal truths (which are lies for Nietzsche)—, then Nietzsche cannot be a perfectionist. Though Nietzsche might have held opinions in his personal life that sound elitist or perfectionistic, I do not *read* such ideas in his philosophy. For example, allow me to briefly review the passage that Rawls cites to show Nietzsche's apparent perfectionism: "Mankind must work continually to produce individual great human beings . . . how can your life, the individual life, retain the highest value, the deepest significance? . . . Only by your living for the good of the rarest and most valuable specimens." I interpret this kind of passage to be a call to each and every one of us to fulfill our potential and live our dreams to our fullest. Since Nietzsche argues violently against Darwin's views, his use of "specimens" cannot mean individuals of a greater species; rather, it should be *read* as the particular manifestation of the *Übermench*, the existential attitude or choice to create through and beyond human life.

30. Henry Rosemont, Jr., "Why Take Rights Seriously? A Confucian Critique," in *Human Rights and World's Religions*, L. Rouner, ed. (Notre Dame, Ind.: University of Notre Dame Press, 1988), 175.

31. LSCQ, 76; cited above in Chapter 2. He Lingxu, and Tian Fengtai analyze the political implications of this expression.

32. Hall and Ames, *Thinking through Confucius*, 180.

33. LSCQ, 896; cited above in Chapter 2.

34. Y. P. Mei, "The Status of the Individual in Chinese Social Thought and Practice," in *The Status of the Individual in East and West*, C. A. Moore, ed. (Honolulu: University of Hawaii Press), 334.

35. Ronald Dworkin, *Law's Empire* (Cambridge, Mass.: Belknap Press of Harvard University, 1986), 14.

36. Ibid., 52, 53.

37. Ibid., 36.

38. Ibid., 57.

39. Ibid., 67.

40. Ibid., 164–65.

41. Ibid., 166.

42. Ibid.

43. Ibid., 176.

44. Ibid., 216.

45. Philip Soper, "Dworkin's Domain," *Harvard Law Review* 100:1166: 1180–81 (1987).

46. Ronald Dworkin, *Law's Empire*, 359–60.

47. Ibid., 379–80.

48. Ibid., 398.

49. Andrew J. Nathan, *Human Rights in Contemporary China*, (New York: Columbia University Press, 1986), 78.

50. Nathan, *Human Rights*, 121–22.

51. A. John Simmons, *Moral Principles and Political Obligations* (Princeton, N.J.: Princeton University Press, 1981), 101 ff, and 143 ff.

52. Recall the examples of human children raised by nonhuman animals, and the inordinate, if not impossible, task of reintroducing them into human society. The Tarzan myth is part of the Romantic image of the noble savage ideal (i.e., that uncultured and untutored people living alone as rugged individuals can achieve true humanity). There is no evidence for this ideal. In fact, the evidence shows that without appropriate human contact, psychological and sociological pathologies develop.

53. Hall and Ames utilize Mead's understanding of the social self in *Thinking from the Han*, 41–43. For works by L.S. Vygotsky, see *Mind and Society* (Cambridge, Mass.: Harvard University Press, 1978), and *Thought and Language* (Cambridge, Mass.: MIT Press, 1962).

54. Alasdair MacIntyre has made his own comparisons. See "Incommensurability, Truth, and the Conversation between Confucians and Aristotelians about the Virtues" in *Culture and Modernity: East-West Philosophic Perspectives* Eliot Deutsch, ed. (Honolulu:

University of Hawaii Press, 1991). Hall and Ames have pointed out some of the difficulties and ironies in MacIntyre's approach. See *Thinking from the Han*, xii–xv.

55. Rawls, *A Theory of Justice*, 410.

56. Ibid., 547.

57. Possibly Rawls prefers "position" to "role," because it emphasizes the contractual-game connotation of social interaction, whereas "role" carries the conservative organic connotations, not to mention the team "positions" that athletes, baseball players in particular, hold.

58. Rawls, *A Theory of Justice*, 110. Of course much has been said about the etymology of "person" being derived from the Latin *persona*, the actor's mask. The word "person," then, carries the connotation of playing a role. However, this should not be taken in its modern pejorative sense, where "game playing" or "role playing" and "wearing a mask" are considered artificial and dishonest, but rather it should be considered positively, as when Shakespeare proposes that all the world is a stage and we are but its actors. Namely, to be human is to be damned to choose (to paraphrase Sartre) to perform social roles (i.e., to be human is to interact with other humans, and our interaction is primarily fulfilled through social roles). The person-as-social-role-player wears a costume (uniform/distinguishing dress) and a mask (bears a certain public appearance and attitude—note that traditional drama masks did not cover up, but displayed the attitude, for instance, of tragedy or comedy) and performs a certain part that allows others to play their parts.

59. Rawls, *A Theory of Justice*, 110.

60. Ibid., 128.

61. Rawls argues against special types under the topic of "perfectionism"; see *A Theory of Justice*, 414 f, 325–32.

62. Ibid., 55.

63. Ibid., 511.

64. Ibid., 462–67.

65. Ibid., 467.

66. Ibid., 468.

67. Ibid.

68. Ibid., 471.

69. In classical Chinese, "parent" is expressed as *fumu* (father-mother) and "children" as *zinu* (sons and daughters); there is a generic for "close blood relatives"—*qin*, which can mean "parents" in some contexts, notably in the *Mozi*.

70. Mengzi, *Mengzi yinde*, 20/3b/4; Lau, *Mencius*, 102.

71. Hsü, *The Political Philosophy of Confucianism*, 33–37; and see my "The *Lü-shih ch'un-ch'iu*'s Proposal of Governing by Filial Piety," 44–45.

72. Rawls, *A Theory of Justice*, 571.

73. See the *Daxue* (*Great Learning*) formula, where the person and the state are coterminous, so that the empire is set in order by one putting one's own life in order (*Daxue*, in *Sishu guangjie*, Chen Jizheng. ed. (Tainan: Zonghe publishers, 1981).

74. Jean-Paul Sartre, "Existentialism is a Humanism," in *Existentialism from Dostoyevsky to Sartre* (New York: New American Library, 1975), 350.

75. A draft of this section was published as part 3 of "Eco-Ethics: A New Perspective from Guam," *Asian Culture Quarterly* 21:3:47–51.

76. See Tom Regan, "The Case for Animal Rights," in *Morality in Practice* (Belmont: Wadsworth, 1984), 319–326. H.J. McCloskey, "Moral Rights and Animals," in *Today's Moral Problems* (New York: Macmillan, 1985). 479–505. Joel Feinberg, "The Rights of Animals and Unborn Generations," in *Moral Dilemmas* (Belmont: Wadsworth, 1985), 408–16.

77. Eugene C. Hargrove, "Forward," in *Nature in Asian Traditions of Thought: Essays in Environmental Philosophy*, (Albany: State University of New York Press, 1989), xix.

78. Roger T. Ames, "Putting the *Te* Back into Taoism," in *Nature in Asian Traditions of Thought: Essays in Environmental Philosophy* (Albany: State University of New York Press, 1989), 124ff.

79. Ames, "Putting the *Te* Back into Taoism," 118; LSCQ, 540.

80. Richard DeGeorge, "The Environment, Rights, and Future Generations," in *Moral Dilemmas* (Belmont: Wadsworth, 1985), 418, 419.

81. J. Baird Callicott and Roger T. Ames. eds., "Introduction," to *Nature in Asian Traditions of Thought: Essays in Environmental Philosophy* (Albany: State University of New York Press, 1989), 6.

Appendix I

1. J. L. Austin, "A Plea for Excuses," 149, in *Philosophical Papers* (Oxford: Clarendon Press, 1961), cited in Hall and Ames, *Thinking through Confucius*, 4. Paul Ricoeur has undertaken a similar project in Western philosophy. See *Time and Narrative*, 3 vols.

2. James L. Kinneavy, "*Kairos*: A Neglected Concept in Classical Rhetoric," in *Rhetoric and Praxis*, Jean Dietz Moss, ed. (Washington, D.C.: The Catholic University of America Press, 1986), 81.

3. Ibid., 82.

4. Smith, "Time and Qualitative Time," 5.

5. Graham, "The Background of the Mencian Theory of Human Nature," 8.

6. *Zhi* 之 is used as a loan for the indexical "this," and *shi* 時 is also used as a loan for "this," *shi* 是.

7. Claude Larre, "The Empirical Apperception of Time and the Conception of History in Chinese Thought," in *Cultures and Time* (Paris: Unesco Press, 1976), 36.

8. Tse-tsung Chow argues that poetry (*shi*) was originally interchangeable with "intention" (*zhi*). See "The Early History of the Chinese Word *Shih* (Poetry)," in *Wen-lin* . . . (Madison: University of Wisconcin Press, 1968) 155–66.

9. LSCQ, 56, cited in Chapter 4. See the discussion of Zen master Dōgen's emphasis on the interdependency of time and activity in Chapter 5.

10. Liezi, *Liezi duben*; see A. C. Graham, trans., *The Book of Lieh-tzu* (London: John Murray, 1960), 109–110. Another version of this story appears in the *benwei* chapter of the LSCQ, 537.

11. Fagg, *Two Faces of Time*, 155, and chapter 7.

Appendix II

1. Tang Junyi, "The *T'ien Ming* in Pre-Ch'in China," 195.

2. Following Bi Yuan's commentary which interprets *yuan* (far reaching) as *da* (to penetrate).

3. LSCQ, 685–86, cited above in Chapter 4. Again the text reads *yuan* (far reaching). Wang Niansun notes that the same passage in the *Xinxu* reads *tong*. Bi Yuan notes that *yuan* should be *da*. Their interpretations are synonymous. In fact, a similar passage in the LSCQ uses *da*, p. 68, and another uses *tong*, 1130-31.

4. LSCQ, 68, cited in Chapter 2.

5. The Chinese concept of *ming*, like the Buddhist teaching of interdependent causation, is both psychological and physical—the full notion of interpenetration requires a blending of inner psychological states and outer physical manifestations, not only in the physical body but also in nature itself. *Ming* differs from the Buddhist theory, in that it is less general and far more concrete and determinative of the particular.

6. LSCQ, 940.

7. By suppressing the particle *yu*, this line could be rendered as "The interaction of yin and yang makes heaven and is completed."

8. LSCQ, 940–41.

9. Ibid., 753.

10. Tao Hungqing's commentary interprets *zhidao* (the Way of proper rulership) to mean *zhidao* (to know the Way).

11. Richard Wilhelm ends the quote here; see *Frühling und Herbst des Lü Bu We*, 277. Chen Qiyou takes the quote to the end of the paragraph.

12. LSCQ, 772–73.

13. Ibid., 1130, 1131.

14. Ibid., 766.

15. Hsiao cites three key elements in the LSCQ's art of rulership: to comply with the mind of the people, to accept remonstrance, and to regulate the desires (p. 565).

16. Gao You's commentary suggests reading *fan* (return) as *ben* (root).

17. LSCQ, 510.

Bibliography

Ahern, E. 1981. *Chinese Ritual and Politics*. Cambridge: Cambridge University Press.

Allan, Sarah. 1979. "Shang Foundations of Modern Chinese Folk Religion." Pp. 1–21 in *Legend, Lore, and Religion in China*, ed. Sarah Allan and Alvin P. Cohen. San Francisco: Chinese Materials Center.

———. 1997. *The Way of Water and Sprouts of Virtue*. Albany: State University of New York Press.

Ames, Roger T. 1983. *The Art of Rulership*. Honolulu: University of Hawaii Press.

———. 1983. "Is Political Taoism Anarchism?" *Journal of Chinese Philosophy* 10:1:27–47.

———. 1984. "Religiousness in Classical Confucianism: A Comparative Analysis." *Asian Culture Quarterly*, 12/:2: 7–23.

———. 1985. "The Common Ground of Self-Cultivation in Classical Taoism and Confucianism." *Tsinghua Journal* (December): 65–79.

———. 1989. "Putting the *Te* Back into Taoism." Pp. 113–44 in *Nature in Asian Traditions of Thought: Essays in Environmental Philosophy*, ed. J. Baird Callicott and Roger T. Ames. Albany: State University of New York Press.

———. 1991. "The Mencian Conception of *Ren Xing*: Does It Mean 'Human Nature'?" Pp. 143–75 in *Chinese Texts and Philosophical Contexts*, ed. H. Rosemont. La Salle, Ill.: Open Court Press.

Ames, Roger T., and Henry Rosemont Jr., trans. 1998. *The Analects of Confucius: A Philosophical Translation*. New York: Ballantine Books.

Analects, see *Lunyu yinde.*

Aristotle. 1941. *The Basic Works of Aristotle*, ed. Richard McKeon. New York: Random House.

Austin, J. L. 1961. "A Plea for Excuses." In *Philosophical Papers*, Oxford: Clarendon Press.

Benn, S. I. and R. S. Peters. 1969. "Justice and Equality." Pp. 54–81 in *The Concept of Equality*, ed. W. T. Blackstone. Minneapolis: Burgess Publishing Co.

Berdyaev, Nikolai. 1962. *The Meaning of History*, trans. George Reavy. Cleveland: Living Age Books.

Blackstone, W.T., ed. 1969. *The Concept of Equality*. Minneapolis: Burgess Publishing Co.

Bloom, Irene. 1994. "Mecian Arguments on Human Nature (*Jen-hsing*)." *Philosophy East and West* 44:1:19–53.

Bodde, Derk. 1961. "Myths of Ancient China." Pp. 369–408 in *Mythologies of the Ancient World*, ed. S.N. Kramer. New York: Anchor Books.

———. 1967. *China's First Unifier, A Study in the Ch'in Dynasty As Seen in the Life of Li Ssu.* Hong Kong: Hong Kong University Press.

Bodde, Derk, and Clarence Morris. 1967. *Law in Imperial China.* Philadelphia: University of Pennsylvania Press.

Brashier, K. E. 1996. "Han Thanatology and the Division of 'Souls'." *Early China,* 21: 125–58.

Brumbaugh, Robert S. 1984. *Unreality and Time.* Albany: State University of New York Press.

Callicott, J. Baird, and Roger T. Ames, eds. 1989. *Nature in Asian Traditions of Thought: Essays in Environmental Philosophy.* Albany: State University of New York Press.

Carson, Michael F. 1985. *A Concordance to Lü-shih ch'un-ch'iu.* Taibei: Chinese Material Center.

Carson, Michael, and Michael Loewe. 1993. "*Lü shih ch'un ch'iu.*" Pp. 324–30 in *Early Chinese Texts A Bibliographical Guide,* ed. Michael Loewe. Early China Monograph Series No. 2. Berkeley: The Society for the Study of Early China and the Institute of East Asian Studies.

Chan, Wing-tsit. 1963. *A Source Book in Chinese Philosophy.* Princeton, N.J.: Princeton University Press.

Chang, Kwang-chih. 1980. *Shang Civilization.* New Haven: Yale University Press.

———. 1983. *Art, Myth, and Ritual: The Path to Political Authority in Ancient China.* Cambridge, Mass.: Harvard University Press.

Chang, Leo S. and Yu Feng. 1998. *The Four Political Treatises of the Yellow Emperor: Original Mawangdui Texts with Complete English Translation and an Introduction.* Monograph No. 15, Society for Asian and Comparative Philosophy. Honolulu: University of Hawaii Press.

Chen, Ning. 1997. "The Concept of Fate in Mencius." *Philosophy East and West,* 47:4: 495–520.

Cheng, Chung-ying. 1980. "On Timeliness (*shih-chung*) in the *Analects* and the *I ching*: An Inquiry into the Philosophical Relationship between Confucius and the *I ching.*" Unpublished manuscript prepared for the International Sinological Conference at Academica Sinca, Taibei, August 15–20.

Cheng, Te-k'un. 1966. *New Light on Pre-historic China* England: Cambridge University Press.

———.1959, 1960, 1966. *Archaeology in China,* vols. 1–3. Cambridge: Cambridge University Press.

Chow, Tse-tsung. 1968. "The Early History of the Chinese Word *Shih* (Poetry)." Pp. 151–209 in *Wen-lin: Studies in the Chinese Humanities,* ed. Chow Tse-tsung. Madison: University of Wisconsin Press.

Chuang Tzu. See Zhuangzi.

Cook, F. H. 1977. *Hua-yen Buddhism: The Jewel Net of Indra.* University Park: Pennsylvania State University Press.

Cook, Scott. 1997. "Zhuang Zi and His Carving of the Confucian Ox." *Philosophy East and West* 47:4:521–53.

Creel, H. G. 1974. *Shen Pu-Hai: A Chinese Political Philosopher of the 4th Century B.C.* Chicago: University of Chicago Press.

Crump, James. I., trans. 1970. *Chan kuo ts'e.* London: Oxford University Press.

Curtis, Michael, ed. 1961. *The Great Political Theories,* vol. 1. New York: Avon Books.

Daxue. 1981. Pp. 1–19 in *Sishu guangjie*, ed. Chen Jizheng. Tainan: Zonghe Publishers.

DeGeorge, Richard T. 1985. "The Environment, Rights, and Future Generations." Pp. 416–25 in *Moral Dilemmas: Readings in Ethics and Social Philosophy*, ed. Richard L. Purtill.

Deutsch, Eliot. 1982. *Personhood, Creativity, and Freedom*. Honolulu: University of Hawaii Press.

———. 1992. *Creative Being: The Crafting of Person and World*. Honolulu: University of Hawaii Press.

Dōgen. 1979. "Being Time *Shōbōgenzō Uji*." trans. N. A. Waddell. *Eastern Buddhist* 12:1 (May) p. 114–29.

Dong, Zhongshu. 1936. *Chunqiu fanlu*. in *Sibubeiyao*. Shanghai: Zhonghua.

Dubos, René. 1962. *The Torch of Life*. New York: Pocket Books.

Duyvendak, J.J.L., trans. 1963. *The Book of Lord Shang*. Chicago: University of Chicago Press.

Dworkin, Ronald. 1986. *Law's Empire*. Cambridge, Mass.: Belknap Press of Harvard University.

Eliade, Mircea. 1974. *The Myth of the Eternal Return, or Cosmos and History*. Trans. Willard Trask. Princeton, N.J.: Princeton University Press.

Elton, L. R. B., and H. Messel. 1978. *Time and Man*. Oxford: Pergamon Press.

Fagg, Lawrence W. 1985. *Two Faces of Time*. Wheaton, Ill.: Theosophical Publishing House.

Feifel, Eugen. 1975. "Review of *Frühling und Herbst des Lü Bu We*." *Philosophy East and West*, 25:1: 112–13

Feinberg, Joel. 1985. "The Rights of Animals and Unborn Generations." Pp. 408–15 in *Moral Dilemmas: Readings in Ethics and Social Philosophy*, ed. Richard L. Purtill. in *Morality in Practice*. Belmont, Calif.: Wadsworth Publishing Co.

Fu, Sinian. 1980. *Xingming guxun bianzheng*. Pp. 161–263 in *Fu Sinian quanji*, vol. 2, ed. Kong Decheng. Taibei: Lianjing Publishing.

Fung, Yu-lan. 1952. *A History of Chinese Philosophy*, vols. 1, 2, trans. Derk Bodde. Princeton, N.J.: Princeton University Press.

———. 1983. *Zhongguo zhexueshi xinbian*, vol. 1. Beijing: Renmin Publishing.

Gadamer, Hans-Georg. 1977. *Philosophical Hermeneutics*, trans. and ed. David E. Linge. Berkeley: University of California Press.

Geertz, Clifford. 1986. "The Uses of Diversity." Pp. 235–75 in *The Tanner Lectures on Human Values*, vol. 7, ed. Sterling M. McMurrin. Salt Lake City: University of Utah Press.

Gernet, Jacques. 1985. *China and the Christian Impact*, trans. Janet Lloyd. Cambridge: Cambridge University Press.

Giles, H. A. 1928. *A History of Chinese Literature*. New York: Grove Press.

Girardot, N. J. 1983. *Myth and Meaning in Early Taoism: The Theme of Chaos (hun-tun)*. Berkeley: University of California Press.

Graham, Angus C. 1979. "The *Nung-Chia* 'School of the Tillers' and the Origin of Peasant Utopianism in China." *Bulletin of the School of Oriental and African Studies*, 42:1:66–100.

———. 1986. "The Background of the Mencian Theory of Human Nature." Pp. 7–76 in *Studies in Chinese Philosophy and Philosophical Literature*, Singapore: Institute of East Asian Philosophies.

———. 1986. *Yin-Yang and the Nature of Correlative Thinking*, Monograph no. 6. Singapore: The Institute of East Asian Philosophies.

———. 1989. *Disputers of the Tao*. La Salle, Ill.: Open Court Press.

———, trans. 1960. *The Book of Lieh-tzu*. London: John Murray.

———, trans. 1981. *Chuang-tzu: The Seven Inner Chapters and Other Writings from the Book Chuang-tzu*. London: George Allen & Unwin.

Guanzi. 1982. in *Sibu beiyao*. Taibei: Chung Hwa Book Co.

Guo, Moruo. 1962. *Shi pipanshu*. Peking: Koxue chubanshe.

Gurwitsch, Aron. 1964. *The Field of Consciousness*. Pittsburgh: Duquesne University Press.

Hall, David L. 1986. "Logos, Mythos, Chaos: Metaphysics As the Quest for Diversity." in *New Essays in Metaphysics*, ed. Robert Neville. Albany: State University of New York Press.

Hall, David L. and Roger T. Ames. 1987. *Thinking through Confucius*. Albany: State University of New York Press.

———. 1995. *Anticipating China: Thinking Through the Narratives of Chinese and Western Culture*. Albany: State University of New York Press.

———. 1998. *Thinking from the Han: Self-Truth and Transcendence in Chinese and Western Culture*. Albany: State University of New York Press.

Hamowy, Ronald. 1987. *The Scottish Enlightenment and the Theory of Spontaneous Order*. Carbondale: Southern Illinois University Press.

Hanfeizi. 1979. ed. Shi Zhao, trans. Burton Watson. Taibei: Confucius Publishing Co.

Hanfeizi. 1982. *Hanfeizi jinzhu jinyi*, ed. Shao Zengjin. Taibei: Taiwan Commercial Press.

Hargrove, Eugene C. 1989. "Forward." Pp. xiii–xxi in *Nature in Asian Traditions of Thought: Essays in Environmental Philosophy*, ed. J. Baird Callicott and Roger T. Ames. Albany: State University of New York Press.

He, Lingxu. 1970. *Lüshi chunqiu de zhengzhililun*. Taibei: Taiwan Shangwu yinshuguan.

Hirth, Friedrich. 1908. *The Ancient History of China*. New York: Columbia University Press.

Hobbes, Thomas. 1964. *Leviathan*. New York: Washington Square Press.

Hsiao, Kung-chuan. 1979. *A History of Chinese Political Thought*, trans. F. Mote. Princeton, N.J.: Princeton University Press.

Hsü, Leonard Shih-lien. 1932. *The Political Philosophy of Confucianism*. New York: E. P. Dutton & Co.

Hsu, Wen-ying. 1979. *The Ku-ch'in*. Taibei: Central Book Co.

Hu, Shi. 1961. "Du *Lüshi chunqiu*" in *Hu Shi wencun*, vol. 3, ed. Pu Jialin. Taibei: Far Eastern Book Co.

Huainanzi. 1974. ed. Gao You. Taibei: World Books Publishing Co.

Hume, David. 1980. *A Treatise of Human Nature*, ed. L. A. Selby-Bigge. Oxford: Oxford University Press.

Jan, Yün-hua. 1980. "Tao, Principle, and Law: The Three Key Concepts in the Yellow Emperor Taoism." *Journal of Chinese Philosophy*,7:3:205–28.

Jensen, Lionel M. 1997. *Manufacturing Confucianism: Chinese Traditions and Universal Civilization*. Durham, N.C. and London: Duke University Press.

Kant, Immanuel. 1965. *The Metaphysics of Morals*, trans. John Ladd. Indianapolis: Bobbs-Merrill Educational Publishing.

Karlgren, Bernhard. 1946. "Legends and Cults in Ancient China." *Bulletin of the Museum of Far Eastern Antiquities*, 18:199–365.

Kinneavy, James L. 1986. "*Kairos*: A Neglected Concept in Classical Rhetoric." Pp. 79–105 in *Rhetoric and Praxis*, ed. Jean Dietz Moss. Washington, D.C.: The Catholic University of America Press.

Knapp, Keith N. 1995. "The *Ru* Reinterpretation of *Xiao*." *Early China* 20: 195–222.

Laozi. 1968. *Konkordanz zum Lao tzu*, ed. C. C. Müller, and R. G. Wagner. München: E. Schmitt.

Larre, Claude. 1976. "The Empirical Apperception of Time and the Conception of History in Chinese Thought." Pp. 35–62 in *Cultures and Time*, ed. L.Gordet, et al. Introduction by P. Ricoeur. Paris: The UNESCO Press.

Lau, D.C. 1953. "Theories of Human Nature in Mencius and Shyuntzy [Xunzi]." *Bulletin of the School of Oriental and African Studies*, 15:3:541–65.

———, trans. 1970. *Mencius*. Middlesex, England: Penguin Books.

———, trans. 1979. *The Analects (Lun Yü)*. Middlesex, England: Penguin Books.

Lau, D. C., and Fong Ching Chen, eds. 1996. *A Concordance to the Lüshi chunqiu*. Taibei: Taiwan Commercial Press.

Lau, D. C., and Roger T. Ames, trans. 1996. *Sun Pin, the Art of Warfare: A Comprehensive Translation of the Fourth-Century B.C. Chinese Military Philosopher and Strategist*. New York: Ballantine Books.

———. trans. 1998. *Yuan Dao: Tracing Dao to Its Source*. New York: Ballantine Books.

Le Blanc, Charles. 1985–1986. "A Re-examination of the Myth of Huang Ti." *Journal of Chinese Religion* 13–14:45–63.

Legge, James, trans. 1885. *The Li Ki, Sacred Books of the East*, vols. 27, 28. Oxford: Oxford University Press.

Li, Liu. 1996. "Mortuary Ritual and Social Hierarchy in Longshan Culture." *Early China* 21:1–46.

Liji jijie. 1980. ed. Xi Dan. Taibei: Wenshizhe Publishing Co.

Liezi. 1981. *Liezi duben*, ed. Zhuang Wanshou. Taibei: San Min Publishing Co.

Liu, Xiang. 1975. *Xinxu jinzhu jinyi*, ed. Lu Yuanjun. Taibei: Taiwan Commercial Press.

Liu, Yuanyan. 1992. *Zajia diwangxue: Lüshi chunqiu*. Beijing: Sanzong shudianchuban.

Lloyd, Geoffrey E. R. 1996. *Adversaries and Authorities*. Cambridge: Cambridge University Press.

Locke, John. 1952. *The Second Treatise of Government*. Indianapolis: Bobbs-Merril Co.

Loewe, Michael. 1993. *Early Chinese Texts: A Bibliographical Guide*. Early China Monograph Series No. 2, Berkeley: Society for the Study of Early China and Institute of East Asian Studies.

———. 1994. *Ways to Paradise: The Chinese Quest for Immortality*. Taibei: SMC Publishing.

Loewe, Michael, and Edward L. Shaughnessy, eds. 1999. *The Cambridge History of Ancient China from the Origins of Civilization to 221 B.C.* New York: Cambridge University Press.

Louton, John. 1981. *The Lü-shi chun-qiu: An Ancient Chinese Political Cosmology*. University of Washington, unpublished dissertation.

Loy, David. 1997. *Nonduality: A Study in Comparative Philosophy*. Atlantic Highlands, N.J.: Humanities Press.

Lü, Buwei. 1977. *Lüshi chunqiu jishi deng wushu* (cited as LSCQ in text), ed. Yang Jialuo. Taibei: Ding Wen Publishing Co. Contains Xu Weiyu's commentary.

———. 1984. *Lüshi chunqiu jiaoshi*, ed. Chen Qiyou. Shanghai: Xuelin Publishing Co.

———. 1979. *Lüshi chunqiu jiaoshi*, ed. Yin Zhongrong. Taibei: Guoli bianyi.

———. 1986. *Lüshi chunqiu shizhu*, ed. Chang Shuangdi, et al. Gulin: Gulin wenshi Publishing Co.

Lunyu yinde. 1941. In *Shisanjing yinde*, ed. Zhao Fengtian. Taibei: San Min Publishing Co.

MacIntyre, Alasdair. 1991. "Incommensurability, Truth, and the Conversation between Confucians and Aristotelians about the Virtues." Pp. 104–22 in *Culture and Modernity: East-West Philosophic Perspectives*, ed. Eliot Deutsch. Honolulu: University of Hawaii Press.

Major, John S. 1987. "The Meaning of *Hsing-te*." Pp. 281–91 in *Chinese Ideas about Nature and Society: Studies in Honour of Derk Bodde*, eds. Charles Le Blanc and Susan Blader. Hong Kong: Hong Kong University Press.

Maspero, Henri. 1924. "Légendes mythologiques dans le *Chou king*." *Journal Asiatique* CCIV: 1–100.

Mbiti, John S. 1970. *African Religions and Philosophy*. New York: Anchor Books.

McCloskey, H. J. 1985. "Moral Rights and Animals." Pp. 479–505 in *Today's Moral Problems*, ed. Richard A. Wasserstrom. New York: Macmillan Publishing Co.

Mei, Y. P. 1968. "The Status of the Individual in Chinese Social Thought and Practice." in *The Status of the Individual in East and West*, ed. C. A. Moore. Honolulu: University of Hawaii Press, 1968.

———, trans. 1980. *The Works of Motze*. Taibei: Confucius Publishing Co.

Mencius see Mengzi.

Mengzi. 1941. *Mengzi yinde*, in *Shisanjing yinde*, ed. Zhao Fengtian. Taibei: San Min Publishing Co.

Mill, John Stuart. 1979. *Utilitarianism*. Indianapolis: Hackett Publishing Co.

Moore, C. A., ed. 1968. *The Status of the Individual in East and West*. Honolulu: University of Hawaii Press.

Mote, Frederick W. 1972. "The Cosmological Gulf between China and the West." Pp. 3–21 in *Transition and Permanence: Chinese History and Culture*, eds. David C. Buxbaum and F. W. Mote. Hong Kong: Cathay Press Limited.

Munro, Donald J. 1979. *Concept of Man in Contemporary China*. Ann Arbor: University of Michigan Press.

———. 1988. *Images of Human Nature—A Sung Portrait*. Princeton, N.J.: Princeton University Press.

Nathan, Andrew J. 1986. *Human Rights in Contemporary China*. New York: Columbia University Press.

Needham, Joseph. 1956. *Science and Civilisation in China*, vol. 2. Cambridge: Cambridge University Press.

Newton-Smith, W. H. 1980. *The Structure of Time*. London: Routledge & Kegan Paul.

Nivison, David S. 1996. *The Ways of Confucianism: Investigations in Chinese Philosophy*. ed. Bryan W. Van Norden. Chicago and La Salle, Ill.: Open Court Press.

Nowotny, Helga. 1994. *Time: The Modern and Post-modern Experience*, trans. Neville Plaice. Cambridge, U.K.: Polity Press.

Pankenier, David W. 1995. "The Cosmo-Political Background of Heaven's Mandate." *Early China* 20:121–76.

Pelliot, Paul. 1930. "Review of Richard Wilhelm's *Frühling und Herbst des Lü Bu We*." *T'oung Pao*, 27:68–91.

Purtill, Richard L., ed. 1985. *Moral Dilemmas: Readings in Ethics and Social Philosophy*. Belmont, Calif.: Wadsworth Publishing Company.

Qian, Mu. 1956. *Xian Qin zhuzixinian*. Hong Kong: Hong Kong University Press.

———. 1977. "Lü Buwei zhushukao." Appended to the editor's preface in *Lüshi chunqiu jishi deng wushu*, ed. Yang Jialo. Taibei: Ding Wen publishers.

Rawls, John. 1971. *A Theory of Justice*. Cambridge, Mass.: Belknap Press of Harvard University.

Regan, Tom. 1984. "The Case for Animal Rights." Pp. 319–26 in *Morality in Practice*, ed. James P. Streba. Belmont, Calif.: Wadsworth Publishing Company.

Reischauer, Edwin O., and John K. Fairbank. 1958. *East Asia: The Great Tradition*. London: George Allen & Unwin.

Rickett, W. Allyn. 1985. *Guan tzu: Political, Economic, and Philosophical Essays from Early China. A Study and Translation*. Princeton, N.J.: Princeton University Press.

Ricoeur, Paul. 1984. *Time and Narrative*, 3 vols. Chicago: University of Chicago Press.

Riegel, Jeffrey. 1995. "Do Not Serve the Dead as You Serve the Living: The *Lüshi chunqiu* Treatises on Moderation in Burial." *Early China* 20:301–30.

Robinet, Isabelle. 1997. *Taoism: Growth of a Religion*, trans. Phyllis Brooks. Stanford, Calif.: Stanford University Press.

Rosemont, Henry Jr. 1970–1971. "State and Society in the *Hsün Tzu*: A Philosophical Commentary." *Monumenta Serica* 29:38–78.

———. 1988. "Why Take Rights Seriously? A Confucian Critique." in *Human Rights and World's Religions*, ed. L. Rouner. Notre Dame, Ind.: University of Notre Dame Press.

———, ed. 1991. *Chinese Texts and Philosophical Contexts: Essays Dedicated to Angus C. Graham*. La Salle, Ill.: Open Court Press.

Rousseau, Jean P. 1967. *The Social Contract and Discourse on the Origin of Inequality*, ed. Lester G. Crocker. New York: Pocket Books.

Ryden, Edmund. 1997. *The Yellow Emperor's Four Canons: A Literary Study and Edition of the Text from Mawangdui*. Taibei: Guangji Press.

Sartre, Jean-Paul. 1975. "Existentialism Is a Humanism." Pp. 345–8 in *Existentialism from Dostoyevsky to Sartre*, ed. Walter Kaufmann. New York: New American Library.

Sellmann, James. 1983. "The 'Cosmic Talisman' of Liturgical Taoism: An Analysis of the Structure and Content of the *Ling-pao chen-wen*." *Chinese Culture*, 24:3:57–69.

———. 1983. "On Mobilizing the Military: Arguments for a Just War Theory from the *Lü-shih ch'un-ch'iu*." *Asian Culture Quarterly*, 11:4:26–43.

———. 1985. "The *Lü-shih ch'un-ch'iu*'s Proposal of Governing by Filial Piety." *Asian Culture Quarterly*, 13:1:43–61.

———. 1987. "Three Models of Self-Integration (*tzu te*) in Early China." *Philosophy East and West* 37:4:372–91.

———. 1990. "Seasonality in the Achievement of *Hsing* in the *Lü-shih ch'un-ch'iu*." *Asian Culture Quarterly*, 18:2: Pp. 42–68.

———. 1993. "Eco-Ethics: A New Perspective from Guam." *Asian Culture Quarterly*, 21:341–51.

———. 1995. "Lü Buwei." Pp. 39–43 in *Great Thinkers of the Eastern World*, ed. Ian McGreal. New York: HarperCollins.

———. 1995. "On the Myth of Cosmogony in Ancient China." Pp. 211–220 in *Analecta*

Husserliana. "Oriental/Occidental Phenomenology." Book 6, ed. A. T. Tymieniecka. Boston: Mass.: Kluwer Academic Press.

———. 1998. "*Lüshi chunqiu.*" Pp. 864–65 in *Routledge Encyclopedia of Philosophy*, ed. E. Craig, London and New York: Routledge.

———. 1999. "The *Lüshi chunqiu* on the Ruler's Use of Proper Timing." *Asian Culture Quarterly*, 27:1:59–71.

———. 1999. "The Origin and Role of the State According to the *Lüshi chunqiu.*" *Journal of Asian Philosophy*, 9:3:193–218.

Shang, Yang. 1979. *Shangjunshu jiegudingben*, ed. Yang Jialo. Taibei: Ting Wen Publishing Co.

Shaughnessy, Edward L., ed. 1997. *New Sources of Early Chinese History: An Introduction to the Reading of Inscriptions and Manuscripts.* Berkeley: The Society for the Study of Early China.

———. 1997. "Western Zhou Bronze Inscriptions." Pp. 57–84 in *New Sources of Early Chinese History: An Introduction to the Reading of Inscriptions and Manuscripts*, ed. Edward L. Shaughnessy. Berkeley: The Society for the Study of Early China.

Sherover, Charles M. 1975. *The Human Experience of Time: The Development of its Philosophic Meaning.* New York: New York University Press.

Shi, Jiao. n.d. *Shizi* in *Baibu congshu jicheng*, vol. 7, ed. Yan Yiping. Taiwan: Yiwen yinshuguan.

———. 1997. *Xinyi Shizi duben*, eds. Shui Weisong and Chen Manming. Taibei: Sanmin.

Shujing yinde. 1941. in *Shisanjing yinde.* Taibei: Sanmin Publishing Co.

Sima, Qian. 1975. *Shiji xuan.* "Lü Buwei *liezhuan.*" Taibei: Wenyi Publishing Co.

———. 1979. *Selections from the Records of the Historian*, trans. Yang Xianyi and Gladys Yang. Peking: Foreign Language Press.

Simmons, A. John. 1981. *Moral Principles and Political Obligations.* Princeton, N.J.: Princeton University Press.

Smith, John E. 1969. "Time, Times, and the 'Right Time': *Chronos* and *Kairos.*" *The Monist* 53:1:1–13.

———. 1986. "Time and Qualitative Time." *Review of Metaphysics* 40 (September):3–16.

Soper, Philip. 1987. "Dworkin's Domain." *Harvard Law Review* 100:1166–1186.

Streba, James P., ed. 1984. *Morality in Practice.* Belmont, Calif.: Wadsworth Publishing Company.

Sun, Bin. 1984. *Sun Bin bingfa jiaoli*, ed. Zhang Zhenze. Peking: Zhonghua.

T'ang, Chün-yi, or T'ang, Chun-i. See Tang Junyi.

Tang, Junyi. 1962. "The *T'ien Ming* (Heavenly Ordinance) in Pre-Ch'in China." *Philosophy East and West* 11:4:195–218.

———. 1968. *Zhongguo zhexue yuanlun: Yuanxingpian.* Hong Kong: New Asia Press.

Thompson, P. M. 1979. *The Shen Tao Fragments.* Oxford: University of Oxford Press.

Tian, Fengtai. 1979. *Lüshi chunqiu yanjiu.* Taiwan: Chengzhi Daxue, unpublished dissertation.

———. 1986. *Lüshi chunqiu tanwei.* Taibei: Taiwan Xueshengshuju.

Twitchett, Denis, and Michael Loewe, eds. 1986. *The Cambridge History of China*, volume 1, *The Ch'in and Han Empires.* Cambridge: Cambridge University Press.

Vico, Giambattista. 1948. *The New Science*, trans. Thomas Goddard Bergin. Ithaca, N.Y.: Cornell University Press.

Vygotsky, L.S. 1962. *Thought and Language*. Cambridge: MIT Press.
———. 1978. *Mind and Society*. Cambridge, Mass.: Harvard University Press.
———. 1985. *Pensée et langage*. Paris: Editions sociales.
Wang, Fanzhi. 1993. *Lüshi chunqiu yanjiu*. Inner Mongolia: Neimenggudaxue chubanshe.
Wang, Zongfei. 1988. "*Lüshi chunqiu*: Zhengzhi falu sixiang chutan." *Beifang luncong*. Vol.4:39–44 Peking.
Wasserstrom, Richard A., ed. 1985. *Today's Moral Problems*. New York: Macmillan.
Watson, Burton. 1962. *Early Chinese Literature*. New York: Columbia University Press.
———, trans. 1967. *The Basic Writings of Mo Tzu, Hsün Tzu*, and *Han Fei Tzu*. New York: Columbia University Press.
———, trans. 1968. *The Complete Works of Chuang Tzu*. New York: Columbia University Press.
White, Hayden. 1978. "The Burden of History." in *Tropics of Discourse*, Baltimore: Johns Hopkins University Press.
Wilhelm, Richard, trans. 1979. *Frühling und Herbst des Lü Bu We*. Introduction by Wolfgang Bauer. Düsseldorf: Eugen Diederichs Verlag.
Wilhelm, Richard, and Cary F. Baynes, trans. 1978. *The I ching*. Princeton, N.J.: Princeton University Press.
Wood, Douglas K. 1982. *Men sgainst Time*. Lawrence: University of Kansas Press.
Wu, John C. H. 1968. "The Status of the Individual in the Political and Legal Traditions of Old and New China." in *The Status of the Individual in East and West*, ed C. A. Moore. Honolulu: University of Hawaii Press.
Wylie, A. 1970. *Notes on Chinese Literature*, reprint. Taibei: Bookcase Shop.
Xu, Fuguan. 1963. *Zhongguo renxinglunshi*. Taizhong: Donghai University Press.
———. 1982. *Lianghan sixiangshi*, vols. 1–3. Taibei: Student Book Store.
Xunzi. 1981. *Xunzi duben*, ed. Wang Zhonglin. Taibei: San Min Publishing Co.
Yanzi. 1981. *Yanzi chunqiu jiaozhu*, ed. Yang Jialo. Taibei: World Books Publishing Co.
Yates, Robin D. S. 1997. *Five Lost Classics: Tao, Huang-Lao, and Yin-Yang in Han China*. New York: Ballantine Books.
Yin, Guoguang. 1997. *Lüshi chunqiu cileiyanjiu*. Beijing: Huafu chubanshe.
Zhang, Dainian. 1982. *Zhongguo zhexue dagang*. Peking: Chinese Academy of Social Sciences Press.
Zhanguoce. 1978. ed. Gao You. Taibei: Shang Wu Publishing.
Zhongyong. 1981. Pp. 20–59 in *Sishu guangjie*, ed. Chen Jizheng. Tainan: Zonghe Publishers.
Zhouyi benyi. 1975. Taibei: Hua Lian Publishing Co.
Zhouyi yinde. 1941. Vol. 1, pp. 1–185 in *Shisanjing yinde*, ed. Nie Chongqi. Taibei: Sanmin Publishing Co.
Zhuangzi. 1956. *A Concordance to Chuang tzu*. Harvard-Yenching Index Series No. 20. Cambridge, Mass.: Harvard University Press.

Index